The Visitor's Guide
to
FLORENCE & TUSCANY

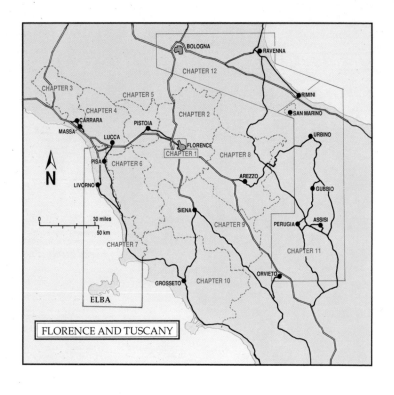

CHAPTER 3

CHAPTER 5

CHAPTER 4

MASSA

CARRARA

LUCCA

PISTOIA

CHAPTER 2

CHAPTER 12

BOLOGNA

RAVENNA

RIMINI

SAN MARINO

URBINO

FLORENCE

CHAPTER 1

CHAPTER 8

CHAPTER 6

PISA

LIVORNO

N

0   30 miles

50 km

CHAPTER 7

AREZZO

SIENA

CHAPTER 9

GUBBIO

PERUGIA   ASSISI

CHAPTER 11

GROSSETO

CHAPTER 10

ORVIETO

ELBA

FLORENCE AND TUSCANY

THE
VISITOR'S GUIDE TO
FLORENCE &
TUSCANY

PHIL WHITNEY

MPC
HUNTER
PUBLISHING INC

Published by:
Moorland Publishing Co Ltd,
Moor Farm Road West,
Airfield Estate,
Ashbourne,
Derbyshire DE6 1HD
England

1st edition published 1986
2nd edition revised and enlarged
1990, 1993

ISBN 0 86190 375 7 (paperback)

Colour origination by:
Scantrans, Singapore

Printed in Hong Kong by
Wing King Tong Co., Ltd.

Published in the USA by:
Hunter Publishing Inc,
300 Raritan Center Parkway,
CN 94, Edison, NJ 08818
ISBN 1 55650 282 6 (USA)

British Library Cataloguing in
Publication Data:
Whitney, Phil
   The visitor's guide to Italy.
   -2nd ed. - (Visitor's guides).
   Florence and Tuscany
   1. Italy. Tuscany - Visitor's
   guides I. Title II. Whitney. Phil.
   Visitor's guide to Florence and
   Tuscany, 1986 III. Series
   914.5504929

Illustrations have been supplied as
follows: H. Alcock: pp 14, 19, 30
(both), 31 (both), 35 (both), 59
(bottom), 62 (bottom), 70, 71 (both),
83 (bottom), 86, 87, 98, 99, 103, 106,
107, 130 (both), 131, 147, 150
(bottom), 151, 154 (top), 155, 175,
182 (both), 183, 186, 187 (bottom),
190, 191 (both), 194, 198, 199 (both),
202, 203 (top); Azienda di
Promozione Turistica di Assisi:
p187 (top); Azienda di Promozione
Turistica, Rimini: p203 (bottom);
Ron Scholes: pp 62 (top), 67 (top),
150 (top). All other illustrations
supplied by the author.

CONTENTS

Key to Symbols Used in Text Margin and on Maps

Recommended walk

Archaeological site

Nature reserve/Animal interest

Skiing facilities

Garden

Sports facilities

Cave

Church/Ecclesiastical site

Building of interest

Castle/Fortification

Museum/Art gallery

Beautiful view/Scenery, Natural phenomenon

Other place of interest

Watersports

Park

Key to Maps

Main road

Motorway

River

Town/City

Town/Village

Lake

Provincial Boundary

Note on the maps

The maps drawn for each chapter, while comprehensive, are not designed to be used as route maps, but rather to locate the main towns, villages and places of interest.

INTRODUCTION

In the eighteenth and nineteenth centuries, when foreign travel was the prerogative of a privileged minority, it was necessary for well-bred young men to undertake the 'Grand Tour' to complete their education. The idea of the tour was to visit the major European cities, including Paris, Munich, Berlin, Madrid, Athens, Rome, Naples, Venice and Florence. Many young men never completed the tour, but fell in love with one of the cities along the way and stayed there. Of all these cities, perhaps the most inviting was Florence, with its mild climate and cultured atmosphere. Indeed, so many Englishmen decided to spend their lives in Florence that a new monumental cemetery was built which, even today, is known as the English Cemetery.

Florence (Firenze in Italian) is the capital of Tuscany, the triangular area of central Italy limited by the Apeninnes, the Apuan Alps and the Tyrrhenian Sea. The word tuscan, however, originally described anything derived from the Etruscans, and this is the reason why nine of the most interesting places in Italy, situated just outside the region's official boundaries, have been included in this book. There are two chapters on these places and one chapter on each of Tuscany's nine provinces: Arezzo, Florence, Grosseto, Livorno, Lucca, Massa, Pisa, Pistoia and Siena, as well as a chapter on the city of Florence.

Much of the area is best visited by car, but there is so much to see that even those who rely on the buses and trains will be spoilt for choice of places to visit.

For those interested in history, art or archaeology the area will seem like paradise. It is possible to get a good idea from most of the area's towns of how modern civilisation has developed. Bologna, for example, can boast remains from the neolithic, Etruscan, medieval and Renaissance periods, while the origins of Florence are only slightly more recent. The museums and galleries of the various towns and cities contain works by all the most famous artists, and even the most modest village church may house an altarpiece worthy of any of the world's great collections.

The large number of visitors in search of sun, sea and sand will be more than satisfied by the Tyrrhenian Coast, and by the stretch of the Adriatic covered by the guide. Resorts such as Rimini on the Adriatic are famous throughout Europe, while Forte dei Marmi and Viareggio on the Tyrrhenian Sea are also extremely popular with holidaymakers. Although much of the coast is fairly commercialised, there are still some places which offer a relatively quiet holiday if the visitor is prepared to look for them.

In the winter, the area can also offer winter sports in several resorts in the Apennines and the Apuan Alps. In summer these become centres for less demanding pursuits, such as walking, climbing or just relaxing in the pure mountain air.

These then are the basic attractions of the area: sea, sun, mountains and history, but they are not the only ones. Even if few people outside Italy speak Italian, there must be very few, if any, who have never heard the words Chianti and spaghetti bolognese. Chianti, the rich red wine produced in the region of the same name, between Florence and Siena, is considered by many to be one of the best in the world. The visitor will be pleased to find that a glass of this wine costs little more than a glass of mineral water.

Situated just outside Tuscany, but easily reached from Florence, Bologna has prided itself for centuries on its skills in the culinary arts. The famous sauce is only one of the many local specialities which visitors will be tempted to try if they visit this historic city. Other cities and towns in the area have their own gastronomic delights and local wines which will please the palate.

The geography of the area, with hills and mountains crisscrossed by many rivers, has limited the choice of sites for human settlements, with all their pre-requisites, such as an adequate water supply, defensibility, and good communication routes. As a result of this, the sites of the towns today are very often the sites of those of our early ancestors. This, together with the fact that the region was the most advanced in Europe during the Middle Ages and the Renaissance, has left a great legacy of historical interest in the region.

Before the growth of Roman power, the leading people in Italy were the Etruscans who, from the seventh century BC, were a trading nation, only slightly less important than the Greeks and the Phoenicians. Many of the towns in the region have Etruscan origins, and in some, such as Volterra, there are significant remains.

Six hundred years of Roman wealth and culture provided a further stimulus to development in the area and, when the Empire split into eastern and western sections, the western capital was, for a time, nearby Ravenna.

At the end of the Dark Ages the Italian cities re-emerged as *comuni* over which Church and Empire constantly struggled for supremacy. As the struggle became more intense, the leading families in many of the towns allied themselves with either the Guelphs (those who accepted the temporal authority of the Pope) or the Ghibellines (the supporters of the rights of the Holy Roman Emperor in Italy). Usually this was merely an excuse to improve the standing of their own family and, in the thirteenth and fourteenth centuries, the *comuni* were racked by a succession of fierce civil wars.

As the Papacy gradually established its national supremacy, the more important of the *comuni* became independent duchies or city-states, paying no more than lip-service to spiritual or temporal powers. In time, some states came to dominate large areas, and the country remained divided like this until Unification in 1860. One of these small independent states, San Marino, has survived as an anachronism until the present day, and a visit there is well-worth-while.

The most important period in the area's history was the Renaissance, when Florence, stimulated by the arts patronage of the Medici family and the riches accrued for the city by its skilled textile workers, could justly claim to be the cultural centre of Europe. Other cities in the region, such as Urbino and Perugia, were also great centres of learning.

Whichever way visitors decide to approach their visit to Tuscany, they are assured of a holiday full of interest and variety.

1
THE CITY OF FLORENCE

The city of Florence is situated at the first crossable point on the River Arno, after the Arno Valley emerges from the Apennines and opens up to form a wide plain. As a result of this, it has always been a properous city, as the point where the north-south and east-west routes meet in Italy.

The first people to recognise the importance of the site were the Villanovians, who established a primitive settlement there despite the marshy nature of the ground. Two hundred years after this, settlement seems to have been abandoned; the Etruscans, with defence uppermost in mind, founded Fiesole on the hill overlooking Florence. It was not until 59BC, when the Romans established a colony for Caesar's veterans, that the site was occupied again. The rectangular plan of the Roman colony is still evident in the centre of the city and excavations have revealed important remains.

Events in Florence during the Dark Ages are obscure, but when Charlemagne visited the city in AD780, the Battistero (Baptistry) di San Giovanni was already in existence, and several other churches date back to the Carolingian period.

Florence expanded in the eleventh and twelfth centuries, rapidly becoming the most powerful of the *comuni* in the area and crushing the power of the feudal barons in the surrounding countryside. The first notable Florentine works of art date from this period, with the construction of several Romanesque churches. In the following two centuries, the *comune*, although constantly in a state of near civil war between supporters of the Papacy and of the Empire, enjoyed such a literary boom that the Tuscan language gradually became adopted as the model for a standardised form of Italian.

The literary prowess of the Florentines is first seen in the poetry of Guido Cavalcanti (1255-1300) but it was the fourteenth-century

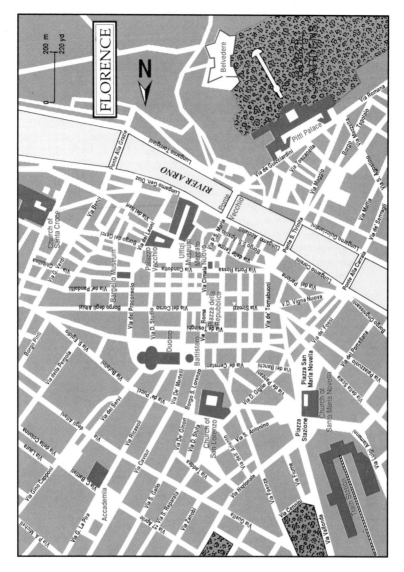

writers who really established Florence as the centre of Italian literature. Dante Alighieri, epic poet and politician (1265-1321), is one of the best-known poets in history, and his masterpiece is *The Divine Comedy (La Divina Commedia)*. For visitors with a little time to spare, it is well-worth reading the Comedy, as it mentions many of the places they will visit.

Giovanni Boccaccio (1313-75) and Franco Sacchetti (1332-1400) picture contemporary life vividly in their marvellous short stories, while the poetry of Francesco Petrarch has influenced succeeding generations of poets.

As happened in most of the *comuni* where deep divisions arose between various factions, the majority of the people longed for stability at any cost. This eventually led to power being vested in the hands of one family; in the case of Florence, it was the Medici.

Of relatively humble origins, in the Valle del Mugello, the Medici family rose to be one of the most highly regarded ruling families in Europe, with three popes and numerous cardinals among other ruling figures. The Medici, who had become extremely rich in the world of commerce, gained popular support, not only because of their generosity and fairness, but also because of their munificence towards artists. Their contribution to the arts, however, was not only in the guise of patrons; several members of the family were talented writers (notably Lorenzo the Magnificent and Lorenzino). Later generations made important contributions to scientific research.

During the Medicean period most of Italy's great men were either Florentines or passed a considerable amount of time at the Medici court. The Medici palaces in and around Florence are full of works by Florentines such as Michelangelo and Leonardo, by 'foreigners' such as Raphael, and by others such as Rubens and Durer whose works were acquired by the Grand Dukes.

The Medici ruled Florence from 1434 until 1743, when the line became extinct and the House of Lorraine then governed the Duchy until the Unification of Italy.

From 1865 to 1870, when Unification was completed with the taking of Rome and the Papal States, Florence was Italy's provisional capital. After the transfer of the capital, Florence expanded rapidly without any real planning, and a period of neglect and decadence followed. However, a new upsurge of intellectual activity in the 1920s, coupled with a rapid growth in tourism, reversed the trend. Now, despite the damage inflicted by World War II, Florence is again one of the most rewarding places in the world to visit.

The Museums of Florence

Not counting the various Medicean villas, there are about forty museums and galleries to visit in Florence. Very few people will have time to visit them all, but it is possible to see a fair selection. Therefore, an indication of what each museum contains has been included, with some explanation of the meaning of some of the pictures and the uses of some of the objects.

The Uffizi

Asked to name the five most important museums in the world, it is fairly certain that ninety-nine people out of a hundred would include the Uffizi on their list. Although two periods of exile between 1494 and 1527 caused the dispersal of much of the original Medici collection, the impetus given by Cosimo I (1537-74) and maintained by his successors meant that the former riches were soon far surpassed by the acquisitions.

The building of the Uffizi was ordered by Cosimo to centralise the Florentine administration archives and courts. In 1581 Cosimo's son, Francesco I, reorganised the third floor to house a part of the family collection, which was almost immediately opened to the public.

During the Medicean period the Uffizi collection was made up of every imaginable type of collectable item. The arrival of the 'Age of Reason' and the Lorraine Dynasty in 1743 saw the Uffizi limited to painting and sculpture, while other more specialised museums were opened to house the rest of the collection.

Designed and initiated by Giorgio Vasari in 1560, the building is a masterpiece of the late Renaissance. The statues which adorn the niches of the building were added in the nineteenth century, and represent prominent Florentines from the fields of history, culture and science. The only sculpture conceived as part of the original design is that of Cosimo I, above the archway at the river end of the building. This sculpture is the work of Giambologna and was intended to give an impression of Cosimo's dominance over the city.

During the summer, especially on days when admission is free, the visitor may have to queue for some time. However, do not be deterred by this, or by the high admission price, as visiting the Uffizi forms an essential part of any visit to Florence.

The only part of the ground floor open to the public is the recently restored Romanesque Church of San Pier Scheraggio, which Vasari adapted into the structure of the new building. Students of architecture will find the remains fascinating. However, the attention of the layman is more likely to be attracted by Andrea del Castagno's detached frescoes of *Famous Men*, which include many of those whose statues appear in the niches outside the building. Besides the *Famous Men*, the other important fresco exhibited here is Botticelli's *Annunciation*, one of the masterpieces of the Renaissance.

The first floor houses the prints and drawings section, containing over 104,000 examples. This collection is only open to those with a letter of introduction but the room on the left at the top of the stairs houses continual public exhibitions of parts of the collection.

The major collection is housed on the second floor, and even a

The Uffizi: detail of Spring *by Botticelli (right) and* The Virgin Mary on the Throne *by Domenico Ghirlandaio (below)*

←*A panorama of Florence with Giotto's Tower in the foreground*

fairly superficial visit to this floor requires at least 2 hours. This floor consists of three corridors devoted to marbles and sculpture, around which there are a large number of rooms devoted to painting.

The first corridor contains many Roman busts and sculptures of emperors and mythological subjects (many copied from Greek originals). There are also some excellent tapestries (mainly of the sixteenth-century Florentine school). Just below the ceiling, the corridor is lined with a series of portraits of famous men. It is difficult to make out the names under most of the portraits but the keen-eyed visitor will be able to pick out Thomas More and Henry VIII, among others.

The second (shortest) corridor is again filled mainly with Roman copies of Greek originals. Both sides of this corridor are full of windows, and the extra light makes the statues here look more impressive. The windows provide excellent views of the Ponte Vecchio in one direction and the Palazzo Vecchio in the other.

More Roman sculptures (including the excellent *Hanging Marsia*) are to be found in the third corridor, along with more fine tapestries. The visitor should spare a glance for the ceiling in this corridor, as each section is devoted to a group of famous Florentines — artists, architects etc — and shows them against the background of the city.

The rooms housing the collection of paintings are set out chronologically for the Florentine paintings, and geographically for the others. Each room is clearly numbered.

Room II is devoted to the thirteenth century and Giotto. In the thirteenth century all art was religious and the emphasis was, above all, on spiritual qualities. It would have been considered almost sacrilegious to produce what we would now call a realistic image. For example, in many of the pictures Christ is represented as much larger than the saints, who, in turn, are larger than the ordinary people. Gold backgrounds and haloes emphasise the excellence of Divine nature. The most important thirteenth-century artists were Cimabue and Duccio. Giotto, active in the first part of the following century, began to break away from tradition, with a more realistic representation of figures and an understanding of perspective.

Room III shows the fourteenth-century Sienese school. This group of painters achieved an expressiveness of line and colour that had never been seen before. Particularly notable is the *Annunciation of the Saints* by Simone Martini, the leader of the group.

Room IV is devoted to fourteenth-century Florentine painting. Although Florentine painting was generally shadowed by the Sienese in this period, the tryptich *St Nicholas of Bari, Virgin and Child with Saints, and St Procolo*, by Ambrogio Lorenzetti, is a masterpiece.

Rooms V and VI contain the Florentine Gothic: Lorenzo Monaco and Gentile da Fabriano are the most important artists represented here.

Room VII shows the developments of the early fifteenth century. The most important works in this room are Paolo Uccello's *Battle of St Romano*, Piero della Francesco's portraits of the Duke and Duchess of Urbino, and the *Virgin and Child with St Anne* by Masaccio and Masolino, which show that private patrons demands for pictures of non-religious subjects was now becoming as important as religious art.

Room VIII is given to works by Filippo Lippi. Of particular note is the *Coronation of the Virgin*.

Room IX offers an interesting contrast between Pollaiolo's series, shown in this room, of *Faith, Hope, Charity, Temperance, Fortitude* and *Justice*, and Botticelli's *Fortitude*. The expressiveness of the face and the detail of the throne just give Botticelli the verdict.

Rooms X, XI, XII, XIII and XIV are actually one large room displaying works by Botticelli. The magnificent *Birth of Venus* and *Spring (Primavera)* are mythological subjects drawn from Apuleius' *The Golden Ass*, and selected by the philosopher Marsilio Ficino as aids to the education of Lorenzo di Pierfrancesco dei Medici. Filippino Lippi, whose *Madonna of the Eight* contains a fine example of *trompe l'oeil* (the towel overhanging the edge of the stage) and Ghirlandaio's *Enthroned Virgin with Child and Saints* stand up well to comparison with their great contemporary. Also interesting is the comparison between restored and unrestored works.

Room XV is devoted to Leonardo da Vinci. *The Baptism of Christ* was painted by Leonardo and Verrocchio while Leonardo was a pupil of the latter. The left hand side, painted by Leonardo, is so superior that it is said Verrocchio gave up painting in despair. *The Adoration of the Magi*, left unfinished when the artist was sent to Milan in 1481, is extremely interesting because it shows how Leonardo constructed a painting.

Room XVIII, which is known as the Tribuna, once held the most important works of the Medici collection. It now holds a collection of sixteenth-century portraits (mainly of the Medici) grouped around the Medici Venus, an excellent first-century Greek marble copy of a bronze original.

Room XX shows works of Durer and the Germans, who were more analytic but less fluent than their Italian contemporaries.

Room XXI is given to paintings by the Venetians Bellini and Giorgione; note the more realistic landscape background of the Venetians.

In Room XXIV, the round *Holy Family* is the finest of all Michelangelo's paintings.

Room XXVI has works which were recently restored for the 500th anniversary of Raphael's birth. Particularly outstanding is his triple portrait of Leo X, his cousin Giulio (later Clement VII) and his nephew Cardinal Luigi Rossi.

Room XXVII is devoted to Titian, who reveals a perfect understanding of the human figure and a powerful use of colour, particularly, in *The Venus of Urbino* and *Venus and Cupid*.

Room XXVIII shows some of Parmigianino's works, including *Madonna of the Long Neck*. This demonstrates how the idealisation of the Renaissance gave way to Mannerism — a spirit of pure decorativeness.

Room XLI has good examples of the Flemish painter Rubens' ability to paint on a monumental scale, and of his voluptuous use of paint.

Room XLIV has examples of Rembrandt and Caravaggio, the two greatest exponents of chiaroscuro, the dramatic effect of contrasting light.

Vasari's Corridor, for which visits must be booked in advance with the secretary of the Uffizi, links the gallery to Palazzo Pitti. Exhibited along the corridor is a long series of portraits executed in various periods.

The Bargello

The Bargello was built in 1255 as the seat of the *Podestà* (governor) and then, in 1574, adapted for the captain of the *Bargello* (police) from whom it derives its name. In 1857, the cells which had been added were demolished and the building restored to its original state, to be opened 2 years later as a museum devoted mainly to sculpture.

While most museums dedicated to sculpture do little to inspire the onlooker, the quality of the exhibits in the Bargello is so high as to make it one of the world's most interesting museums. The exhibits around the central courtyard begin by whetting one's appetite.

Room I, to the right of the entrance, houses the work of Michelangelo and other sixteenth-century Florentines. To pick out individual works in this room is pointless, as all of them are exceptional. However, those who have read Cellini's autobiography may wish to dwell a little on his *Narcissus*, carved from a defective piece of marble given to him by his less talented rival Baccio Bandinelli. These sculptures represent the ultimate in the representation of the human body achieved by the Renaissance artists.

Contemporary mouldings and church sculptures are conserved in rooms II and III across the courtyard.

Artist painting the panoramic view from the Church of San Miniato →

On the first floor, the largest room, directly above the room of sixteenth-century sculpture, contains the best works of Donatello and other fifteenth-century sculptors. It was Donatello who, more than any other artist, was responsible for the development of Renaissance sculpture, reaching and even surpassing the level of the ancient Greeks. The marble *St George* (from the Church of Orsanmichele) and the bronze *David*, the first free-standing bronze of the Renaissance, dominate the room. On the wall are the bas-reliefs of the *Sacrifice of Isaac*, Brunelleschi's and Ghiberti's entries for the competition to decide who should be given the job of making the doors for the Battistero.

In the opposite corner of the first floor is the Chapel of St Maria Maddalena, where prisoners made their last confession before being executed. The remainder of the first floor and the second are devoted to interesting collections of objects in ceramics, terracotta, ivory and gold. There are also arms, and a vast number of small bronzes amongst which those by Giambologna and Verrocchio are outstanding. Cellini's bronze bust of Cosimo I is probably the finest representation of the Duke, and is certainly amongst the artist's best works.

The Pitti Palace

Begun in 1457, following a design by Brunelleschi, the palace was built by Luca Pitti, who was at first a friend of the Medici and later hoped to supplant them. The building was regularly enlarged until the beginning of the nineteenth century, luckily always remaining faithful to the original Brunelleschian concept. A royal residence until 1919, it was then given to the state by King Vittorio Emanuele III, along with other Medicean villas.

Behind the main entrance is a magnificent courtyard designed by Bartolomeo Ammanati in the second half of the sixteenth century. The rear of the courtyard is interrupted by two niches and a central grotto, 'The Grotto of Moses', which contains a central pool and a large statue of the prophet.

On the right hand side of the courtyard is the Palatine Chapel, frescoed by Luigi Ademollo, and containing many other more portable works of art.

By 1620 the number of paintings owned by the Medici had grown to be so large that Cosimo II decided to dedicate several rooms on the first floor to house the collection. As the collection grew, more and more rooms were allocated until it became the now splendid Palatine Gallery. The pictures are not laid out to strict chronological order, or even to geographical criteria, but mingle in with the decoration of each particular room according to the taste of the various Grand Dukes.

Priceless works of art by Raphael, Rubens, Titian, Van Dyck, Veronese, Bronzino and Tintoretto are mixed with works by other, lesser known, artists. Many of the paintings, particularly the portraits, are by Justus Sustermans, court painter to the Medici for over 60 years. So numerous are the great works of art in this gallery that there is little point in picking out individual paintings, although perhaps Rubens' *The Consequences of War* and Titian's *Maddalena* should be given special attention.

The ex-royal apartments, also on the first floor, are richly furnished, and contain still more fine pictures. Sustermans' portrait of Cardinal Carlo dei Medici, in the small, private chapel, is particularly interesting.

Although it is called the Silver Museum, the first few rooms of this section of the palace are reception rooms where the story of the Medicis' rise to power and of their cultured tradition are represented by enormous frescoes. The later rooms house what may be considered as the Florentine 'Crown Jewels' and also a vast collection of objects made from precious or semi-precious materials.

The Gallery of Modern Art houses a large and interesting collection from the neo-Classical period onwards. The bulk of the exhibits are by Tuscan artists. Among the sculptures, those by Canova — *Napoleon* and *Calliope* — and those by Medardo Rosso — *Laughing Girl*, *Man Who Reads* and *The Porter* — are exceptional, while the gems amongst the paintings are those by Giovanni Fattori and Camille Pissarro. Also in this collection is one of Gericault's preliminary studies for the *Raft of the Medusa*.

The Costume Museum and the Contini-Bonacossi collection are housed in the Meridiana Pavilion at the rear of the palace. The costumes consist of various items, mainly of women's clothing, dating back several centuries. The clothes are wonderfully situated in the spacious residence favoured by of King Vittorio Emanuele II during Florence's period as capital.

The Contini-Bonacossi collection consists of 144 items of great value, donated to the state in 1969. Painters represented in the collection range from Cimabue and Duccio, through Veronese to Velasquez and Goya. The most important piece of sculpture is the *Martyrdom of St Lawrence* by Bernini.

The Carriage Museum, housed in the projecting right wing of the palace, contains carriages formerly belonging to the houses of Medici, Lorraine and Savoy.

The Porcelain Museum is housed in the Casino del Cavaliere, at the top end of the Boboli Gardens. The collection mainly consists of the tableware of the various dynasties, including some very fine pieces from the Napoleonic period when his sister was Grand Duchess. Many of the services were specially made to celebrate family weddings.

At the beginning of the Boboli Gardens, in the square behind the projecting right wing of the palace, is Buontalenti's Grotto, a group of three fantasy grottoes, with fine statues by Bandinelli and Giambologna. The group of *Prisoners* by Michelangelo in the first grotto are copies of the originals, which are now in the Academy Museum.

Directly behind the house is the seventeenth-century amphitheatre, where a 3,500-year-old Egyptian obelisk can be seen. Busts and statues are placed around the edge of the theatre.

Going up the steps behind the amphitheatre, one arrives at Neptune's Pond, presided over by Stoldo Lorenzo's bronze *Neptune*. Turning to the left, there is a raised round garden house, with beautiful views of Florence and Fiesole, which now serves as a café.

Further up and to the right, near to the Porcelain Museum, is the Garden of the Cavaliere, with the Monkey's Fountain by Tacca. Leaving the garden on the other side, one descends by the statue lined *viottolone* (avenue) to the Piazzale dell' Isolotto where several fine fountains play. The Ocean Fountain by Giambologna is outstanding.

Palazzo Vecchio

The front part of the *palazzo* and the tower were begun in 1299, and sections were added on behind over the next 300 years. Part of the building is still used as Florence's administrative centre, but the four courtyards and the monumental apartments are open to the public.

At the top of Vasari's monumental staircase is the Salone del Cinquecento, which is magnificently frescoed and housed the Italian parliament from 1865-71. This room, like many others in the palace, was designed and frescoed by Cosimo I's great favourite, Vasari. Particularly notable is the *Studiolo* (small study) of Francis I. Many of the sculptures in the palace are by Cosimo's other favourite, the far less talented Bandinelli.

The Mezzanine quarters, constructed by Michelozzo and later adapted for Cosimo's mother, contain important paintings by Masolino (*Humble Virgin*), Bronzino (*Pygmalion and Galatea*), Rubens (*Judith and Holofernes*), Tintoretto (*Leda*) and Veronese (*Nymph and Satyr*), to name but a few. The clock on the tower dates from 1667, and is still in perfect working order.

In front of Palazzo Vecchio is the Loggia dei Lanzi, built in the late

Palazzo Vecchio

fourteenth century for the public ceremonies of the government. The loggia is now an open-air sculpture museum. *Rape of the Sabine Women* and *Hercules and Nessus* by Giambologna are exceptional, while Cellini's *Perseus* is one of the finest pieces of sculpture ever produced.

Ammanati's *Fountain of Neptune*, and Giambologna's equestrian monument to Cosimo I, are the most important monuments in the *piazza.* The others are Bandinelli's *Hercules and Cacus* and a copy of Michelangelo's *David.* An inscribed granite disc marks the spot where the Dominican monk Savonarola was burnt for heresy in 1498.

The Alberto Della Ragione Collection
On the opposite side of Piazza della Signoria to the Loggia dei Lanzi, this collection, donated to the city in 1970, contains some of the most important examples of Italian twentieth-century art. This gallery does not get crowded, even when the nearby Uffizi is bursting at the seams.

The Accademia
This gallery houses a collection of fine Renaissance paintings by

artists such as Ghirlandaio, Fra Filippo and Filippino Lippi and Bronzino. However, the paintings are overshadowed by the sculpture gallery, which contains many of Michelangelo's works. The unfinished *Prisoners*, designed for the tomb of Giulio II, form an avenue leading up to the *David*, his masterpiece. This work, originally sited in Piazza della Signoria, was carved out of a piece of abandoned marble, considered useless by other sculptors.

Museo dell' Opera del Duomo

Situated below the Duomo, this museum contains works of art which were originally part of the Duomo, the Battistero and the bell tower, including parts of the original façade of the Duomo, demolished in 1587.

The most important exhibits are the choir balconies by Luca della Robbia and Donatello; sixteen statues from the bell tower, of which six are by Donatello; and the panels by Giotto, also originally from the bell tower. Michelangelo's *Pietà* has also recently been transferred from the Duomo and given a room to itself.

The museum has also been designated as the new home for Ghiberti's bronze doors (*The Door of Paradise*) which are being replaced on the Battistero by copies. Also housed here are some of the original tools with which the Duomo was built.

The Bardini Museum and Corsi Gallery

The *palazzo*, which uses fragments of old churches and villas for its doors and windows, was bequeathed to Florence in 1923 by Stefano Bardini along with his vast and varied art collection. On the second floor, the Corsi Gallery consists of another collection left to the city in 1937.

Both collections contain high quality works by well-known artists, but are under-publicised and never very crowded.

The Opificio delle Pietre Dure

The former Grand Ducal workshops were world famous for their work in hard and semi-precious stones. Some restoration work is still carried out by the workshops, but the main part is now a museum exhibiting former productions.

Palazzo Davanzati: Museum of the Florentine House

Architecturally, this fourteenth-century house represents the transition between the fortified tower house and the Renaissance palace. Restored at the beginning of the century, the house has been completely redecorated in original Florentine style.

The Stibbert Museum

An Englishman with an Italian mother, Frederick Stibbert fought alongside Garibaldi and then settled in Florence. Widely travelled, he assembled a large collection of arms, furniture, clothes and antiques in general from all over the world. He left his villa and collection to the British government, who renounced the inheritance in favour of the city of Florence.

The arms collection is one of the most important in the world, while the villa's gardens are among the finest in Florence.

Florence As It Was

This museum, in the ex-convent of the Oblate Sisters, contains paintings, drawings and prints of Florence and Florentine customs of the last 500 years.

Museum of Prehistory

Situated on the other side of the convent, the two floors consist of a general teaching section and collections from primitive societies.

The Gallery of the Hospital of the Innocents

Forming one side of the Piazza Santissima Annunziata, this fine fifteenth-century Brunelleschian building was originally an orphanage. The gallery, which contains fine Renaissance paintings, is situated in the loggia above the cloister. The most important picture is Ghirlandaio's *Adoration of the Magi*.

The Horne Museum

A little known museum of great interest, very near the centre of the city. The English art historian, H.P.Horne, left his collection of paintings, drawings, sculpture and antique objects to the Italian state in 1916. Highlights of the collection are Gozzoli's *Deposition from the Cross* and Giotto's *St Stephen*.

The Medici Riccardi Palace

Built by Michelozzi between 1444 and 1460, the palace was greatly enlarged (without altering the style) after it passed to the Riccardi family in the late seventeenth century. The palace now contains government offices, but the original courtyard, and the small chapel frescoed by Gozzoli, may be visited free of charge. Gozzoli's frescoes of the *Procession of the Magi* contain portraits of the Medici and their land in the Mugello.

The History of Science Museum

Both the Medici and Lorraine Dynasties took a great interest in science and scientific instruments. Galileo, whose instruments form part of the collection, was one who benefited from their patronage.

Anthropology and Ethnology Museum
Housed in the sixteenth-century 'Unfinished' Palace, the museum contains material relating to customs all over the world. A collection of musical instruments is included.

The Botanical Institute
Around the Botanical Gardens are situated the Botanical Museum, The Museum of Palaeontology and Geology, and the Institute of Mineralogy, Lithology and Geochemistry, each of great importance in its field.

The Archaeological Museum
This museum, which contains collections of Greek, Roman and Egyptian relics, is particularly important for its Etruscan section. The most notable exhibits are the three large bronzes; *The Wounded Chimera*, *Minerva* and the *Orator*. The Egyptian section is also of great interest, being the second largest in Italy, and containing a range of mummies and sarcophagi.

The most important item in the large collection of ceramics is the celebrated François Vase, of Etruscan origin, which depicts six mythological scenes.

The Churches of Florence
Like most Italian cities, Florence is full of fine churches. When one considers that many of the sixty-nine churches are situated in the older central part of the city, where some of the more noble houses were furnished with their own private chapels, the number seems even more amazing.

Some of the churches are world famous, such as the Duomo, which is the world's fourth biggest church, after St Peter's in Rome, St Paul's in London, and the Duomo of Milan. Others, such as the Badia, are equally interesting, both historically and artistically. However, because they do not open on to a *piazza*, and are therefore almost impossible to photograph adequately, they tend to be neglected by most guidebooks and hence by tourists. While the Duomo and Santa Croce have not been neglected, churches such as the Badia, and many of the smaller churches which are also of great interest, have been given more prominence, as otherwise they may be missed.

Descriptions of the better known churches are more abbreviated, as information on them is readily available in the free hand-outs at tourist information centres, and also from the recorded information machines in the churches themselves.

Battistero di San Giovanni

The oldest building in Florence, probably built in the fourth century, then covered in marble in the twelfth, the Battistero (Baptistry) is particularly famous for its bronze doors. The southern set (now the entrance) by Andrea Pisano is the oldest, being distinctly medieval in style. The north door, by Lorenzo Ghiberti, dates from 1403-1424 and shows the new ideas of the early Renaissance.

The east door facing the Duomo is Ghiberti's masterpiece: known as the Door of Paradise, it was made between 1425 and 1452, and must be the best-known door in the world. The three doors represent the life of St John the Baptist (south); the New Testament (north); and the Old Testament (east).

Inside the Battistero, the funeral monument to the antipope John XXIII (1419) by Donatello (statue) and Michelozzi (base), is exceptional not only in artistic terms, but also because its erection almost led to a war between Florence and the Papal States. The inside of the roof is almost entirely covered by mosaics of biblical stories, the work of late thirteenth-century Venetian masters.

From 1059 and 1128, the Battistero served as Florence's cathedral, while Santa Reparata was being enlarged.

The Duomo

The Duomo, or Cathedral, of Santa Maria del Fiore, with its magnificent dome, dominates the city and is visible from several kilometres down the Arno Valley. Begun in 1296 on the site of the former Cathedral of Santa Reparata, it was not until the eighteenth century that the building was finally completed, with the addition of the mock Gothic façade.

Many famous artists and architects were involved in the construction. The most important were Arnolfo del Cambio, who began the work; Giotto, who was responsible for the bell tower (1334); and Brunelleschi, whose dome, finished in 1434, had been considered by many to be impossible to build.

Outside, the structure is covered with three colours of marble and complements the Battistero. The inside, having had many of the most precious works of art moved to the Museo dell' Opera del Duomo, is something of a disappointment by contrast. However, the altar by Benedetto da Maiano, the statues in the niches around the altar, and the 'New Sacristry' with its beautiful fifteenth-century woodwork, are all masterpieces.

It is possible to go up the bell tower, and to the top of the dome (the highest point of the city), while the remains of the Crypt of Santa Reparata may also be visited.

Santa Croce

Santa Croce is by far the most interesting church in Florence, and really deserves a guide book to itself. However, the following brief summary should help the visitor avoid the confusion encountered by E.M. Forster's Lucy in *A Room With A View*. Apart from the nineteenth-century marble façade, a gift from the Englishman Sir Francis Sloane, the outside is bare of decoration, but still majestic.

Inside, the church is richly decorated with numerous funeral monuments by Canova and Vasari among others, and many private chapels, including one belonging to the Bonaparte family. Two of the chapels near the altar are decorated by Giotto.

Having passed through the Sacristy on the right at the rear, one arrives at the Santa Croce leather school, where very high quality leather goods can be bought at fairly reasonable prices. Outside, to the right of the façade, is the entrance to the rest of the complex, which consists of two fine cloisters, the Pazzi Chapel, and the Santa Croce Museum. The first cloister has been freed of a mass of eighteenth-century tombstones, and is now splendid in its original thirteenth-century appearance.

At the end of this cloister is the famous Pazzi Chapel, designed and begun by Brunelleschi in 1443; it is one of the finest examples of Renaissance chapel architecture. The inside is decorated with Della Robbian earthenware, coloured marble, and a series of frescoes representing the signs of the zodiac.

To the right is the museum, containing many fine paintings and sculptures by Cimabue, Donatello, and Bronzino among others. The outstanding exhibit is Donatello's bronze St Ludovico, one of his first Renaissance works (1423).

The second, or large cloister is another of Brunelleschi's masterpieces of early Renaissance architecture.

Santa Maria Novella

This was begun in 1246 on the site of an earlier tenth-century church. Its fine oval *piazza* (designed in 1563, to host chariot races) was the home of the papal court for several years. The Council of Florence took place here in the fifteenth century to establish unity between the Roman and Greek churches.

The church, which is entered through the magnificent doorway by Leone Battista Alberti, contains many chapels dedicated to the leading families of Renaissance Florence, who employed the best available artists to decorate them.

On the right-hand side of the transept, the Rucellai Chapel contains a marble statue by Nino Pisano and a bronze by Ghiberti. The Chapel of Filippo Strozzi, immediately to the right of the altar, is frescoed by Filippino Lippi, while the tomb of its patron is by Benedetto da Maiano.

The Altar Chapel was frescoed by Ghirlandaio for the Tornabuoni family, of whom many of the figures are portraits. To the left, the Gondi Chapel contains Brunelleschi's only known wooden sculpture, sculpted to prove to Donatello that idealisation was as effective as a more realistic depiction of suffering.

In the third chapel on the left-hand side is Masaccio's *Trinity, Mary, and St John*, while the crucifix on the entrance wall is one of Giotto's earliest works.

Outside the main entrance, a side entrance leads to the monastery and the cloisters. The smaller 'green' cloister was formerly decorated with frescoes by Paolo Uccello depicting *The Great Flood* and *The Sacrifice of Noah*, which have been detached and are now exhibited in the refectory, on the other side of which is the 'large' cloister.

On the first floor of the old monastery (now a police training school) is the Pope's Chapel, frescoed by Pontormo in 1515.

San Lorenzo and The Medici Chapels
Surrounded by the tourist market, San Lorenzo and its *piazza* form one of the most picturesque sights in Florence. A church has existed on the site since AD393. The actual construction dates from 1420, when the Medici, whose local church it was, increased their patronage. Designed by Brunelleschi, the inside of the façade was added later by Michelangelo, who was also responsible for the unfinished outer façade.

The two bronze pulpits are the last works of Donatello (1460) while the *Annunciation with two Angels* by the altar is one of Filippo Lippi's best works. The Old Sacristy to the left of the altar is a fine example of the combined talents of Donatello and Brunelleschi. The tomb of Piero and Giovanni de' Medici is by Verrocchio. Above the fine cloister is an open loggia offering interesting views as well as access to the Laurentian Library, where the Medici collection of antique manuscripts is housed.

The Medici Chapels represent the most impressive mausoleum since Classical Rome. The ground floor contains the tombstones of the Medici, while above, the domed Chapel of the Princes recalls the Pantheon in Rome, with its monuments to each of the Medici Grand Dukes. The New Sacristy was designed by Michelangelo for the Medici Popes Leo X (1513-21) and his cousin Clement VII (1523-34). It is outstanding for the monuments to Lorenzo and Giuliano de' Medici (nephew and brother to Leo X) which are decorated with Michelangelo's *Dawn and Dusk* and *Day and Night*.

The ceiling of the Battistero di San Giovanni

The doors of the Battistero are a major attraction

A close-up of one of the Battistero's door panels reveals a wealth of carving

Intricately carved door panel, the Duomo

Orsanmichele

This was originally built as an open loggia for the sale of grain in 1337, on the site of an eighth-century church. In 1380 the arches were filled in, and the building became a church again. Two more stories were added to store grain in case of emergencies. In place of the archways, each of the Florentine guilds commissioned statues of their patron saints. St Mark, St Peter and St George are by Donatello, St Matthew and the Baptist by Ghiberti.

The interior of the church is interesting for its unusual architecture, which is due to its original function as a market. The major work of art is the magnificent marble tabernacle by Andrea Orcagna. The upper storeys are occasionally used to house exhibitions.

San Carlo

Facing the entrance to the Orsanmichele, this fourteenth-century church is unusual in Florence for its simplicity, although it does contain some excellent works of art, such as Rosselli's *Glory of St Carlo Borromeo*.

The Church and Monastery of San Marco

The complex was built in 1299, and later enlarged for Cosimo il Vecchio de' Medici, by Michelozzi. Inside, the church is richly decorated with excellent if not famous paintings. It is remarkable that the older ones have survived, as the prior of San Marco in the 1490s was Savonarola, the Dominican monk who incited the Florentines to throw out the Medici and burn many books and works of art in Piazza della Signoria.

The major part of the monastery, which is built around two fine Michelozzian cloisters, is a museum of the paintings of Fra Angelico who resided there. Almost one hundred of his best works have been collected together there.

Santissima Annunziata

Like many other important Florentine buildings, this church was rebuilt by Michelozzo in the fifteenth century. In front of the church, but behind the porticoed façade, is the Cloister of Vows, frescoed by several artists, the most outstanding being Andrea del Sarto. Inside the church, the most noteworthy of the works of art are Bandinelli's marble *Pietà* and the frescoes by Andrea del Castagno of *The Holy Trinity* and *The Saviour and St Julian*, which are in the first and second chapels on the left. To the left of the church is the large Cloister of the Dead where another fine fresco by del Sarto is to be found, *The Virgin of the Sack*.

St Michael Visdomini
Situated on the corner of Via dei Servi and Via Bufalini, this church contains a *Sacred Family and Saints* by Pontormo.

Santo Spirito (Holy Spirit)
The bare yellow façade hides one of Brunelleschi's purest Renaissance creations, begun in 1444. The bell tower was added in 1490. It has a marvellous sense of harmony and sobriety; forty decorated side chapels give the church the look of a museum. The paintings date mainly from the sixteenth and seventeenth centuries. The sacristy and the cloister are entered from the left-hand side of the nave.

The refectory (entered separately to the left of the church) contains fourteenth-century frescoes of the *Cruxifixion* and the *Last Supper* by Andrea Orcagna.

Santa Maria del Carmine
Begun in 1268, much of the interior was destroyed by fire in 1771. The Brancacci Chapel at the end of the right-hand arm of the transept was spared, with its scenes from the life of St Peter, and depiction of the original sin; frescoes begun in 1425 by Masaccio and Masolino and completed 50 years later by Filippino Lippi. The frescoes represent the highest achievement of early Renaissance painting and are notable for the early use of perspective and chiaroscuro. *The Expulsion from Paradise* and *The Tribute Money* are the most important.

The Badia
Built in 978 and enlarged in 1282, the addition of surrounding buildings in 1627 made the church virtually unrecognisable from the outside. A door opposite the Bargello leads to a small courtyard, and the church is entered from there. The courtyard is the best place from which to view the superb hexagonal bell tower.

Inside, to the left of the entrance, is the *Appearance of Mary to St Bernard*, one of the finest works of Filippino Lippi. In the left-hand arm of the church are fragments of the original late thirteenth-century frescoes. A door from the sacristy leads to the fifteenth-century Cloister of the Oranges.

Santa Maria Maddalena dei Pazzi
The archway of No 58 Borgo Pinti gives onto a fine courtyard, beyond which is Sangallo's late fifteenth-century church of St Mary Magdalen. Originally the setting for Botticelli's *Annunciation* (now in the Uffizi), the church is now notable for its architecture and, above all, for Il Perugino's frescoes of the Crucifixion which may be visited in the crypt.

Santa Maria dei Ricci

This sombre, Baroque church is notable mainly for the vandalised wooden crucifix, which took on an agonised expression in front of the cameras after being damaged. The photographs are exhibited with the crucifix on the left of the nave.

San Filippo Neri

The left wing of the building known as San Firenze which houses the law courts, this church is the finest example of seventeenth-century religious architecture in Florence. The marble bas-reliefs tell the story of the church's patron saint.

San Frediano

Another example of seventeenth-century Baroque architecture, decorated by the best Florentine artists of the period. The church across the river stands out for its graceful dome.

Ognissanti (All Saints)

Built in 1256 and reconstructed in 1627, this was the church of the Vespucci. A portrait of Amerigo Vespucci is believed to be included in the fresco of the *Merciful Madonna* by Domenico and Davide Ghirlandaio, in the second altar on the right. When Vespucci landed in America he named the bay where he landed Baia Todos Santos (All Saints Bay in Spanish).

The greatest assets of the church are Ghirlandaio's *Last Supper* and *Study of St Gerolamo* and Botticelli's *Study of St Augustine* which are situated in the old refectory, behind the cloister.

Santa Trinità (Church of the Holy Trinity)

This church was built in the eleventh century, and enlarged in the Gothic style in the fourteenth. The fourth chapel on the right is frescoed by Lorenzo Monaco, but by far the most outstanding works in the church are the frescoes of the Sassetti Chapel (at the front on the right) by Ghirlandaio. These frescoes are full of portraits of contemporary Florentines, although officially they tell the story of St Francis of Assisi. The beautiful altarpiece *The Adoration of the Shepherds* is also by Ghirlandaio.

San Miniato al Monte

Near the panoramic Piazzale Michelangelo, this ancient church, which was rebuilt in the eleventh century, dominates the city. The inside of the church is stupendous, being almost entirely constructed of coloured marble. Fragments of frescoes by Paolo Uccello and Andrea del Castagno can be seen in the cloister.

A copy of Michelangelo's David and other statues in the Piazza della Signora

A statue of Neptune in the Boboli Gardens

The *Last Supper (Il Cenacolo)* of San Salvi

Andrea del Sarto's *Last Supper* can be seen in the refectory of a former convent at 16 Via San Salvi.

The *Last Supper* of San Apollonio

Andrea del Castagno's *Last Supper* can be seen at 1 Via XXVII Aprile in the former refectory of the nuns of St Apollonio.

The *Last Supper* of the Conservatory of Foligno

Painted by il Perugino, this *Last Supper* is to be found in Via Faenza 42.

The Cloister of the Scalzo

This 1376 cloister at 42 Via Cavour is decorated with sixteen frescoes by Andrea del Sarto.

A relaxing alternative to the cultural pilgrimage around the churches and museums is a slow walk around the old centre. The narrow streets often open out into fine squares with great potential for interesting and unusual photographs.

The most popular Florentine view of all is that from Piazzale Michelangelo. It overlooks the city from near the Church of San Miniato. This large square, which has a copy of Michelangelo's *David* in the centre, is well-provided with bars and stalls selling every kind of souvenir. To get to the square, most people take a No 13 bus, but it is reached just as quickly on foot by the steps leading up to the church. At the bottom of these steps a little lane (Via di Belvedere) follows the old city wall up the adjacent hill to the Fort of Belvedere, which is often the site of both indoor and outdoor exhibitions.

It is possible to enter the top end of the **Boboli Gardens** from the fort, and a relaxing afternoon can be spent here either sunbathing on the grass by the fountains or sitting in the shade under the trees. Leaving the gardens by the Palazzo Pitti exit, the visitor will pass over the Ponte Vecchio (Old Bridge) while returning to the centre. This bridge, lined on both sides by small shops, was built in the fourteenth century. Apart from the addition of Vasari's Corridor linking The Uffizi with Palazzo Pitti in the sixteenth century, it has changed little since then. The shops were originally butchers' until Grand Duke Ferdinando I decreed that only goldsmiths be allowed to work there: they are still all run by goldsmiths and silversmiths, although a profusion of street vendors and buskers often provides variety.

Eating in Florence

The Italians have a reputation for eating well, and the many restaurants and snack-bars in tourist cities such as Florence make the most of this.

For devotees of fast food there are now several burger bars in Florence; try the one just over the river by the Ponte Vecchio, the one at the junction of Via Cavour and Via Guelfa, or the one opposite the station.

Most of the snack bars in the centre offer a selection of inviting rolls (*panini*) and slices of pizza. As a rule, those between the station and the Duomo are the best value; those on Via de'Calzaiuoli (linking the Duomo to Piazza della Signoria) tend to be expensive. Best value of all are the two little bars under the arch at the junction of Borgo degli Albizzi and Via dei Palmieri which sell made to order hot and cold sandwiches. Hot tripe sandwiches are sold on stalls near the central market and in Piazza dei Cimatori: these are a local speciality and any prejudices you may have against tripe should be firmly set on one side.

Pizzas are a Southern Italian speciality and none of the Florentine pizzerias comes up to the standard of those in the South. They are, however, far better than those available outside Italy. Several pizzerias are located in Borgo San Lorenzo, the best of which is Nuti, not only for quality, but also for price. For the visitor on a tight budget, the best-value pizzas are those of the Pizzeria-Spaghetteria La Porta Gialla at the end of Via Sant Egidio. More upmarket pizzerias which can be recommended are La Bussola in Via Porta Rossa, and da Pepe at Ponte al Pino near Campo di Marte station.

There are well over a hundred restaurants in Florence covering the whole of the price range. Only general advice and a few recommendations can be offered here. Look at several price lists before choosing your restaurant, as similar dishes may be offered in similar places for greatly differing prices. Remember to take the cover charge (*coperto e pane*) and the service charge into account. It is also important to remember that any vegetables, salad or potatoes must be ordered separately, because they are classed as extras.

Local specialities are tripe (*trippa alla fiorentina*) and charcoal-grilled T-bone steaks (*bistecca alla fiorentina*). The price shown on the menu for the *bistecca* is per 100g ($3^1/_2$ oz) uncooked weight, so the actual price will be seven or eight times that on the menu. Unless you are a connoisseur it is usually best to order the house wine, particularly when the menu says *vino sfuso* as this usually means they bring you a very large bottle and then charge you for the amount you drink.

The Enoteca on Via Ghibellini is reputedly one of Italy's best restaurants; it is certainly one of the most expensive.

The Osteria da Quinto in the Volta de' Peruzzi is a good restaurant; fairly expensive but excellent value. Traditional live music is always provided, and Quinto himself, who used to be an opera singer, is apt to burst into song without warning.

I Paoli in Via dei Tavolini is an excellent restaurant with fourteenth-century decoration. This is one of the few top class restaurants to offer a set menu at a reduced price.

Of the many cheap restaurants, the most highly recommended are the Trattoria da Carlo in Via delle Stinche and La Maremmana in Via dei Macci. These offer plentiful helpings of good food at reasonable prices, as do most of the little restaurants in the back streets south of the river.

For visitors with their own cooking facilities, the Central Market is by far the most economical place to shop in Florence itself. In the outskirts, large new supermarkets have been opened by the Co-op, Esse-lunga, and Super Al which are much cheaper than other shops.

One gastronomic delight at which the Florentines really excel is making ice-cream. The city is full of *gelaterias*, the best of which are Vivoli in Via delle Stinche, whose claim to make the finest ice-cream in the world is seldom disputed, and Gailli near the Ponte Vecchio. Best value are the tubs, for which one may select several different flavours.

Shopping

Italian clothes enjoy a high reputation, but the visitor to Florence will be surprised to find that even in large stores such as Standa and Upim the price of most items is prohibitively expensive.

Shoes tend to be more economical than clothes as leather is a local speciality. However, beware of bargain-price men's shoes, as they tend not to last too long.

The city, particularly the area between Piazza San Firenze and Santa Croce, has many leather goods shops which sell wares, ranging from full length coats to lipstick holders. The quality in these shops, which usually have their own workshops on the premises, is generally excellent. On average, there is not much difference between prices in the various shops, although perhaps the best value is to be found at CAD on Via dell'Anguillara.

Gold and silver are also good value in Florence, particularly in Cellini's, The Gold Market, and The Gold Corner, around Piazza Santa Croce. All the gold sold is eighteen carat, and the jewellery is generally priced by weight.

Ornate chess sets on fine leather or marble bases are some of the reasonably priced specialities of Florence. The best place to buy one is on the street stalls where appearing to loose interest on hearing the price can often lead to considerable reductions.

Most credit cards are widely accepted in Florence. Showing your credit card when making a purchase and then asking if there is any reduction for cash can often save you about ten per cent on the marked price.

Florentine Festivals

Almost every Italian town has at least one traditional festival on a religious or folkloristic theme. Some of these celebrate patron saints, while others recall the historic subdivisions of each town.

Florence itself has a number of these festivals, the most important of which is the Calcio Storico (historic football). These games, which are played in traditional costume, take place in June; the first on one of the first Sundays, then on 24 and 28 June, in one of the city's principal squares. The Calcio Storico was banned for a while in the late 1970s after one of the players' ears was bitten off by an oponent. A procession of over 500 men in medieval costumes precedes and follows each of the games, each man is dressed in the colourful livery of his zone of the city.

The most important religious ceremony takes place on Easter Sunday. A burning model pigeon slides down a wire from the altar of the Duomo to a chariot covered in fireworks, which is placed between the Duomo and the Battistero. The ceremony dates from the first crusade, when Pazzino de'Pazzi was chosen to relight the sacred flame. Tradition says that if the pigeon negotiates the wire without assistance, the year to come will be prosperous for the Florentines.

On Ascension Day the Florentines celebrate the Festival of Crickets in the Cascine Park. Traditionally damaging to agriculture, the crickets were formerly hunted and then taken home in cages. Nowadays the festival consists of a carriage race through the park.

The patron saint of Florence is St John. On St John's Day (24 June) a large firework display is set off from Piazzale Michelangelo, creating fantastic reflections on the Arno.

Musical May, which actually lasts until the end of June, consists of musical performances in various public places throughout the city.

The Suburbs of Florence

The Florentine suburbs consist mainly of uninteresting modern buildings, but fine Medicean villas can still be found in some of them. These were originally country retreats or hunting lodges.

Careggi is best-known for the large hospital there. Originally,

Careggi was the country estate of the Lippi family, until it was bought by the Medici in 1417. In 1457 the villa was enlarged by Michelozzi for Cosimo 'il Vecchio' and hosted Lorenzo the Magnificent's Platonic Academy. Many of the art treasures were destroyed by fire after the expulsion of the Medici in 1494. The villa is now a nurses' hall of residence but may be visited with the permission of the hospital.

Not far from Careggi is the somewhat more pleasant suburb of **Castello**, where three Medicean villas are to be found. Villa la Quiete, given to the *condottiero* Niccolo da Tolentino in 1438, later became a Medici hunting lodge. Now a convent and a church-run primary school, the villa houses many fine paintings including several by Ridolfo Ghirlandaio.

One kilometre ($^1/_2$ mile) away is the Villa of Petraia. Originally the medieval castle of the Brunelleschi, it was transformed into a villa by Buontalenti in the seventeenth century. It is one of the best of the Medici villas, and was favoured by King Vittorio Emanuele II. It has beautiful gardens and is decorated with paintings relating episodes from the history of the Medici.

The fourteenth-century Villa of Castello, bought by the Medici in 1480, was originally decorated by Pontormo, but his frescoes were lost when the villa was set on fire in 1494. The villa was restored by Vasari for Cosimo I, and for a long time housed some of the Medicis' most precious works of art.

Sesto Fiorentino, just outside Florence, developed as a centre for porcelain and ceramics. The Ginori family began production in 1737, and in 1965 a Porcelain Museum was set up to house the Ginori collection.

Poggio Imperiale, less than 2km (1 mile) outside Porta Romana, is now a school. The villa was gradually developed from a medieval castle. It passed through various hands before taking its name from Cosimo II's widow, a member of the Austrian imperial family. From then on the villa was a favourite residence of the Medici princesses. Free classical concerts are given on Sunday mornings between October and April.

Galluzzo, to the south of Florence, has grown up around the magnificent Certosa (Monastery). The Certosa, begun in 1341, is outstanding not only for the works of art it contains but also for its architecture. The monks' cells give it an unusual profile. Inside the monastery are a church, some chapels, an art gallery and several cloisters. The underground Capella di Sant' Andrea, which contains monuments to the Accaiuoli family, is exceptional. The gallery contains fine Renaissance works; five frescoes by Pontormo are outstanding.

2

THE PROVINCE OF FLORENCE

Overlooking Florence and the Arno in one direction and the Valley of the Mugnone in the other, the town of **Fiesole** is Florence's nearest and most attractive neighbour. The site, chosen by the Etruscans in the seventh century BC with defence uppermost in mind has, more recently, protected the town from a much greater peril than originally envisaged. While other towns such as Bagno a Ripoli and Peretola have been entirely swallowed up by Florence's suburban sprawl, the steep hill separating the city from Fiesole makes building so difficult that a handful of magnificent villas are all that have been constructed.

Fiesole was subdued by the Romans in 90BC and then colonised by them 10 years later. From then on it was to follow the usual history of towns in the area, passing through the hands of the Goths and the Longobards before finally becoming a fairly important free *comune* in the early middle ages. Its close proximity to Florence meant that there was great rivalry between the two towns, and by 1125 the newer town's greater potential for expansion had tipped the balance of power far enough in its favour to allow the complete subjection of Fiesole. Since then Fiesole has only entered the history books as the birthplace of several fine artists and sculptors, and as host to a great many others.

Whether going to Fiesole by car or taking the No 7 bus from Piazza San Marco, the visitor would be well-advised to stop for a while in the little village of **San Domenico**. This has a splendid view and two very interesting churches which should be visited. The first of these, on the main road, is the Church of San Domenico, built in the early fifteenth century, and enlarged in the seventeenth. Some of the more important works of art have been removed and can now only be seen in the Prado (Madrid) and in the Louvre (Paris). However, several important works, by Lorenzo di Credi and Fra Angelico (who took orders in the neighbouring monastery) still remain to make it well-worth visiting. Down the side road to the left is the Badia Fiesolana, which until destruction in 1026 was the cathedral of Fiesole. Although it was previously rebuilt, Cosimo il Vecchio provided new impetus in 1456 and is responsible for the magnificent Brunelleschian structure of the church as it is now. Most of the paintings are by Francesco Ferrucci and Francesco di Simone Ferrucci, two of the more important Fiesolan artists of the period.

Another $2^1/_2$ km ($1^1/_2$ miles) brings you to Fiesole itself and immediately into the central square, formerly the site of the Roman Forum. The bottom (east) end of the square consists of a seventeenth-century seminary and the eleventh-century Bishop's Palace, the façade of which is more modern, dating from 1675. On the north side of the square is the Duomo, built between 1024 and 1028 and then added to in 1213. Apart from a bust by Mino da Fiesole in the Salutati Chapel, the works of art are by lesser known, though still excellent artists, amongst whom various members of the Ferrucci family figure prominently. Pleasant bars and pizzerias (where it is possible to eat outside until about 1am) complete the north side.

The top end of the square is composed of the fourteenth-century Palazzo Pretorio, decorated with the coats of arms of many of its former incumbents, and the Church of Santa Maria Primerana. The latter was built in the sixteenth century and contains a self-portrait of Francesco da San Gallo, in marble bas-relief. The bronze equestrian statue in front of the Palazzo Pretorio represents the meeting of Garibaldi and Vittorio Emanuele and dates from 1906.

Five roads lead out of the *piazza*; one is the road to Florence, and the other four all deserve to be explored on foot before leaving the town. The first of these rises sharply between the Bishop's Palace and the seminary, and is the most spectacular. After a short distance the visitor will reach a terrace on the left with extensive views over Florence and far down the Arno Valley. A little further on, in a small square where the road turns to the right, there is the little Church of Sant' Alessandro. This church was built by the Romans on the site of an Etruscan temple, and since then it has been modified at regular intervals throughout the centuries. The key is available from the sacristan of the cathedral.

Overlooking this church, 45m (50yd) higher up at the end of the road, is the Church of San Francesco; built in 1330 and enlarged in 1407. This was largely restored at the beginning of this century. The

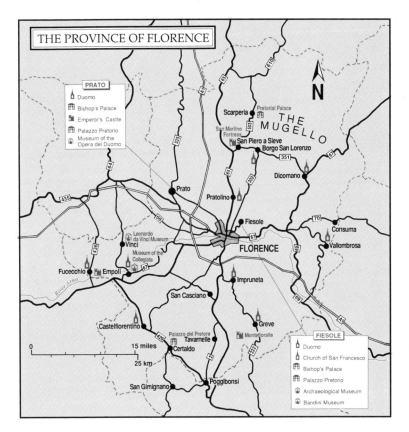

site occupied by the church is the most imposing in the area; it was originally the site of the Etruscan Acropolis, then that of the Romans, and finally of the medieval fortress, until this was dismantled by the Florentines in 1125. From the interior of the church it is possible to pass into the Sacristry Cloister and from there into the Ethnological Museum which contains interesting collections of Chinese, Etruscan and Egyptian objects. Outside the church door is the entry to the Cloister of San Bernardino, above which one can visit the cell of the saint, who was abbot here for 4 years. Beyond the Cloister of St Bernardino is the fifteenth-century Choir Cloister and the seventeenth-century Cloister Grande.

After visiting the Church of San Francesco, instead of descending by the road, take the path through the Public Gardens which rejoins the road just above the *piazza*. The next exit from the *piazza* leads to the Archaeological Museum and archaeological area which have a combined entrance. The Roman theatre was excavated in 1873 and is occasionally the site of open-air classical representations. To the left of the theatre is the Roman temple, built on the remains of its Etruscan predecessor, while to the right are the remains of the Roman baths. The museum contains all the objects found on the site, and is one of the best laid-out in Central Italy.

Opposite the entrance of the archaeological complex, in Via Dupre 1, is the Bandini Museum which houses interesting thirteenth- and fourteenth-century Florentine panel paintings, and a collection of Byzantine ivory objects, among other interesting articles.

If you follow the main road out of the north-eastern corner of the square, you will come to an excellent pizzeria (La Terazza). About 90m (100yd) further on there is a left turn, down which there are several Etruscan chamber tombs.

Another pleasant walk is to take the road from the south-east corner of the square, which is signposted as a panoramic walk. The route is circular, takes about 20 minutes, and brings you back into the square.

For those who have visited Fiesole by bus, a pleasant alternative route back is to walk down the steep Via Vecchia Fiesolana and then take the bus from San Domenico. Some of the most impressive of Fiesole's villas are along this quiet lane, and at one point there is a small panoramic terrace where one can rest on the bench placed there for Queen Victoria's use.

Archaeological evidence has shown that **Prato** — 'Tuscany's Manchester' — was originally a late Etruscan settlement. The origins of the present city date back to the late eighth century. Built up around the Duomo, it is only recently that the city has spilled outside its original thirteenth-century hexagonal walls.

Famous as a textile centre, the city is neglected by tourists, rather unfairly, as a day in Prato is surprisingly pleasant. The new blends in unexpectedly well with the old here, and life seems much less hurried than in nearby Florence.

The principal attraction is the Duomo. Like many Tuscan churches, little remains of the original tenth-century structure, but a series of excellent additions make it worth a visit. The most important of these is the thirteenth-century exterior pulpit by Donatello and Michelozzi, one of the finest examples of this kind of structure.

Inside the Duomo, the general impression is one of lofty severity, although the choir behind the altar is frescoed by Filippo Lippi. Among the frescoes, *Herod's Banquet*, which is modelled on a typical, boisterous Renaissance feast, is of great interest for the insight it gives into how the wealthy lived.

Next to the church, one of the sides of the original twelfth-century

Cloister can still be seen. The adjoining Bishop's Palace and the Museum of the Opera del Duomo should also be visited.

Frederick II's Emperor's Castle was built in the 1230s and is unique in Central and Northern Italy. The interior was left unfinished after Frederick's death and is now often a venue for plays and concerts.

The Communal Gallery is housed in the picturesque thirteenth-century Palazzo Pretorio, built in the manner of the contemporary tower houses. The *palazzo* was the centre of government until the city was sold to the Florentines in 1351 by its theoretical ruler Queen Giovanna of Naples. The gallery holds one of the more important of Tuscany's minor collections and includes several works by Filippo Lippi, who lived in Prato for many years.

The Mugello

This is essentially an excursion for the motorist, although a less demanding itinerary could be followed by bus.

Leave Florence on the SS65 Via Bolognese; excellent views of Fiesole and the Mungone Valley can be had soon after leaving Florence. Thirteen kilometres (8 miles) further on, at the top of a steep hill, is the village of **Pratolino**. Next to this village is the park of the former Medicean villa of Pratolino, built in 1569 and demolished in 1820 as an economy measure. Although the marvellous villa has been lost, the park, with its grottoes and sculptures by Giambologna (*Mungone* and *The Apennine*), gives some idea of the former nature of the site.

From Pratolino take the road to the right signposted Bivigliano and then follow the signs for the Convento di Monte Senario. The monastery is at a height of 808m (2,649ft) and is reached up a steep, fir-lined avenue. It was established in 1241 by several holy men who founded the Order of the Servants of Mary. The order now has monasteries in several countries but the headquarters has always remained at Monte Senario. The monastery contains some fine paintings and has outstanding views over both the Mugello and Arno Valleys. Several grottoes which served as shelters for the first monks may be seen in the mountainside just below. The monastery was rebuilt in the sixteenth century under the patronage of the Medici.

Come down the mountainside through the modern village of **Bivigliano**, where many Florentines have second houses which allow them to escape the heat of the city during the hot summer months. After passing the large campsite, the road rejoins the main Florence-Bologna road at Vaglia. Turn right towards Bologna and continue for 7km (4 miles) until the right hand turn for **San Piero a Sieve.**

Leave the car in San Piero a Sieve and, after looking at Luca della Robbia's font in the parish church, walk for about 2km (1 mile) to the Medicean fortress of San Martino, which dominates the town. You can drive up to the fortress, but the attractive scenery, and a consideration for the car suspension, make walking the best alternative.

The fortress, which was constructed as an irregular pentagon, was built in 1569 by Lanci and Buontalenti for Cosimo I to defend the Florentine state from invasion from the north. The formidable bulwark was considered expendable by Leopold I in the late eighteenth century, and the military installations were turned into farmhouses. It is only possible to visit a small part of the fortress, but the beauty of the surroundings makes up for any disappointment. The Medicean Villa of Cafaggiolo can be clearly seen in the valley below.

From San Piero a Sieve take the SS503 to **Scarperia**, where the Pretorial Palace, built in 1306, is one of the finest examples of early thirteenth-century Tuscan civil architecture. Both the main churches, the Oratorio della Madonna di Piazza and the Oratorio della Madonna dei Terremoti, contain important works of art; in particular, the second church contains a fresco by Filippo Lippi. Just outside Scarperia is the Mugello International Autodrome, an ultra-modern circuit which hosts the Italian leg of the World Formula 2 Championship.

Leave Scarperia by the same road on which you entered, then turn right just before re-entering San Piero a Sieve to head for the Convento di Bosco ai Frati. Restructured around 1440 by Michelozzo for Cosimo il Vecchio, the church is a charming example of early Renaissance simplicity combined with a basically medieval structure. A fine crucifix by Donatello is the most important work of art in the church, but for some, the most impressive is the terracotta bas-relief in the Refectory; it is of the Last Supper and was sculpted by Father Rossi in 1934.

Keep on the same road, and follow the signs to the SS65. Turn left towards Florence until the magnificent Medicean Villa of Cafaggiolo is reached, on the right. This fortified villa was constructed by Michelozzo in 1451, together with a moat and a castellated tower. Bought by the Prince Borghese in the second half of the last century, the moat was filled in and the tower pulled down. The villa is now closed and has an air of melancholy.

Two kilometres (1 mile) further on, as the road climbs a hill, is a small sign to the right for Il Trebbio, pointing up what seems to be a

*Medicean Villa of
Cafoggiolo, the
Mugello*

*Fresco in the
Convento di Monte
Senario, the
Mugello*

cart track. Follow this to the top where you will find another Medicean villa, constructed about 10 years before Cafaggiolo. **Il Trebbio**, like its neighbour, was designed by Michelozzo and still has the air of an impregnable fortress, although it is lived-in and beautifully kept. Visits to the gardens can be arranged on certain days of the month by the Ente Provinciale per il Turismo in Florence. For those who like walking, leave the car at Il Trebbio and follow the track to the right for 2km (1 mile) until the eleventh-century Church of San Giovanni in Petroio is reached.

Back on the main road, driving another 1km ($^1/_2$ mile) towards Florence brings the visitor to the San Piero a Sieve turn-off again. Take the turning and, immediately after, take the right hand turn towards Borgo San Lorenzo.

Borgo San Lorenzo is the main town in the Mugello, a busy market town with some light industry. Scattered amongst the mainly unremarkable buildings are a few which are exceptional. One such is the magnificent Romanesque Church of San Lorenzo which dates from the thirteenth century. The three-naved church is probably the finest of its kind in Tuscany but one of the least visited even though it would grace many a cathedral city.

The next town along the valley is **Vicchio**, a very pleasant town to use as a base for walking in the surrounding hills on the well-marked footpaths. The area was the birthplace of both Giotto di Bondone and the Beato Angelico. The house where Giotto was born can be visited on Thursday, Saturday and Sunday afternoons in the nearby hamlet of Vespignano. A number of small restaurants in the area provide excellent food at prices much lower than those to be found in better-known tourist centres. However, beware of small restaurants which do not have written menus as they tend to charge higher prices to tourists.

Further down the valley is the small town of **Dicomano**. Take a few minutes to look at the thirteenth-century Church of Santa Maria which, amongst other works of art, contains a Madonna del Carmine attributed to Giorgio Vasari.

Typical of the Mugello are the many little hillside villages where simple, old churches are surrounded by a few cottages. One of these which is easily accessible is **Cistio**. It faces Vicchio from the hill on the other side of the valley. After the turning to Cistio the next sideroad off the Vicchio-Sagginale road leads to the lonely Church of Barbiana, parish church to a number of farms in the hills. In the 1950s and 60s, however, this church became the centre of a movement which brought together the church and the working classes against the establishment. Father Milani, a young priest from a converted Jewish family, was posted to the isolated church by the Bishop of Florence as a result of his having sided with the working class reform movements in the poorer suburbs of Florence. Far from marginalising Don Milani, the move made him a centre of attention. Many of his former parishioners, together with the intelligentsia of the city, travelled to Barbiana to hear him preach and he set about giving the children of the isolated farmers an education that the Italian education system of the time denied them.

Don Milani and his helpers built a swimming pool at Barbiana to teach the youngsters to swim, arranged for them to travel in Europe and North Africa, and for conferences to be given at Barbiana by like-minded persons from all over Italy and Europe. The community has declined since Don Milani's death and the church is only opened for a visiting preacher to address the occasional local farmer. However, the empty swimming pool near the church is a reminder of the rebel priest.

An Excursion West of Florence

The Florentine Province stretches out westwards for almost 50km (30 miles), encompassing some important historical sites.

Follow the signs for Siena in order to leave Florence, then turn right in Galluzzo for Castelfiorentino. The road is hilly with spectacular views and one can catch glimpses of medieval churches and fortified villas. Of particular note is the Castle of Montegufoni between Cerbaia and Montespertoli, which dates from the thirteenth century.

Castelfiorentino, a lively agricultural centre, is on two sites; a modern centre and a small medieval hilltown. The Baroque Church of Santa Verdiana was entirely rebuilt around 1700, but from the nave one may descend to the cell where the saint (1178-1242) was walled in with two snakes for 34 years. The adjoining vicarage contains a small art gallery containing interesting works by the workshops and followers of leading Renaissance artists. From Castelfiorentino, take the main road (the SS429) north to Sant'Andrea, then turn right along the minor road to Empoli.

Empoli developed in the twelfth century around the Church of Sant' Andrea, and almost immediately pledged loyalty to Florence. It was here, in 1260, that Farinata degli Uberti's speech to the Ghibelline Parliament saved Florence from being destroyed after the Battle of Montaperti.

Sant' Andrea, now known as the Collegiata, was rebuilt in its original Romanesque style after suffering severe damage in World War II. To the right of the church is the Museum of the Collegiata, with six rooms, two formed by the Baptistry. Among several fine works are Filippo Lippi's *Madonna and Child with Angels and Saints* and Mino da Fiesole's *Virgin and Child* marble bas-relief. While you are in Empoli, the fourteenth-century Church of St Stefano is also worth a visit.

From Empoli take the road to **Fucecchio**. Fucecchio is typical of many Tuscan towns; its nucleus is a pleasant, medieval hilltown, surrounded by a modern town. The old town was independent until 1330, when a pact was made with Florence. In the old town is the spacious tenth-century Church of St John the Baptist. The square to the left of the church offers a fine view of the lower Arno Valley. Other places to visit include a small museum, Castruccio's Tower (ruined in the last war), and the fairly well-preserved medieval castle 'la Rocca' built in 1323.

After visiting Fucecchio, the next place of interest is **Vinci**, the birthplace of Leonardo, whose birthdate is celebrated by festivities every 15 April. Take the road towards Empoli for 7km (4 miles) and then turn left. This quiet town, surrounded by vines and olives, is built around a thirteenth-century castle. In the castle is a museum dedicated to the town's most famous son, housed next to the Leonardo Library. Next to the castle is the church where the font in which Leonardo was christened can be seen. The rustic cottage in which he is said to have been born can be visited 3km (2 miles) to the north at Anchiano on the road to Pistoia.

From Vinci, follow a small scenic road signposted Vitolini; after about 8km (5 miles) turn right along the minor road at Verghetto which leads to **Artiminio**. The beautiful white Villa of Artimino was built as a hunting lodge for Ferdinando I by Buontalenti in 1594. This is one of the most beautiful of Medici villas.

Five kilometres (3 miles) to the north is the Villa of Poggio a Caiano, bought by the Medici from the Strozzi in 1480, and rebuilt by Sangallo. The villa has had a chequered history. In 1587, Grand Duke Francesco I and his second wife Bianca Capello died there within 24 hours of each other, amid rumours of poisoning. Later, Cosimo III's estranged wife was kept virtually a prisoner there before the intervention of her cousin Louis XIV obtained her return to France. The magnificent interior is decorated by paintings relating to glorious episodes from the history of the Medici. Outside, the villa has a well laid-out garden and a large area of parkland.

South and East of Florence

To the south of Florence is the famous wine-producing area of Chianti. The bulk of this area lies in the Province of Siena, but enough is in the Province of Florence to provide a pleasant afternoon's excursion.

Shortly after Tavarnuzze, on the SS2 to Siena, a small road leads up a hill to the right. At the top of the hill is the tiny hamlet of **Sant'Andrea in Percussina**. It was in his family home here that Machiavelli wrote his most important works, while in exile from Florence. Tradition has it that he spent the afternoons playing cards with the locals in the inn across the road. The inn is probably 50 years too recent for this to have been the case, but after a glass of local wine and an excellent and reasonably priced meal, one tends to succumb to the more romantic viewpoint.

Continue to the end of the small road and then turn left to San Casciano, a quiet country town which comes alive in February for the annual carnival. After San Casciano the SS2 twists downwards over the Florence-Siena superstrada towards the Chianti Classico area. After about 5km (3 miles), a left turn leads to **Sambuca** where there is an excellent pizzeria in the Gramsteda complex. This also includes an outdoor swimming pool, tennis courts and a pleasant hotel.

Just before Sambuca a narrow road leads up into the Chianti hills to the Badia di Passignano and then Greve in Chianti. The Badia di Passignano is a splendid tenth-century abbey which was sumptuously decorated in the late Renaissance period. A *Last Supper* by the Ghirlandaio brothers can be seen in the old refectory of the former monastery which faces the Badia. The monastery is now a beautifully situated, luxury hotel. Continuing along the road from the Badia for about 15 minutes brings the visitor to the early medieval castle of Montefioralle which dominates the western approach to Greve.

Greve itself claims to be the capital of the Chianti Classico wine-producing area. The centre of the town, which is a lively mixture of the old and the new, is the asymmetric Piazza Matteotti. Three sides of the *piazza* are lined with imposing colonnaded porticoes while the southern end is taken up by the Church of Santa Croce. A number of festivals are held in Greve throughout the year, but the most important of these is the Mostra Mercato del Chianti which is held in mid-September. South of Greve the road climbs steadily for several kilometres to the village of Panzano and then falls steeply into a wooded valley. In the bottom of the valley, immediately after having crossed the bridge, take the small right turn signposted La Piazza. This will take the visitor through one of the most beautiful parts of the Chianti.

The hamlet of La Piazza is precisely what its name suggests; a few houses around a *piazza*. One of these houses, however, sells delightful homemade chestnut honey (*miele di castagne*). After La Piazza the road climbs gently to another small hamlet, Sicelle, after which it is no longer tarmac. The scenery continues to be spectacularly beautiful and it is hard not to feel envious of the fortunate people who own the splendid villas which can be glimpsed occasionally.

The road rejoins a main road in a small group of houses known as **La Madonnina** just outside San Donato in Poggio. The hamlet takes its name from the late Renaissance sanctuary of the Madonna di Pietracupa. The church is fairly dimly lit behind its impressive colonnaded porch, which is a pity as it contains an interesting altarpiece by Paolo Schiavo.

Until very recently, **San Donato in Poggio** had changed little since the Middle Ages when it was a Florentine border fortress town during the almost continual wars against the Sienese. The town has now been discovered by quality tourist operators and improvements in communications have brought it within daily commuting distance of both Florence and Siena. The additions which have been made, however, are mainly in good taste and the old centre is unscathed. The main monuments of the town — Palazzo Pretorio and Palazzo Malaspina — are grouped around the small central *piazza*. Both can usually only be visited around 24 June when the town celebrates its patron saint. The festivities also include a donkey derby (*palio dei ciuchi*) and a procession of vintage vehicles. The town can also boast a fine Romanesque church on its northern edge but it is usually only possible to view this fine building from the outside.

Eight kilometres (5 miles) to the west of San Donato, past the delightful fifteenth-century Pieve di Morrocco with its external frescoes and terracotta *Annunciation* by Andrea della Robbia, is the busy market town of **Tavarnelle**. For those visitors self-catering in the area, the Co-op here is by far the best place to shop. From Tavarnelle take the road to Marcialla and from there to **Certaldo** which is known mainly for its association with Boccaccio, the thirteenth-century author of the *Decamerone*. There are two distinct parts to Certaldo, a newer town on the floor of the valley and an old, medieval centre high on an outcrop above. It is possible to drive up to the old centre but as there are already far too many vehicles up there, it is far better to leave your vehicle in the new town and walk the last 270m (300yd). Were it not that parking is allowed within the walls, the town would be as typically medieval as San Gimignano, the towers of which can be seen on a hilltop in the distance (see Chapter 9 for more details about San Gimignano). It does, however, have the compensating advantage of attracting fewer tourists.

Certaldo consists of a main street and a number of little alleyways which wind around it. At the head of the street is the Palazzo del

Pretore which now houses a small but interesting museum (this is open most mornings). Half way down the street there is a building with a tower; it houses the town library and was the home of Boccaccio. He played a major role in developing the short story as a form of writing and was a great influence on Chaucer.

For those staying in Florence, Certaldo is not easily reached on public transport although there are regular organised trips during the peak season. For those who do make it, the best of a number of small trattorias, all of which offer excellent food at reasonable prices, seems to be La Tinaia, down an alleyway below Boccaccio's house.

After Certaldo, those travelling by car should head for **Montespertoli**; a small hilltown which was a free city until being over-run by the Florentines in the sixteenth century. Some Renaissance works of art can be seen in the Church of Sant 'Andrea and in the nearby eleventh-century Pieve di San Pietro in Mercato. Works of art which should not be missed include the thirteenth-century marble font and the mid-fourteenth-century tryptich in Sant' Andrea, while the Romanesque architecture of San Pietro is impressive.

To return to Florence, follow the road through Chiesanuova until it drops down into **Galluzzo** on the outskirts of Florence. The fine villa on the right hand side, about 1km ($^1/_2$ mile) after Chiesanuova, is said to have been the home of Mona Lisa and the setting for Leonardo's painting. Before the edges were trimmed off the painting by one of its previous owners, more of the villa could be seen on it.

Another attractive little town is **Impruneta**, 7km (4 miles) southeast of Galluzzo. First inhabited by the Etruscans, Impruneta became important as a sanctuary in the early medieval period. Many of the fine buildings were badly damaged in World War II, but have since been fully restored. The Church of Santa Maria dell' Impruneta merits a visit, but Impruneta (which means 'in the pines') should be visited, not for its individual buildings, but for its general atmosphere of picturesque tranquillity.

To the east of Florence, the province consists mainly of heavily forested hills and valleys. The few roads offer an attractive drive to nature lovers, with the chance of sighting wild boar amongst other flora and fauna. There are also some small centres of particular interest in these hills.

Consuma, on the SS70, is a small but well-known centre for winter sports, ideally placed for quick access from Florence. The road which leads from Consuma to Vallombrosa is possibly the most beautiful in this area, passing through a forest of beech, pine and fir. **Vallombrosa** itself is a quiet, summertime mountain resort which has developed around an imposing monastery.

The origins of the monastery can be traced to the beginning of the eleventh century when two monks from the Abbey of Settimo, just outside Florence, left their monastery to live as hermits. For their hermitage they chose this wild, wooded area on the slopes of the Pratomagno. The two monks were forgotten about for 20 years until they were discovered by Giovanni Gualberto Visdomini, who was fleeing from Florence after one of the regular Guelph-Ghibelline power struggles. Giovanni constructed a small church in the woods and huts for the original hermits and others who can to join them, attracted by their simple lives and their vows of silence and chastity. The group was recognized by Pope Victor II in 1055 and Giovanni was canonized in 1093, 20 years after his death. The monastery itself is basically a fifteenth-century building, although it was heavily restored after being badly damaged by the troops of Charles V of Spain in 1529.

The woods around the monastery are excellent for pleasant walks, particularly to places associated with the life and religious mythology of Giovanni. A large rock by the side of the road leading to the monastery contains what, with a little imagination, can be seen as the impression of a man's body. It is said that as Giovanni was tempted by the devil, the rock against which he pressed himself softened and held his body until the temptation was past.

Another walk with a less tenuous connection with the saint begins from the road leading to Saltino. Part way along a footpath that leads from the road into the woods is a large beech tree known as il Faggio di San Giovanni Gualberto next to the spot where he had the first church built. The path continues over the Torrente Vicaro with its waterfalls to Il Paradisino, a chapel built on the site of a hermitage where monks from the main monastery went for periods of penitence in the eleventh and twelfth centuries. There is a magnificent view from the chapel over much of Tuscany: on a clear day it is possible to see Portoferraio on the Island of Elba.

Back down at the monastery, those interested in architecture will be able to see examples of the Romanesque, Renaissance, Classical and Baroque in its structure as it has gradually been enlarged or restored through the centuries.

Close to Vallombrosa is the small village of **Saltino**, a well-known winter resort owing to the close proximity of Monte Secchietta with its three ski runs. A *rifugio* (refuge) at the top of Monte Secchietta offering warmth and simple meals can be reached by car. The pistes are ideal for non-expert skiers as they are neither too long, nor particularly taxing.

3
MASSA AND THE PROVINCE OF MASSA-CARRARA

The Province of Massa-Carrara forms the northern tip of Tuscany, bordering the regions of Liguria and Emilia-Romagna. It can be split into two distinct parts; the well-known southern area where the cities of Massa and Carrara separate the province's 10km (6 mile) coastline from the northern section of the Apuan Alps, and the somewhat neglected interior, the Lunigiana.

For more than 2,000 years the Apuan Alps have supplied man with marble. The Romans quarried there; most of the marble used by Michelangelo was Carrarese, and even today the area is the world's most important source of marble. Several of the quarries in the mountains and the workshops on the coastal plain may be visited by those wishing to learn more about the production of marble. The mountains are also popular with climbers and mountaineers, for whom expert information is readily available locally.

One effect of the quarrying of marble is that even from quite close by, the mountains appear to be capped with snow throughout the year. This adds to the magnificent effect the mountains have as a backdrop to the seaside towns below. The province's coastline forms part of the Versilian Riviera, with a continous wide beach of fine, white sand.

Marina di Carrara and Marina di Massa are the province's resorts. In both of them, groups of buildings alternate with conserved sections of pine forest which once covered the whole of the coastal plain. Both resorts are well-provided with bathing establishments, cafés and shops selling equipment for the beach. They are virtually indistinguishable from each other, both having been developed in the post-war period.

The province's capital, **Massa**, was first recorded in the ninth century. Possession was disputed by Lucca and Pisa until 1442 when, along with Carrara, it became an independant duchy ruled by the Cybo-Malaspina family. In 1741 the duchy passed under the control of the Este family of Modena and, apart from the Napoleonic period when it formed part of Elisa Bonaparte's Cisalpine Republic, it remained in their hands until Unification.

The heart of the city is Piazza degli Aranci, which is dominated by the fine fifteenth-century Palazzo Malaspina. The courtyard, with its beautiful marble-decorated double loggia, is particularly impressive, and hosts a number of cultural events in the summer. The battlements, added in the sixteenth and seventeenth centuries, offer excellent views of the city and the coast.

The area immediately around Piazza degli Aranci forms the fifteenth-century nucleus of the city and it is this area, with the old medieval town just below the fortress, which should hold the attention of the visitor.

The medieval fortress (*rocca*) once formed the highest point of the defensive system surrounding the medieval Castello di Massa which preceded the city. The walls of the fourteenth-century fortress offer good views over the city and the coastline, while a covered loggia connects it to a princely residence erected by the Malaspina in the sixteenth century as a symbol of their power.

Other important buildings to visit while in Massa are the Churches of San Rocco and the Carmine. San Rocco is situated at the centre of the quarter closest to the fortress and contains a crucifix which is believed to be an early work by Michelangelo. The Carmine is on the visitor's right as he or she descends the Via della Rocca to return to the centre. The church contains several fifteenth-century paintings by the Lombardian school and sixteenth-century choir stalls. Of minor interest are the Malaspina villas around the edges of the city, the best of which are the Villa della Rocca and the Villa della Cuncia which were originally intended as hunting lodges.

Behind Massa the main road for Castelnuovo di Garfagnana climbs steeply up the marble Apuan Alps. The road passes two towns, the small spa of San Carlo Terme and the village of Altagnana which appears to be clinging precariously to the mountainside. A large statue of a Pope blessing the towns below signals that the summit has almost been reached. Towards the top of the mountains, and on the descent on the other side, the visitor has a close view of the vast scale of the marble works in the area. At several points on the road, small restaurants advertise *salsicce e polenta*; a wonderfully tasty and filling dish which is a local speciality.

The province's second city, **Carrara**, is actually slightly larger than Massa, although this is due mainly to its greater number of marble works. Historically, the two cities have followed much the same path. First recorded in the tenth century, Carrara has been linked to Massa for over 500 years.

Fewer old buildings have been preserved in Carrara than in Massa, owing to the demands of a continually flourishing industry, but some are still to be seen around the Cathedral and Piazza Alberica. The former residence of the Cybo-Malaspina, built in the sixteenth century around an older medieval castle, is one of these. The building was given to the Academy of Fine Arts by Elisa Bonaparte and houses their headquarters and training school. The art and sculpture galleries may be visited with the permission of the director.

The lower part of the marble cathedral, which was built between the eleventh and fourteenth centuries, is in the Romanesque style, but higher up it changes to the Gothic. The façade dates from the twelfth century and is a fine example of the Pisan style. The upper section consists of a large rose window flanked by seven pillars on each side. Inside, the architecture is severe and fairly plain, though the marble pulpit in the Presbytery should not be missed.

In Via Santa Maria, the fine thirteenth-century building known as the House of Emanuele Repetti is believed to have housed the city's administration in the medieval period and, more importantly, to have been the home of Petrarch.

For those interested in learning more about the marble industry, Carrara offers two possibilities. The first, and less strenuous alternative is to visit the large Mostra Nazionale del Marmo (open to the public during the summer). This has been opened by the local Chamber of Commerce as a permanent exhibition of all aspects of marble production, including its history.

The second method is to visit the quarries themselves. The best place to do this is **Collonnata** which is 8km (5 miles) from the centre of the city and takes its name from a column of slaves brought in by the Romans to work in the quarries.

For the hardy visitor, Carrara is a base for a number of walks up the Apuans. Mounts Spallone, Borla, Sagro, Foce di Vinca and Torre di Monzone, all of which are well over 1,000m (3,500ft), can be ascended from the town.

Three kilometres (2 miles) west of Carrara, just over the Ligurian border, are the ruins of the Roman city of *Luni*. During the Roman period the city was the most powerful in the area, dominating the coastal route and having a flourishing trade in marble. However, its

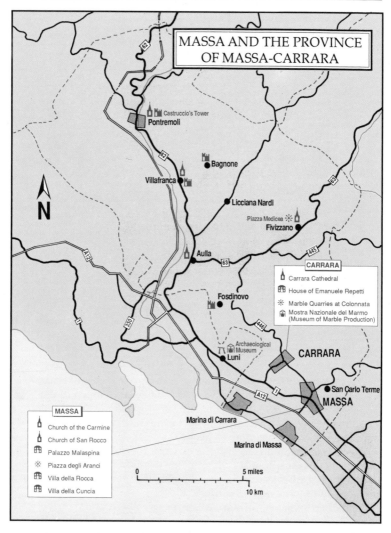

MASSA AND THE PROVINCE OF MASSA-CARRARA

Pontremoli
Castruccio's Tower

Bagnone

Villafranca

Licciana Nardi

Piazza Medicea
Fivizzano

Aulla

Fosdinovo

CARRARA
- Carrara Cathedral
- House of Emanuele Repetti
- Marble Quarries at Colonnata
- Mostra Nazionale del Marmo (Museum of Marble Production)

Archaeological Museum
Luni

CARRARA

San Carlo Terme

MASSA

Marina di Carrara

Marina di Massa

MASSA
- Church of the Carmine
- Church of San Rocco
- Palazzo Malaspina
- Piazza degli Aranci
- Villa della Rocca
- Villa della Cuncia

0   5 miles

10 km

fine coastal position eventually led to its downfall as it was pillaged first by the Longobards, then by the Normans and then several times by the Saracens while malaria had a constant weakening effect on the population. The city was finally abandoned in the twelfth century and from then until the second half of this century it was largely forgotten about. During the last 40 years, however, a concentrated

The medieval fortress in Massa, backed by the Apuan Alps

The village of Antona with marble slides in the hills beyond

program of excavations has brought much of the old city to light. The most complete building to be excavated so far is the amphitheatre, while an on-site archaeological museum houses articles which have been discovered on the site.

The bulk of the province, which is generally known as the Lunigiana or the 'Land of the Hundred Castles', has little to offer in the way of tourist attractions. However, it is a fascinating area as the gradual rural depopulation has meant that most of the many small villages have remained virtually unchanged for centuries.

The only real sign of the twentieth century is the Parma — La Spezia motorway link which cuts through the middle of the area. As the name of the area suggests, it was originally the territory of *Luni*. In fact, even today, the area has much stronger links with the adjoining regions than with the rest of Tuscany. Those people who have lived and worked their whole lives in the area have little personal contact with other areas while the younger generation, who live in the area but travel out to work, tend to follow the *autostrada* and the railway to the industries of Liguria or Emilia-Romagna.

The area is traditionally insular; the Romans were fiercely resisted, and after Italian Unification the area became a hotbed of anarchy. The many castles which dot the Lunigiana, and which give it its popular name, were not built for military reasons but to exact stiff tolls from those wishing to make the journey between the north and the coast. Unfortunately, only a small minority of these castles are in public ownership and the rest usually cannot be visited.

Pontremoli, in the north, is the main town in the area. As old as Massa, it was allied to Milan for 300 years before being ceded to Florence in 1650. The oldest part of the town is that immediately to the north of Castruccio's Tower. This tower was part of a fortress built in 1332 to separate the original northern part of the town (which was inhabited by the Guelphs) from the newer part of the town which had been built by the Ghibellines.

Other than the tower, the visitor should look at some of the wealthy medieval town houses, many of which are decorated with impressive pieces of sculpture. The seventeenth-century cathedral is something of a disappointment, but the Church of the Annunziata more than makes up for this, with its small octagonal marble temple by Sansovino.

To the north of the town the Castello del Piagnaro, part of the original medieval town, now houses a museum which contains some exceptionally interesting pieces of pre-Roman sculpture.

From Pontremoli head southwards on the SS62 to **Villafranca in Lunigiana**, 13km (8 miles) down the valley, at the confluence of the

Rivers Magra and Bagnone. Of interest in Villafranca are the pictur-esque remains of the medieval Castello Malaspina which was badly damaged during the last war, and the restored sixteenth-century Church of San Francesco.

Five kilometres (3 miles) east of Villafranca is the small town of **Bagnone** which dominates the valley of the same name. An impres-sive cylindrical tower is the best-preserved part of the castle which stands on a spur above the town looking down the valley to Villafranca. In recent years the town has gained popularity as a quiet mountain resort during the summer and a number of excellent walks can be taken in the mountains above it. Of these, perhaps the most interesting is that which eventually leads the visitor to Lago (Lake) Santo, just over the regional border in Emilia-Romagna. The lake is well-stocked with trout and other fish.

On the far side of the lake is a mountain refuge (*rifugio*) run by the Club Alpino Italiano. The shelter, which is open from June to October, offers simple meals and can accommodate up to fifty people per night. It is also possible to hire rowing boats here and there are limited facilities for winter sports. For the latter, however, it is more practical to approach the lake from Lagdei in the Province of Parma.

Head south on the minor road which twists its way along the face of the mountains to **Licciana Nardi** which is an attractive village. The second part of its name was added after the Unification of Italy in honour of Anacarsi Nardi who was shot in 1844 while leading an uprising in the South of Italy. His remains are housed in a large sarcophagus at the centre of Piazza del Municipio.

Another 16km (10 miles) of minor roads with panoramic views brings the visitor to **Fivizzano**, the second largest town in the Lunigiana. Fivizzano was acquired by Florence from the Malaspina in the middle of the fifteenth century and fortified to become the seat of the governor of Lunigiana in the seventeenth century. The town has declined greatly in importance over the last 100 years. This is mainly due to its distance from all the major cities. However, its previous status has left it with an enviable artistic and architectural patrimony which survived the earthquake that hit the town in 1920. The central square of the town, Piazza Medicea, is surrounded by Renaissance *palazzi* and the Church of Saints Jacopo and Antonio. The church contains an impressive walnut choir stall by Pisanino and several fine paintings, notably a *Resurrection of Lazarus* by Pietro Sorri in the last side chapel of the right-hand nave.

For several hundred years the region was dominated by the Abbey of San Caprasio, 18km (11 miles) to the west of Fivizzano where the River Taverone meets up with the Magra. The apse of the original

Carved marble blocks illustrating the quarrying process, Carrara

Marble blocks cut from the Carrara quarries

eighth-century abbey has been incorporated into the parish church of Aulla which grew up around the abbey. Unfortunately, this is now the only thing worth visiting in Aulla as the small medieval centre was totally destroyed during the war. There are a large number of attractive little villages in the Lunigiana. The visitor may be particularly interested in the small winter sports centre of **Zum Zeri**, 26km (16 miles) west of Pontremoli. It is also worth visiting **Fosdinovo**, at the southern tip of the area; Dante was once a guest in the castle here. More winter sports facilities are situated by the Lago del Cerreto just over the border in Emilia-Romagna, 24km (15 miles) north-east of Fivizzano over the spectacular Passo del Cerreto.

4
LUCCA AND ITS PROVINCE

T he city of **Lucca** was probably founded by the Ligurians and passed through the hands of the Etruscans before becoming a Roman Colony in 180BC. Situated at the crossing point of the Via Cassia and the Via Aurelia, Lucca became an important centre of communications. Its chief early claim to fame is that in 56BC the triumvirate of Caesar, Pompey and Crassus met there to decide the future of the Empire.

Under the Longobards, and then the Carolingian Empire, Lucca was an important city, being the then capital of *Tuscia* (Tuscany). In the early years of this millenium, the city's flourishing silk and banking industries made it important enough to be accorded the status of a free *comune* with free trading rights by the Empire.

The usual Guelph/Ghibelline confrontation then weakened the city, giving power to a succession of *signori* (lords). The most important of these was Castruccio Castracani, who, but for his early death in 1328, would probably have made Lucca the most powerful city in Tuscany once again.

In 1369 the city became an independent republic, and resisted all the attempts at takeover by its larger neighbours, Pisa and Florence, remaining independent until 1805. The successful defence of the city in this period was mainly due to the strength of its city walls, particularly the second, medieval wall. The latter, which dates from the thirteenth century, withstood many drawn-out sieges. Only two impressive gateways remain of the medieval wall, whose function was superseded by the superb Renaissance equivalent, completed in 1650. This wall still encloses the city, having been preserved in its original condition, with large storerooms set into the inside, and a road around the top which was added in the Napoleonic period.

Inside the walls, virtually nothing has changed since 1650 and, were it not for the vast number of vehicles which afflict all Italian towns, a visit to the city would be like stepping back in time.

Throughout the city, public and private secular and religious buildings, homes and workplaces are all jumbled together in what might be best-described as a harmonious anarchy of town planning. A green belt around the wall separates them from the dull modern houses and factories which have been built around the city in this century. Interestingly, it is this virtually unplanned city which has formed the model for the architects working with the Prince of Wales to create a new town near Dorchester in the South of England.

Unjustly neglected by many tourists, the city does not offer a wide choice of hotels, although those available are adequate except in extremely busy periods. Many of the restaurants in Lucca offer a wider variety of traditional local foods than is the case in many of the more tourist-orientated cities. Local specialities are: *Zuppa di magro*, a thick ham and vegetable soup served over a wedge of bread; *Garmucia*, a stew; *risotto al piccione*; *Tordi*, thrush roasted on a spit; and *Agnello*, lamb with olives.

Museums

The Pinacoteca National Art Gallery is housed in the Palazzo Mansi, an elegant seventeenth-century building in Via Galli Tassi which also contains a rich collection of eighteenth-century furniture. Until very recently the gallery was situated on the first floor of the Palazzo della Provincia. This imposing building was begun by Ammanati in 1578 as the seat of government for the republic. The site of the *palazzo* was originally part of the Fortezza Augusta, designed by Giotto and built by Castruccio Castracani when he was at the height of his power. However, after his death, power was gradually usurped by the people and the fortress was demolished as a manifestation of republicanism.

The original art collection was sold off by Duke Carlo Ludovico before ceding the city to the Grand Duchy of Tuscany in 1847. On annexation, however, Leopold II made a donation from the Florentine art reserves which forms the nucleus of the present collection. The overall standard is of a good provincial gallery, with some fine works by lesser known artists and a few high quality paintings which, for one reason or another, did not appeal to Leopold. The best paintings are to be seen in the rooms where several Tintorettos and a Veronese share the space with portraits of the Medici by Sustermans.

As in all the medieval Italian republics, Lucca had some citizens who were more equal than others. The most important of these was the Guinigi family who were responsible for erecting many new buildings in the fourteenth and fifteenth centuries. One of the most attractive parts of the city is that known as the Case dei Guinigi, just to the south of the old amphitheatre.

The most impressive of the *case* (houses) is a three-storey terracotta building with a high fortified tower. The ground floor was originally an open loggia with the upper storeys supported by stone pillars and terracotta arches. Facing this house is another loggia; it is now partially walled up but was originally the meeting place for the people of the quarter.

The Villa of Paolo Guinigi was built in 1418 by the most important Luccan of his time. The building is distinguished by its open, ground floor loggia and surmounting delicate archways in the middle of the façade. It was much altered during the course of the centuries, but has been restored to its original state since World War II.

The villa has housed an important museum since 1968. The ground floor is dedicated to a collection of sculptures and items of archaeological interest, while the upper floor is devoted to paintings, furniture and other Luccan artefacts, dating from the thirteenth century onwards. There is great variety in the collection, the most important exhibit of which is the portrait of Alessandro de' Medici in Room X.

The marketplace is not a museum as such, but an interesting monument whose oval form reveals its origins as the city's Roman amphitheatre. The original floor level is roughly 3m (10ft) below the present surface, but some remnants of Roman masonry can be identified in the walls of the buildings which surround the market.

The Churches

The Duomo

This was built in the sixth century, then rebuilt in 1060 and again at the beginning of the thirteenth century. The exterior is impressive, although the asymmetric Romanesque façade which links up with the bell tower adds to the impression that the church has been squeezed into one corner of the *piazza*.

The façade and the porticoes are decorated with thirteenth-century allegorical carvings by the Comacine guild of masons from Lombardy. The meaning of much of the allegory has been lost or distorted and interpretation is now a matter for conjecture.

The interior of the church is light, spacious and outstandingly beautiful. Most of the side chapels are decorated with Renaissance masterpieces. Tintoretto's *Last Supper* in the third chapel on the right, and Ghirlandaio's *Virgin and Child with Saints Peter, Paul Clement and Sebastian* in the sacristy are the best of the paintings. In the middle

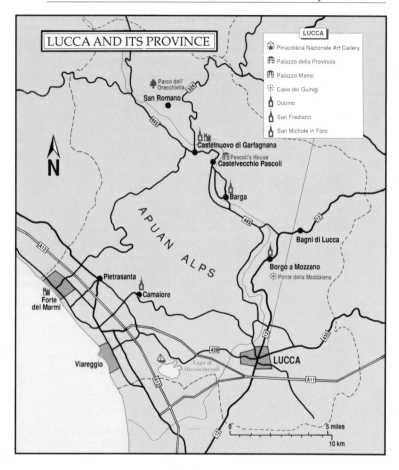

LUCCA AND ITS PROVINCE

LUCCA
- Pinacoléca Nazionale Art Gallery
- Palazzo della Provincia
- Palazzo Mansi
- Case dei Guinigi
- Duomo
- San Frediano
- San Michele in Foro

Parco dell' Orecchiella
San Romano

Castelnuovo di Garfagnana
Pascoli's House
Castelvecchio Pascoli

Barga

APUAN ALPS

Bagni di Lucca

Borgo a Mozzano
Ponte della Maddalena

Pietrasanta
Camaiore

Forte dei Marmi

Viareggio

Lago di Massaciuccoli

LUCCA

0   5 miles
10 km

of the transept is the tomb of Ilaria del Carretto by Jacopo della Quercia, which is one of the finest pieces of Italian sculpture.

A small octagonal marble temple in the middle of the nave contains the famous Volto Santo. This is a wooden crucifix carved by Nicodemus, who helped to bury Christ. After lying hidden in a cave for centuries, the crucifix was found and put onto an unmanned ship, which drifted to *Luni*. At *Luni* the crucifix was put on a cart drawn by unbroken steers which, according to the legend, immediately made their way to Lucca.

A panorama over the rooftops of Lucca

The Duomo with its Romanesque façade, Lucca

San Frediano

This twelfth-century church is dedicated to San Frediano, a sixth-century Bishop of Luccá, who is believed to have been St Finnian of Moville in Ireland. The most important part of the church is the Cappella Trenta, the fourth chapel on the left. The sculpture in this chapel is by della Quercia and his principal assistants. The sarcophagus under the altar contains the bones of St Richard, King of England, thought to have been a son of King Offa of Mercia.

San Michele in Foro

This marble-covered church stands at the centre of the old Roman forum. The large façade seems out of proportion to the rest of the twelfth-century church. This is because the façade was added in the thirteeth century when it was planned to enlarge the church.

Inside, remains of a much older church can be seen under the presbytery. The most important work of art is Filippino Lippi's picture of Saints Jerome, Sebastian, Rocco and Helen.

San Francesco

This largely rebuilt thirteenth-century church contains a cenotaph to Castruccio Castracani, and the tomb of Nino Visconti, who is mentioned by Dante in *The Divine Comedy* (Purgatory VIII 53).

On the weekend of the third Sunday of each month a large, open-air antiques fair is held in the streets of Lucca. The market is the second oldest of its type in Italy and attracts buyers and sellers from far afield. Besides its own intrinsic interest, it also offers an opportunity to see Lucca at its best; the streets and *piazze* involved are cleared of cars.

The Province of Lucca

Like the Province of Massa-Carrara, Lucca is divided in two parts by the Apuan Alps. The larger part of the Province, known as the Garfagnana, is crossed by one major road. The road was once very popular with travellers who wished to avoid the risks of the malaria-infested coastline. Nowadays it is the coastal plain, known as the Versilian Riviera, which has a higher population and receives more visitors.

The most important holiday resort on the Tyrrhenian Sea, **Viareggio**, is one of the most rapidly expanding of Italian towns. In the twelfth century the Luccans erected a tower on the coast to protect travellers on the Via Regia. In time, a small village grew up around the fortifications and began to expand rapidly after a proper drainage system freed the area of malaria in the eighteenth century.

The town became an important fishing port, and in 1861, saw the establishment of the first seaside holiday home for children in Italy. Although lacking in historical interest, the town is pleasant and much more elegant than the majority of modern Italian towns.

It was on the beach at Viareggio, on 16 August 1822, that Byron and a small group of friends arranged Shelley's funeral pyre, after he was drowned in a storm.

The town organises a large number of concerts and cultural events throughout the tourist season. Important sporting events and tournaments are also organised using the town's excellent facilities.

Viareggio's carnival in February is one of the most spectacular in the world, with tens of thousands of people dressed up and dancing in the streets.

The Versilian Riviera's second town, **Forte dei Marmi**, takes its name from the castle in the central square which was built in 1788. The town has grown rapidly since then to become a very popular resort.

Outside the centre, the majority of the houses are very pleasantly set amongst the pine trees. Forte dei Marmi attracts many wealthy Italians looking for second homes, as well as artists and writers who find the surroundings conducive to work throughout the year.

One of the most interesting of the many historical manifestations in the Province of Lucca is held in the little town of **Querceta**, half way between Forte dei Marmi and Pietrasanta. Roughly two thousand people, all dressed in medieval costume, take place in the procession and displays which precede the *palio dei ciuchi* (donkey derby) between the representatives of the eight sections of the town. This represents a very high proportion of the population of the town and the surrounding hamlets. If visitors are passing through the area on the last Sunday in May, they should make a point of seeing this event.

The other towns on the coastal plain are set back from the sea and are of minor interest. For the visitor who wishes to avoid the busy motorway and travel instead along the old Via Aurelia, it is worth making brief stops in some of the towns.

Although it is an industrial centre, **Camaiore** has some interesting old buildings. In particular, the traveller may wish to visit the Collegiata (collegiate church) which dates from 1278, and the eleventh-century Benedictine abbey. Footpaths leading up several of the mountains also begin in Camaiore.

Historically, the most important town in the Luccan part of the coastal plain is **Pietrasanta** which was founded by the Luccans in the thirteenth century. The town reached its zenith a century later at the

A quiet street in Lucca, just off the main square

time of Castruccio Castracani but, with the decline in power of the Luccan state after his death, it passed through several hands before being awarded to Florence by Pope Leo X (Giovanni dei Medici) in 1513. However, this coincided with an increase in malaria on the coastal plain which stifled further development for over 300 years.

Also on the coastal plain is the Lago di Massaciuccoli, a calm, shallow lake which is popular with windsurfers and pleasure boaters, although there have been fears in recent years that the lake is drying up.

Fifty kilometres (30 miles) north of Lucca, where the Rivers of Serchio and Turrite Secca meet, is **Castelnuovo di Garfagnana**. This is the most important centre in the inland half of the province.

The town and its fortress were developed by the Este family of Ferrara, who, with a few short breaks, controlled the area until Unification. Nowadays, the importance of the town lies in its thriving textile industry, but previously it was of great strategic importance as it controlled the main road from Genoa and the north to Lucca and Pisa.

As a result of this strategic importance, the Este often chose their most able men to govern the area. Of these, the most famous is the poet Ariosto who, in true Renaissance style, was not only a poet but also a courtier and soldier. Landscapes which would now be regarded as rugged and beautiful were then seen as wild and inhospitable, and the poet resented the time he spent in the area. Many of the dark and dangerous woods in the *Orlando Furioso* are almost certainly drawn from memories of the Garfagnana.

The fortress (Rocca) still dominates the centre of the town. It dates from the twelfth century and its picturesque, irregular format

Buildings worth visiting in Lucca include the Duomo (above) and the Church of San Michele in Foro (below)

reflects the additions made as the town grew in importance.

The Duomo is built in a simple sixteenth-century style, and is only really noteworthy for a fine Della Robbian terracotta. Many of the town's old buildings were destroyed when it was badly damaged during World War II.

Between the Duomo and the Rocca is a *piazza* with an open loggia at its centre. Every Saturday this loggia houses a small antiques fair.

As the seat of a *comune*, Castelnuovo is also the administrative headquarters of several outlying villages, all of which are attractive and should be visited by those spending more than a short time in the Garfagnana.

Palleroso stands high on a hill to the west of the town in an important strategic position dominating the Serchio Valley and the roads from Lucca and Reggio-Emilia. This led to the village being sacked by the Luccan troops during the wars between Lucca and Ferrara for the possession of the Garfagnana. The village's main church, San Martino, has a fine painting by Lorenzetti in the apse. It is also worth viewing for the fine views over the Apennines, the Apuan Alps, and down the Serchio Valley.

Monterotondo, which takes its name from the form of the hill on whose top it nestles, is the least spectacular of the villages but perhaps the most typical as it and its inhabitants seem to be as much a part of the landscape as the trees and rocks.

The fine portals and arches of some of the buildings in the village of **Gragnanella** hint at a status which has been lost with rural depopulation. This attractive village has an open-air theatre which hosts mainly traditional rural plays during the summer months.

Until the last century, many of the leading citizens of Castelnuovo spent much of their time in houses in the surrounding villages. **Rontano**, just to the south of the town, was the most prestigious of these and this is reflected in the superior architecture of many of the houses and the evident importance of the parish church.

Castelnuovo means new castle and, as its name suggests, it replaces an earlier fortification. The remains of the earlier castle, Castello San Nicolao, stand on a hill to the north of the town. An early seventeenth-century Cappuccin monastery is also situated on the same hill.

A number of roads lead northwards from Castelnuovo and all provide pleasant excursions into the hills. Almost due north of the town is the Passo delle Radici mountain pass which will take the visitor over the Apennines past a large number of holiday homes and various winter sports facilities into Emilia-Romagna. Eight kilometres (5 miles) up the pass is the interesting little town of **Castiglione**

di Garfagnana. The town is completely contained within the limits of a fourteenth-century fortified border village which was built by the Luccans around the thirteenth century Church of San Pietro.

A left turn just to the north of Castiglione leads the visitor to the picturesque village of San Romano di Garfagnana. This still boasts the medieval defensive walls which sucessfully resisted the might of the Florentine army in 1520. The village is an ideal starting point for mountain walks. Beyond the village is the Parco dell' Orecchiella which contains a small holiday village by a lake famous for its trout. The park is also a reserve for deer and wild boar.

Eight kilometres (5 miles) north-west of Castelnuovo, a left hand turn leads up to the *comune* of Vagli Sotto which consists of three attractive mountain villages; Roggio, Vagli Sopra and Vagli Sotto itself. Until 1953 the *comune* consisted of four villages but the fourth, Fabbrica, was submerged when the large Vagli Reservoir was created by the damming of the River Edron.

The creation of the dam and the subsequent development of hydro-electric power brought new life to these mountain communities, giving them the resources to promote tourism in the area. There are many caverns and crevasses in the surrounding mountains and regular courses are run for pot-holers, who come from all over Europe.

The reservoir itself is used for canoeing and for pleasure boats which can be hired in **Vagli Sotto**. Many of the buildings of Fabbrica were left intact when the valley was flooded and the village emerges in the reservoir during exceptionally dry spells.

Vagli Sopra stands 180m (600ft) higher than Vagli Sotto and is the access point for the strangely beautiful glacial Valley of Campocatino with its house-like rock formations. The oldest part of the village is built on a spur which rises out of the wooded mountainside. At the highest point of the spur stands the thirteenth-century Romanesque Church of San Lorenzo with its imposing, grey rectangular tower. The apse of the church contains a fine marble altar table depicting the Twelve Apostles which dates from 1484.

The third of the villages, **Roggio**, is a typical mountain village which seems to be almost lost amongst the chestnut trees. The village has two claims to fame; the first a historic one in that it was the home of Felice Peretti who, on being raised to the Papacy, is said to have chosen the name Sixtus the Fifth because he was sure no later pope would use the name again. The other claim to fame is that Italy's largest chestnut tree grows next to the village. The tree in question has a circumference of 10m (32ft) and is over 26m (85ft) high.

Eight kilometres (5 miles) south-east of Castelnuovo, take the left

The tree-lined Apuan Valley near Gallicano

A picturesque corner of Borgo a Mozzano

The 'Devil's Bridge', built by the people of Borgo a Mozzano →

turn towards Barga. Two kilometres (1 mile) up this road is **Castelvecchio Pascoli**. This gained the second part of its name after the death of the great poet. Pascoli spent much of his life there in a house bought with the gold won in an international competition for Latin poetry. One of his best-known series of poems, *Canti di Castelvecchio*, was written here. Pascoli's House can be seen exactly as it was when he died in 1912. His sister, who outlived him by 40 years, kept the house as a shrine until her death when the municipal authorities took over the responsibility. Both Pascoli and his sister are buried in the chapel of the house.

The older part of **Barga** is a typical hilltown with narrow streets. To see the town it is advisable to leave the car outside the walls, and then just wander around the quiet, little lanes inside.

Of exceptional interest is the Duomo at the top of the town. Building was initiated in the eleventh century and completed in various stages. Outside, it is rich in fine carvings, while inside is one of Tuscany's best-preserved medieval altars.

After visiting Barga, take the pleasant descent down the Tiglio Valley to Fornaci di Barga and there turn back towards Castelnuovo for 4km ($2^1/_2$ miles) until the left turn for **Gallicano** on the other side of the Serchio.

Seven kilometres (4 miles) to the east of Gallicano is one of the most interesting churches in the whole province. At first sight, the Eremo di Calomini appears to be no more than another attractive neo-Classical church set against the foot of a cliff. However, the neo-Classical building was built over a much earlier church which dates from the eleventh century. The church was established by hermits who venerated an image of Mary known as the Madonna della Penna. The first church consisted of little more than a cave in the rocks at the foot of the cliff. Although the cave was enlarged when the neo-Classical exterior was built, the walls and ceilings of the Presbytery, the Sacristy and the hermits cells are still formed of bare rock.

From Gallicano take the road up into the Apuans signposted **Grotta del Vento**. This is an extensive series of caves and underground caverns containing stalactites and stalagmites which is seen by far less tourists than it deserves. There are more than 3km (2 miles) of caves which have been fully explored and mapped out and an unknown quantity which have not.

Three separate guided tours are available, two of 1 hour each, and one of 3 hours. The tours take in underground rivers and waterfalls full of the reflections of a multitude of fossils and crystals, as well as stalactites and stalagmites. Next to the ticket office, a well-stocked shop sells samples of all the different types of crystals and minerals, as well as articles of jewellery. The grottoes are open from the beginning of April until mid-October.

If you do not wish to go underground, you are still highly recommended to take this road as it passes through what is arguably the most beautiful scenery in the whole of Tuscany. After passing the entrance to the caves it is possible to continue right up to the enchanting mountain village of San Pellegrino without seeing another vehicle on the road.

Back in the main valley, the next place of interest for the visitor is **Bagni di Lucca.** This is not so much a town as a collection of small villages which have grown up around the thermal springs. The warm, mildly radioactive waters have been noted since the eleventh century for their therapeutic qualities. They are particularly effective for sufferers of arthritis, rheumatism and liver complaints.

Montaigne devoted several pages of his journal to the Bagni, while other famous visitors include Byron and Shelley. The centre of Bagni di Lucca is Ponte a Serraglio which takes its name from the bridge at its centre which was built by Castruccio Castracani in 1317. A road from the centre of the village leads up the wooded hillside to the main thermal establishments in Bagni Caldi.

The mountain village of **Coreglia Antelminelli** can be reached by taking a turning up into the mountains roughly halfway between Barga and Bagni di Lucca. It was first inhabited during the summers by mesolithic tribes, 7,000 years before Christ. It was fortified in the eleventh century by a feudal lord and then became an important outpost for Lucca in 1272.

The village has many interesting corners and unspoilt medieval and Renaissance streets, while the eighth-century Church of San Martino is pre-Romanesque. The area around the village prides itself on its production of ceramic busts and figurines, many exquisite examples of these can be seen in the Museo della Figurina di Gesso in Palazzo Vanni.

Back in the main valley, 3km (2 miles) from Bagni di Lucca, is the Ponte della Maddalena or 'Devil's Bridge', as it is more usually referred to. This strange, long asymmetric hump-back bridge was built in the fourteenth century by the people of the nearby town of Borgo a Mozzano.

Legend has it that building the bridge proved to be beyond the people of the town and that the only way that they could get the bridge built was by enlisting the help of the Devil. The Devil agreed to build the bridge in exchange for the first soul to cross it. Accordingly, he built the bridge but the townsfolk sent a pig over the

A roadside café in Bagni di Lucca

bridge and thus cheated the Devil of his due.

They affirmed their Christianity by erecting a tabernacle with a statue of Mary Magdalene at one end of the bridge to protect it from the Devil's retribution. Presumably the townsfolk now consider that the Devil has forgotten the matter as the statue has now been moved to the parish church. The church stands at the centre of the town which is bypassed by the main road and has a very sleepy atmosphere.

Roughly half-way between Borgo a Mozzano and Lucca, a left turn leads up the Vinchiana Valley to the twelfth-century Pieve di Brancoli which has a fortified tower. The interior is divided into three naves by Classical pillars while the whole of the church is dominated by the fine, raised stone pulpit whose supporting pillars rest on the backs of two lions.

5

PISTOIA AND ITS PROVINCE

History has not treated **Pistoia** kindly. The Roman town which defended the junction of the Via Cassia, with a road leading to Padua, was razed to the ground by the Longobards around the year 400. In World War II Pistoia suffered again, being the most badly damaged of the major Tuscan cities.

In between, a period of prosperity during the Middle Ages, when the city was an important international banking centre, came to an end with the Guelph/Ghibelline, and then White Guelph/Black Guelph divisions. The effect of these divisions was compounded as the city found itself in the middle of the fierce struggle between Florence and Lucca, which finished with complete subjection to Florence from the fifteenth century onwards.

The Medici never took much interest in Pistoia, and the city declined in importance and prosperity until the Lorraine Dynasty instigated a revival. However, despite all the city's troubles, many fine interesting buildings remain for the visitor. Most of these date from the prosperous medieval period.

Parking is a problem in Pistoia, and visitors will probably find themselves near the edge of the city before they find a space. However, it is possible to reach the central Piazza del Duomo from virtually any point in no more than 15 minutes on foot.

The Duomo was rebuilt in the Romanesque style in the twelfth century after the original fifth-century church was destroyed by fire. Externally, the outstanding feature is the magnificent terracotta bas-relief by Andrea della Robbia which adorns the central arch of the porch. The interior of the Duomo is majestic though simple. Traces of medieval frescoes have been uncovered during recent restorations, and there are also many fine Renaissance paintings around the church. The church's most important work, however, is the silver altar situated in the Chapel of San Jacopo. This was begun in 1287 and gradually added to over the next two centuries. It is thus of exceptional interest as it shows the development in style from medieval to Renaissance.

The Capitolare Museum is reached through the Sacristry, and houses the treasure of the church. This consists of rare manuscripts, paintings, sculptures and medallions, as well as purely devotional works of art.

The bell tower to the left of the Duomo is built over a former military tower and is over 60m (200ft) high.

The nearby Baptistry is a fine octagonal building built in 1388, and is an excellent example of the Gothic style. It is covered with layers of green and white marble which blend in well with the façade of the Duomo and the bell tower. The polychromatic marble font at the centre is older than its environment, bearing the date 1226.

The impressive Palazzo del Podestà, next to the Baptistry, dates from 1367 and is particularly interesting for its pilastered covered courtyard. The upper floors are used as the province's law courts. On the other side of the Palazzo del Podestà is Palazzo Pallavicini, a fine Renaissance house with its own chapel on the first floor.

The fortress-like building of the Palazzo del Comune faces the Palazzo del Podestà across the square. It was begun by the Guelphs in 1294 but not finished until late in the next century. The Medici coats of arms which decorate the façade were erected in the sixteenth century in honour of the Medici Popes.

The interior of the building is built around a central courtyard and stairway resembling those of the Bargello in Florence. The first floor rooms are traditionally decorated administrative rooms. On the second floor is the Civic Museum, which contains many fine sculptures and paintings by local artists. There are also some works by Florentines such as Benedetto da Maiano which have found their way to Pistoia over the years. There are also examples of other schools such as the Flemish and the Lombard. Local archaeological findings and a rich collection of coins can also be seen in the museum.

The Church of San Bartolomeo, built in 1159, is particularly interesting for its carvings and relief sculptures. The figures on the lintel above the central door are inspired by Roman sarcophagi, one of the first examples of a return to Classical values in art. Inside, the visitor will be fascinated by Guido da Como's pulpit, which was sculpted in 1250. The pulpit stands on three columns, two of which rest on backs of lions while the third is supported on the shoulders of a thirteenth-century merchant. No less remarkable are the New Testament stories depicted in relief around the top of the pulpit.

San Giovanni Fuoricivitas earned the name Fuoricivitas in the twelfth century by being built outside the original city wall. The side of the church facing the centre of the city is composed of three rows of blind archways covered with green and white marble. The bas-relief over the door on this side is probably the work of Gruamonte, the artist responsible for the lintel over the door of San Bartolomeo. The stoup is an early work of Giovanni Pisano. Other works of art to which the visitor should pay special attention are the polyptych by Gaddi and the terracotta *Annunication* by Luca della Robbia.

Of all the fine pulpits in Pistoia, the finest is undoubtedly that of Giovanni Pisano in the Abbazia di Sant' Andrea. The pulpit is hexagonal and richly decorated with biblical stories in relief. It is supported by one central pillar which rests on a base of two eagles and a lion, and six outer pillars. Of these outer pillars, two stand on the backs of lions while a third rests upon the back of a kneeling man. A wooden crucifix contained in a tabernacle behind the right hand altar is another of Giovanni Pisano's masterpieces, and the font is also believed to be his work.

The Museo Diocesano is contained in the Bishop's Palace, or Palazzo Vescovile. It contains some interesting Renaissance paintings as well as articles of furniture, cloth and silverware.

The Church of Santa Maria delle Grazie, with its fine portal thrown into relief by a plain façade, was built by Michelozzo in the mid-fifteenth century. Inside the church, the first things to catch the eye are the four columns in the nave supporting an exquisite cupola. The church's most prized relic is a fifteenth-century bed which can be seen in a small side-chapel. It was the sick bed of a poor Pistoian who recovered miraculously from being on the verge of death and attributed his recovery to a visitation by the Virgin Mary. The bed is of interest, not only to believers, but also to the more sceptical as it is almost certainly the only bed of its kind still in existence.

The busts of the funeral monuments on either side of the altar in the right hand transept of the late thirteenth-century Church of San Domenico are believed to be by Bernini. Part of the church and the adjoining monastery were badly damaged during World War II and now only patches remain of the once fine medieval and Renaissance frescoes. Some of the original frescoes which were less badly damaged have been detached from the walls of the church and can now be seen in the monastery. Perhaps the most interesting of these frescoes is a *Journey of the Magi* where two of the wise men are known to be portraits of Dante and Petrarch.

The Madonna dell 'Umiltà' is a Brunelleschian-style church which was completed by Vasari in the sixteenth century. The church

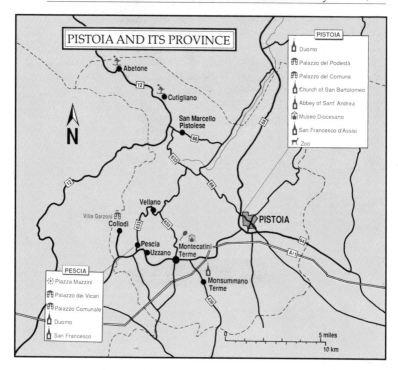

Abetone

Cutigliano

N

San Marcello
Pistoiese

Vellano

Villa Garzoni
Collodi

Pescia
Uzzano

Montecatini
Terme

PISTOIA

Monsummano
Terme

PISTOIA

- Duomo
- Palazzo del Podestà
- Palazzo del Comune
- Church of San Bartolomeo
- Abbey of Sant' Andrea
- Museo Diocesano
- San Francesco d'Assisi
- Zoo

PESCIA

- Piazza Mazzini
- Palazzo dei Vicari
- Palazzo Comunale
- Duomo
- San Francesco

0   5 miles

10 km

is octagonal with a large vestibule serving as the entrance. The vestibule was the first part of the church to be built and used. Its most noteworthy features are a marble altar by Tacca and a fresco which was commissioned in the latter half of the fourteenth century. Work on the octagon was begun in 1509 but suspended in 1522 until Vasari took over 40 years later. Vasari added the third tier of the octagon with the cupola and arranged for the completion of the decoration of the two lower tiers.

The Church of San Francesco dominates Piazza San Francesco d'Assisi. The church has had a chequered history, including spells as a warehouse and as a barrack room before being returned to its original use in 1930. The façade, which is decorated with bands of green and white marble, is striking but the most interesting aspects of the church are the vaulted chapels leading off the large transept. The frescoes in the main chapel are by Puccio Capanna, one of Giotto's closest followers, and depict scenes from the life of St Francis. Many of the other frescoes in the church have suffered the

A sixteenth-century enamelled terracotta frieze on the Ospedale del Ceppo, Pistoia

The Cloisters, Pistoia

ravages of time, but what remains gives a good impression of what the church must have been like during the Renaissance. The Chapter Room which was restored in the late 1960s dates from 1386 and contains more scenes from the life of St Francis, which are almost certainly by Capanna.

Pistoia's biggest tourist attraction for the other residents of Tuscany is its zoo, which is one of the most comprehensive in Italy. It is situated amongst the pines just outside the city.

Like most Italian cities, Pistoia has a traditional sporting event which is competed in once a year by the Quarters of the city. The Giostra dell' Orso, or Bear Joust, was held every year on 9 March from the medieval period until 1666; it was then revived in 1947. Originally the knights representing the various quarters had to hit a target held in the right paw of a bear. Nowadays the bear is a leather shield set up in Piazza del Duomo with two arms which horsemen attacking from different directions attempt to strike.

The Province of Pistoia

For an interesting drive in the Pistoian Mountains, leave the city on the SS64. Soon after leaving Pistoia, the road begins to climb steeply up the mountainside with a series of hairpin bends from which passengers in the car will be able to enjoy magnificent views southwards over the city and the Pistoian Plain. Immediately after the village of Signorino, leave the main road and turn right onto the old road which climbs up to the crest of the Apennine Ridge.

Just before the summit, a small road leads off to the right and follows the crest towards Poggiore. After about 8km (5 miles) a large farmhouse to the left of the road incorporates the remains of the Badia di Taona, an eighth-century Benedictine monastery. An unclassified road leads off to the left here, even further into the mountains. For several kilometres the road is unmetalled, becoming a normal road again when it reaches the tiny mountain village of Torri. Due north of Torri is the large manmade lake of Suviana just over the Tuscan-Emilia Romagnan boundary. The little towns around the lake are quiet summer mountain resorts and it is possible to find places to eat at this stage of the excursion.

Rejoining the SS64 just to the west of the reservoir, the visitor passes through the several small villages which form the mountain *comune* of **Sambuca Pistoiese**. This *comune*, which is centred on the medieval Sambuca Castello, was one of the most important of the Tuscan border posts in the middle ages being fought over for centuries by the city states of Pistoia and Bologna. The castle was virtually impregnable and on the rare occasions when it changed hands it was usually as a result of a wider peace treaty.

The nearby parish church houses a number of interesting seventeenth- and eighteenth-century paintings showing the influence of the Bolognese who were then the most influential of Italian painters.

From Sambuca the main road climbs steadily southwards through attractive scenery for 10km (6 miles), before the visitor has the choice of taking the old road over the summit or the 1960s tunnel through the top of the mountains. On a fine day, the views to be had make it well-worth taking the high road.

A second major excursion from Pistoia heads north-westwards out of the city. Again there is an almost immediate ascent of steep hills with hairpin bends leading up through the forests of chestnut and beech into one of the most beautiful parts of the Apennine Range.

The many villages in these hills are much visited in summer by keen mountaineers and climbers, as well as those just wishing to take pleasant walks in the countryside. One of the most attractive of these villages is **Sammommè**, at the head of the Ombrone Valley, which is surrounded by pleasant chestnut woods. Just outside the nearby village of Piteccio are the ruins of a castle which was the last stronghold of the Pistoian Guelphs after they were driven out of the city in 1305-06.

Other delightful small villages nearby are: Le Piastre, Pracchia on the banks of the River Reno, and Orsigna. The latter is 760m (2,500ft) above sea level and, like the other two, it is a popular starting point for pleasant and not too strenuous mountain walks.

When the main SS66 reaches the village of Le Piastre, take the left turn for **Piteglio** which stands on an outcrop jutting out of the wooded hillside. At the highest point of the town there is an impressively solid looking tower which was originally part of the town's fort and which now acts as the bell tower for the parish church. Just outside the town is an imposing twelfth-century Romanesque abbey.

The main town in the mountainous area of the province is **San Marcello Pistoiese**. Of particular artistic interest in San Marcello is a wax representation of *Pilate Presenting Christ to the Crowds Before the Crucifixion* by Gaetano Gulio (sometimes referred to as Il Zumbo); this is one of the finest surviving examples of the medium. The model can be seen on the second altar on the right in the Romanesque parish Church of San Marcello. Lovers of the Baroque will also find the nearby Oratory of San Marcello interesting.

Three kilometres (2 miles) to the east of San Marcello, along a minor road, is **Gavinana**. Here, in 1530, the defenders of the Florentine

The bell tower with its exterior pulpit, Pistoia

Republic, led by Francesco Ferrucci, fought a last desperate battle against the Imperial troops. The Ferrucciano Museum contains arms and other exhibits relevant to the battle. The village, with its strong Republican associations, became a place of pilgrimage for Italian patriots in the period leading up to the Unification of Italy.

The most famous of the resorts around San Marcello are Cutigliano and Abetone. **Cutigliano**, 5km (3 miles) north-west of San Marcello, is a picturesque medieval town which has developed into a lively and well-equipped mountain resort catering for both winter and summer pursuits. The most impressive building in the town is the Palazzo Pretorio which was built as the overall administrative headquarters of the seven mountain *comuni* in the fourteenth century. The coats of arms of the Capitani di Montagna who resided there can be seen adorning the façade. The parish church contains some interesting paintings, particularly *Saint Bartholemew Carrying Out An Exorcism* by Sebastiano Vini.

The town is linked by a cable car, capable of carrying thirty people, to the ski-slopes of **Doganaccia** 3km (2 miles) to the north. This well-equipped ski-centre can also be reached by car from the

The interior of the world famous Tettuccio Spa at Montecatini Terme →

town, but the 16km (10 mile) drive will take at least 40 minutes, and even longer at weekends, when there can be heavy traffic. A further cable car will take you from Doganaccia to the summit of Monte Croce Arcana.

Well-equipped though Doganaccia is, it is not the area's premier mountain centre; this title belongs unquestionably to **Abetone**, 14km (9 miles) further to the north-west. The name of the town means large fir and is derived from an enormous fir tree which, unfortunately, was chopped down around 100 years ago when the main road was improved and extended to link Tuscany with the Duchy of Modena.

Abetone is the host of important skiing events during the winter, having at its disposal some of the most comprehensive facilities in the whole of Italy. In summer, Abetone is the ideal centre for climbing trips and walking on the well-marked paths through the surrounding forests.

As well as a large number of hotels and boarding houses in the towns and villages, the area is well supplied with *rifugi*. Some of these mountain shelters now offer basic hotel and restaurant services as well as just fulfilling their intended function of giving shelter to mountaineers. The *rifugi* are clearly marked on the low-priced maps of the province which are available in the area.

Other winter sports facilities can be found in the area at Gavinana, which has one ski lift, Maresca which has three, and Val di Luce which has three ski-lifts and a cable car. These smaller centres tend to be less crowded than Cutigliano and Abetone.

During the summer those who decide to walk in this area will come across several small lakes. All of these are well-stocked with trout although it is advisable to check locally whether or not fishing is allowed at any given time.

One of the many cable cars which leaves Abetone goes to the summit of the Alpe delle Tre Potenze (Three Powers Alp), so-called because the summit was the point where the territory of the Grand Duchy of Tuscany met those of the Duchies of Lucca and Modena.

An excellent and reasonably priced restaurant in the area is the Hotel-ristorante La Dogana in the town of the same name just over the boundary in Emilia-Romagna.

Besides Pistoia itself, the main towns on the Pistoian Plain are Pescia and Montecatini Terme. **Pescia** is a pleasant old town at the western extremity of the province and was once important as a border town with the Republic of Lucca. As this role was superseded, the town developed into a major producer and marketer of flowers.

The town itself straddles the river of the same name and, as a result, has developed two distinct focal points: one civil and one

religious. The civil centre of Pescia is, and always has been, Piazza
Mazzini. The most important buildings around the *piazza* are: the
twelfth-century Palazzo dei Vicari which is now the Town Hall, and
the imposing, early thirteenth-century Palazzo Comunale with its
fortified tower. The latter is one of the oldest buildings in the town,
which was almost totally destroyed by the Luccans at the end of the
twelfth century. The town boasts an excellent museum which includes paintings, sculptures and archaeological exhibits. The museum's most notable exhibits are its Etruscan collection and etchings by
Durer and Callot. There is also a library of old manuscripts; both this
and the museum are situated in Palazzo Galleotti.

Pescia is also notable for its fine churches. The Duomo differs
from many others in Tuscany as it is Baroque in style. It was built in
1693 on the site of two older churches, of which some fragments have
been incorporated. The style of the church contrasts with that of the
bell tower, which pre-dates it by almost 400 years.

As far as contents are concerned, the Gothic Church of San
Francesco will be of more interest to the visitor. Of particular interest
is the third altar on the right which is decorated with scenes from the
life of St Francis. These are some of the earliest paintings on this
theme. They were executed only 9 years after the death of the saint
who visited the town and stayed as a guest in a house in Via dei Forni,
the most evidently medieval of all Pescia's streets. However, the
plaque on a house in that street is misleading because the house St
Francis stayed in was an earlier dwelling on that site.

Overlooking the town from the top of the hill immediately
behind the Church of San Francesco is the Convento di Colleviti, a
Renaissance monastery which can be reached by a winding footpath
from the town. The monastery has an attractive Renaissance cloister
and extensive views over the whole of the valley. Also within 3km (2
miles) walking distance of the town is the medieval hill village of
Uzzano which is almost completely unspoilt, with the exception of
the ever-present cars. The village has narrow, winding streets and
there are orchards around the edges of many of the houses so the
village merges almost imperceptibly into the hillside.

Ten kilometres (6 miles) to the north of Pescia is the beautiful
hillside village of **Vellano**, one of the most unspoilt of all the Tuscan
hilltowns. Although people come in summer to enjoy the fresh
mountain air, it is sometimes hard to believe that any other tourist
has ever set foot here. The mountainside on which the village is
situated is so steep that the top of the bell tower of the Church of
Saints Sixtus and Martin, which was established in the tenth century,
is below the floor level of the next building up the slope. Amongst

many fine works of art in the church is a silver reliquary by Benvenuto Cellini, who began his chequered career as a silversmith.

Slightly further to the north is the most impressive of all the Romanesque churches in the Province of Pistoia. The Pieve di Castelvecchio was established in the ninth century, although the bulk of the present building dates from the twelfth. The façade is particularly imposing, with a row of arches surmounted by two tiers of smaller arches. The tripartite design, symbolising the Holy Trinity, is continued inside with triple naves leading up to a raised Presbytery supported by a forest of columns in the crypt. The Pieve's bell tower is detached from the main building which emphasises the fact that this sturdy structure was built with one eye on its defensive possibilities.

Another place worth visiting in this area is Pinocchio's Park. Carlo Lorenzini was born in the town of **Collodi**, just a few kilometres west of Pescia, and took the name of the town as the pseudonym under which he wrote the book. The old hilltown retains much of the charm which inspired Lorenzini to write his book, but around it a whole leisure industry has grown up around his creations. Pinocchio's Park and the adjoining Kingdom of the Toys offer experiences which no child will ever forget. Brightly coloured statues and mosaics in a fantasy setting recreate all Pinocchio's most famous adventures. The Osteria del Gambero Rosso restaurant, just outside the entrance to the park, is one of the finest creations of Italy's leading modernist architect, Michelucci.

The village should not, however, be visited solely for its association with Pinocchio. Besides the characteristic streets of the old hilltown, the grandiose Villa Garzoni, which is the first thing the visitor will see as he approaches the town, is considered to have some of the finest neo-Classical gardens in Italy.

The other main town on the Pistoian plain is **Montecatini Terme**. This famous spa has many springs; their medicinal properties were recognised during the medieval period but it was not until the late eighteenth century that any real commercial exploitation began to take place. In the period from the middle of the last century until the outbreak of World War I, thermal cures were extremely fashionable and, as a result, the town expanded rapidly to become one of the most important spa towns in Europe.

Along with the baths, a large number of parks and a wide range of sporting facilities have been developed to augment the already health-restoring environment. The eight fountains which are used provide different types of water, permitting cures for a variety of ailments. The baths are backed up by modern medical facilities and a scientific research centre. The town's museum has one section devoted to the history of the spa and a second hosting exhibitions.

The old medieval town of **Montecatini Alto** stands at the top of a hill, high (*alto*) above the modern spa town. Once a fortress, fiercely contested by Florence and Lucca, the town had its defences dismantled by Cosimo I in 1554, although the rudiments can still be seen.

The town has not lost its old-world charm, despite the fact that it is generally full of wealthy tourists taking a break from their thermal cures. Several restaurants and well-stocked bars are available to the visitor. The town is reached either by a twisting mountain road, or by a funicular railway which connects it to the spa.

Eight kilometres (5 miles) to the east of Montecatini Terme is another spa, **Monsummano Terme**. The thermal cures take place in the caves of the rocky outcrop behind the town. These cures take a form similar to that of a Turkish bath. The body is made to perspire with the vapour from the hot mineral springs in the caves. The cures are reputed to be particularly effective for the treatment of gout and obesity. The town is mainly modern in aspect, but there is one building which should not be missed. The Church of Santa Maria di Fontenuova, in the central square, is an elegant Baroque structure dating from the first decade of the seventeenth century. Three sides of the church are bordered by loggias under which is a series of fifteen frescoes by Giovanni di San Giovanni depicting the miracles of the Madonna of the Fontenuova (New Bath).

On the top of the outcrop in which the thermal caves are situated is the sadly neglected old hilltown of **Monsummano Alto**. The town developed around a medieval fortress of which the only significant remnant is a crumbling pentagonal tower. The town has been gradually abandoned over the years and the majority of the houses and the Romanesque church with its distinctive fortified bell tower are now in a state of disrepair. However, it is worth taking a walk up to the town, to enjoy the magnificent views down the Nievole Valley.

Another attractive hill village, in a better state of repair, is **Montevettolini**, 5km (3 miles) to the south-east. The most significant aspect of this village is the old fortress which was transformed by Grand Duke Ferdinando I into a hunting lodge for the Grand Ducal court in the late sixteenth century. The lodge was visited regularly by Ferdinando I but was sold, along with the hunting rights, to the Val di Nievole by his grandson Ferdinando II in 1650. Dominating the crest of the ridge which separates the Val di Nievole from the Val d'Ombrone and Pistoia is **Serravalle Pistoiese**. Seen from the nearby motorway, the ruins of the medieval castle which dominate the village offer an invitation to the visitor which is hard to resist.

6

PISA AND ITS PROVINCE

The name **Pisa** immediately conjures up visions of the famous Leaning Tower. There is, however, much more to Tuscany's second largest city than one monument. Despite the considerable damage suffered in World War II, Pisa remains one of Italy's most beautiful cities, with many fine examples of Medieval and Renaissance art and architecture.

The origins of Pisa are uncertain, although it is known that the site, where the Rivers Arno and Serchio flowed into a large lagoon, was inhabited by the sixth century BC. Under the Romans, the town became an important naval base which continued to develop under the Goths and Longobards.

In the eleventh century Pisa became an autonomous *comune* whose policies tended to support the Empire. This loyalty was rewarded by Frederick Barbarossa, who endowed Pisa with large areas of coast. The town was given jurisdiction over the whole coastline from Portovenere to Civitavecchia, as well as feudal rights in Naples, Salerno, Calabria and parts of Sicily. Shortly afterwards, the whole of Sardinia also passed under Pisan rule.

The thirteenth century saw the town almost continually engaged in wars against nearby Lucca, Florence (which needed an outlet to the sea to facilitate her growth as a trading nation) and Genoa which sought to gain dominance over Sardinia and Corsica. In 1284 the Pisan fleet was finally destroyed by the Genoans who took away the heavy chain which had defended the entrance to Pisa's harbour. After the Unification of Italy, the ancient chain was restored to Pisa and is now hung in the Campo Santo. Over six intervening centuries, silt from the rivers had completely filled the lagoon leaving the city in its present position, several kilometres from the sea.

After the loss of its fleet, Pisa was beset by internal strife. This culminated in the famous episode when Count Ugolino della Gherardesca was locked up in a tower with his sons and grandsons and left to starve to death. The episode is recorded by Dante in one of the most powerful passages in the *Inferno*.

The city was taken by Florence in 1406 after a long siege. An initial period of neglect and decadence was followed by a revival under the Medici, particularly in the field of education. The Pisan Study, which had almost disappeared, was revived in 1472 by Lorenzo the Magnificent, who also began building the University. To this day, Pisa retains these two centres of higher education. The Study, known as the Scuola Normale di Pisa, is the most highly regarded educational institution in Italy.

Pisa's Piazza del Duomo is the site of the city's most famous monuments; it is usually known as the 'Field of Miracles'. The *piazza* is formed of a large, well-tended grass lawn, on which are situated the Duomo, the Baptistry, the Bell Tower (better known as the Leaning Tower) and the Campo Santo.

Construction of the Duomo was begun in 1064 and completed towards the end of the following century. Despite this long construction period, the Duomo displays a remarkable degree of architectural unity and harmony. It is without doubt the most beautiful of the many Romanesque cathedrals in Italy.

The three bronze doors of the façade were made in Florence at the end of the sixteenth century after the originals had been destroyed by fire. The doors were considered so fine by the Florentines that they considered altering the front of the Duomo in Florence to keep the doors there. The bronze door opposite the Leaning Tower which is now normally used as the entrance, is also worthy of note.

Inside, the Duomo is rich in works of art. One of the problems of visiting churches in Italy is that so many fine artists have contributed to their decoration that only the professional art historian will have heard of all of them; this is the case in the Duomo of Pisa. Many paintings are by artists who in any other country would be national heroes, but in Italy are overshadowed by contemporaries such as Michelangelo and Leonardo.

The only world famous painter to be represented here is Andrea del Sarto. On the other hand, much of the sculpture in the Duomo is the work of two of the world's famous sculptors; Giovanni Pisano and Giambologna. Amongst these works, the most important is Pisano's Pulpit, similar but superior to that described in the previous chapter.

Construction of the Baptistry was begun in 1152 and finished towards the end of the fourteenth century. During this period the

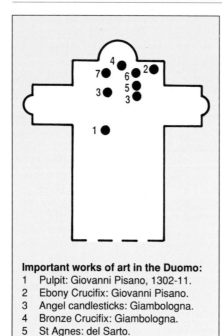

Important works of art in the Duomo:
1 Pulpit: Giovanni Pisano, 1302-11.
2 Ebony Crucifix: Giovanni Pisano.
3 Angel candlesticks: Giambologna.
4 Bronze Crucifix: Giambologna.
5 St Agnes: del Sarto.
6 St Peter and St John the Baptist: del Sarto.

work was supervised by Nicola and Giovanni Pisano, amongst others. The two Pisanos were responsible for much of the sculpture which originally decorated the building. Most of the sculptures which can be seen today are copies of the originals, which have mostly been rehoused in various museums in the city. Some original works remain however, having been transferred from the outside of the building to a more protected situation on the marble seat which runs round the inside of the walls. The following statues can be seen there: *Virgin and Child*, *St John the Evangelist*, a *Prophet*, *David and Prophet with scroll* by Giovanni Pisano; and *Moses*, *St Matthew*, *St Mark*, and *St Luke* by Nicola Pisano.

The most important piece of sculpture, however, is the Pulpit by Nicola Pisano. This pulpit is supported by columns resting on lions and human figures, but is not quite as refined as that by his son inside the Duomo. The contrast between the two gives the visitor the chance to understand the developments in sculpture which took place in the space of one generation.

The Leaning Tower, or Bell Tower, of Pisa was begun in 1173 but abandoned at the level of the third floor when the ground began to subside. Work was started again 100 years later and finished towards the end of the fourteenth century. At the moment the tower leans by just under 3m, at an angle of 55° and this is increasing by 1mm per year.

Each floor level has a marble walkway behind the pillars which support the succeeding floors. Some of these walkways are not

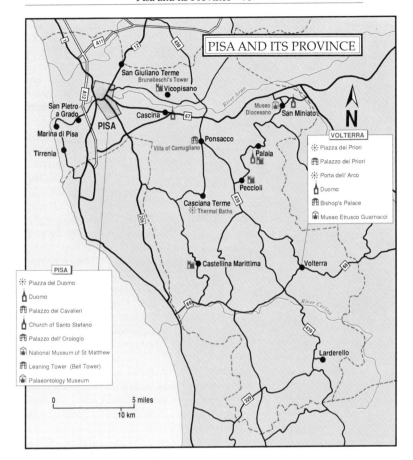

PISA AND ITS PROVINCE

San Giuliano Terme
Brunelleschi's Tower
Vicopisano

San Pietro
a Grado
Cascina
PISA

Marina di Pisa

Tirrenia

Villa of Camugliano

Ponsacco

Palaia

Peccioli

Casciana Terme
Thermal Baths

Castellina Marittima

Museo
Diocesano
San Miniato

N

VOLTERRA
Piazza dei Priori
Palazzo dei Priori
Porta dell' Arco
Duomo
Bishop's Palace
Museo Etrusco Guarnacci

Volterra

River Cecina

Larderello

PISA
Piazza del Duomo
Duomo
Palazzo dei Cavalieri
Church of Santo Stefano
Palazzo dell' Orologio
National Museum of St Matthew
Leaning Tower (Bell Tower)
Palaeontology Museum

0   5 miles
10 km

equipped with handrails, and should be treated with great caution. The top of the tower where the bells are housed is almost straight, having been deliberately finished out of line with the preceding floors. For the visitor who does not suffer from vertigo, and is willing to attempt the 294 steps, there is a magnificent view of the rest of the 'Field of Miracles', and surrounding area.

At the time of writing, the tower is temporarily closed while a major safety review is carried out. It is expected that the tower will be open to the public again when the review is complete.

The rectangular, marble Campo Santo, which dates from 1277, ✳ was a cemetery for the rich Pisan nobles of the late Medieval and

Renaissance periods. To the original funeral monuments and frescoes have been added many other pieces of sculpture from the city and the surrounding area. Over eighty of the sarcophagi are of Roman origin.

Some of the monuments contained in the Campo Santo were destroyed by an American bombardment in 1944. A series of twenty-three frescoes by Benozzo Gozzoli on Old Testament themes was badly damaged by molten lead from the roof in the same raid, but they have been restored as far as possible.

On the south side of the Campo dei Miracoli stands the former Chapterhouse of the Duomo. The building served this purpose from the thirteenth to the seventeenth centuries. At that time the building was given a facelift and became the Diocesan seminary, a function which it performed until passing into private hands in 1784. It was reacquired by the church in 1887, when it became a Capuchin monastery. In 1979 it was taken over by the Cathedral Works Society and in 1986 was opened to the public as the Museo dell' Opera del Duomo. As well as smaller items of value which have been removed from the Duomo and Baptistry for security reasons, the museum also houses many larger works of art which have been removed (and mainly replaced by copies) in order to protect them from air pollution and the gradual erosion caused by the elements.

Rooms one to eight are dedicated to sculptures. In the thirteenth and fourteenth centuries, when many of the works which decorated the Duomo were commissioned, the Pisan sculptors were undisputedly the greatest in Italy (and probably in Europe) so there can be few finer and more homogenous sculpture museums anywhere. The highlights are the sculptures of Nicola and Giovanni Pisano who provided masterpieces for all the major Tuscan Duomo's of the period (with the exception of Pisa's enemy, Florence). The reason why the statues were removed from the exterior of the Duomo and the Baptistry is clear to see when one looks at the large statues which originally stood in the niches around the Baptistry. The once smooth surfaces are badly pitted after centuries of exposure while the occasional head or arm has been lost.

Room seven is dedicated to the works of Tino da Camaiano, the greatest of the thirteenth-century Sienese sculptors who collaborated with the Pisanos on the production of the magnificent pulpit which still stands in the Duomo. Rooms seven and eight consist mainly of works by Nino and Tommaso Pisano, the last of the great Pisan sculptors.

Rooms nine and ten are dedicated to the 'Treasures' of the Duomo which are formed mainly of gold and silver reliquaries. Also housed here are the remnants of the Cintola of the Duomo, a long stretch of cloth decorated with gold, silver and precious stones which was wrapped around the Duomo on the day it was consecrated.

Rooms eleven and twelve contain paintings. Room thirteen contains the few surviving items of the intricately carved fifteenth- and sixteenth-century wooded furniture of the Duomo, much of which was destroyed in a fire in 1595. Room fourteen contains parchments, intricately carved corals and luxuriously decorated wall hangings from the Sacristy. The remaining rooms are devoted to etchings of the Cathedral complex and to archaeological finds from the Campo Santo.

In 1561, Cosimo I created a new order of chivalry in Tuscany, the Order of the Knights of St Stephen. The Order was to a large extent a naval order as its prime concern was to rid the Mediterranean of pirates. As such, the newly developed port of Livorno was the base for its operations, but the adminstrative centre was established in Pisa. Cosimo gave Vasari the task of transforming the medieval Piazza delle Sette Vie into a fitting centre for the Knights. The result was the transformation of the *piazza* into the beautiful Piazza dei Cavalieri.

The sides of the imposing Palazzo dei Cavalieri reveal traces of the medieval architecture of the former Palazzo degli Anziani which Vasari transformed into the headquarters of the new Order. The great beauty of this building lies in its façade, which is completely covered with intricate designs produced entirely by Vasari. The six busts in the niches on the façade represent the first six of the seven Medici Grand Dukes who were Grand Masters of the Order. The statue of Cosimo I in white Luni marble which stands in front of the building was commissioned by Ferdinando I in 1596. The building now houses the Scuola Normale di Pisa.

The Church of Santo Stefano, which stands at the south-west corner of the *piazza*, is basically Vasarian, although the lateral naves were added later. The façade was designed by Don Giovanni de' Medici, Cosimo's illegitimate son, and prominently exposes the Medici arms. Much of the decoration inside the church consists of paintings celebrating the successes of the Order, or of decorations stripped from the pirate ships they captured. In the choir, the gilded bronze reliquary in the shape of a bust of San Rossore is by Donatello.

On the other side of the Palazzo dei Cavalieri is the Palazzo dell' Orologio. This originally comprised two medieval towers with a road running in between. Vasari's linking of the two towers with an archway was a brilliant architectural solution which allowed him to create a Renaissance effect with a minimum of work on the existing

The Baptistry, Pisa

building and without altering the street plan. The clock was added at the end of the seventeenth century.

One of the two original towers is known as the Torre del Fame, (Tower of Hunger) as this is where Count Ugolino and his descendants were left to starve to death.

Pisa's most important museum, the National Museum of St Matthew, is situated in an old Benedictine monastery. The museum houses important examples of Tuscan painting and sculpture dating from the twelfth to the fifteenth centuries.

Room five contains sculptures which have been removed from the Duomo and the Baptistry. Unfortunately, not enough is known about the origins of these sculptures to say definitely if they are by one of the Pisanos, or if they were produced by their followers.

In the glass case separating rooms twelve and thirteen is a gilded bronze bas-relief by Ghiberti of the *Adoration of the Magi*. Guido Reni's *Sacred and Profane Love* is displayed in room seventeen while other important paintings by Tuscan artists can be seen in rooms twenty-one to twenty-five.

Room thirty-five is devoted to paintings by foreign painters. Most of these represented are of the Dutch school, but there is a fine portrait of George IV by Thomas Lawrence.

The Mineralogy and Petrography Museum, which is run by the University, offers the visitor the opportunity to see and understand all the different stones and minerals which are found in Tuscany.

Another part of the University, the Palaeontology Museum, is one of the oldest of its kind in Italy. Tuscany was inhabited by a number of prehistoric peoples so the exhibits are numerous and enlightening. Like the previous museum, the Palaeontology Museum is

The Leaning Tower →

situated in Via Santa Maria 53.

The last of the University-run museums, that of Zoology and Comparative Anatomy, is situated in the old Monastery of Santa Croce in Fossabanda. The museum is of particular interest to ornithologists, osteologists and biologists, but other visitors with a little time to spare may also find it interesting.

The tiny rectangular Gothic Church of Santa Maria della Spina was originally situated on the river bank. Due to the danger of being washed away by the river, the marble building of 1323 was taken down piece by piece in 1871 and reconstructed in its present site on the promenade. The church is no longer in use, the statues by Nino and Tommaso Pisano which adorned the inside have been relocated elsewhere. The unique nature of the exterior, however, makes the church an essential part of any visit to Pisa.

San Michele in Borgo was built in the ninth century over a temple which had been dedicated to Mars. It is situated near the beginning of the city's main street, the finely porticoed Via Borgo Stretto. The interior of the church was damaged during World War II, and only the traces of the antique frescoes remain. Despite the many repairs and alterations which have taken place, the impression given is still one of architectural primitiveness.

Santa Paola a Ripa d'Arno is one of the oldest churches in Pisa, dating from 805. Adaptations over the centuries show the influence which the Duomo has had on the other Pisan churches. The inside was gutted in World War II and has been almost entirely renewed.

The twelfth-century Church of San Nicola contains a wooden statue of the Virgin and Child by Nino Pisano, and a wooden crucifix by Giovanni Pisano. However, the most important thing to see while visiting this church is the bell tower. Leaning slightly, although less than the famous Leaning Tower, it is ascended by a heptagonal open staircase. This staircase is said to have inspired Bramante's staircase in the Vatican, and Sangallo's Pozzo di San Patrizia in Orvieto.

Santa Caterina was built by the Dominicans between 1251 and 1300, in simple Pisan-Romanesque style with a marble façade. The marble statues by the high altar are by Nino Pisano, as is the funeral monument to Archbishop Simone Saltarelli in a side chapel.

The Province of Pisa

The Province of Pisa is made up of two distinct areas. In the north the province consists of the Arno Valley from San Miniato until it reaches the sea, just after Pisa. This area is mainly flat, with older towns on outcrops at either side of the valley, and newer ones along the busy main road near the river.

In terms of size, the south of the province would appear to be the more important, but it is composed of little more than a number of agricultural villages dotted around the hills. The only town of any size is Volterra.

East of Pisa, in the north of the province, the first town of any importance is **Cascina**. The town, which is now an important centre for the manufacture of furniture, was once fiercely contested by Pisa, Lucca and Florence. There is a permanent exhibition of modern furniture in the town, but the real attraction in Cascina is the Pieve di Santa Maria. This twelfth-century abbey is built in the Pisan-Romanesque style with a façade composed of a double row of arches. A small staircase leads up from the left-hand nave to the Baroque Chapel of the Sacrament.

Seven kilometres (4 miles) to the north of Cascina, on the side of Monte Pisano, is the little town of **Vicopisano**. Like Cascina, it was long disputed by the Pisans and the Florentines, changing hands several times before finally being taken by the Florentines in 1498. The town's military importance can be gauged by the remains of the fortifications in the town. The most important of these are 'Brunelleschi's Tower' which dates from the early fifteenth century and the 'Tower with the Four Doors' which originally had to be passed under by anyone wishing to enter the medieval nucleus of the town. At the heart of this medieval nucleus is the fourteenth-century Palazzo Pretorio. It is decorated by numerous coats of arms, some carved out of stone and some in terracotta. The central tower of the medieval fortress is now incorporated in a private house at the highest point of the town.

The most important town east of Pisa is **San Miniato**. This town grew up around an eighth-century church, dedicated to the Florentine martyr, St Miniato. A succession of emperors favoured the town, but in the middle of the thirteenth century it became self-governing. From 1369 onwards, the town became part of the Florentine Republic.

The most interesting building in the town is the Church of San Domenico. The church and its cloister are full of fine works of art. Not far from the Church of San Domenico is the Duomo, which is not as interesting for its works of art, but is more impressive from an architectural point of view. A rich collection of works of art is housed in the Museo Diocesano. Most of the exhibits originate from the area; the most important is a *Crucifixion* by Filippo Lippi.

The town's original eighth-century church was rebuilt in the thirteenth and then in the second half of the fifteenth century, and is now dedicated to St Francis.

Palazzo dei Cavalieri with its intricately designed façade, Pisa

One of the branches of the Bonaparte family originated in San Miniato, and a plaque on the wall of a house in Piazza Buonaparte informs the visitor that Canon Filippo Buonaparte played host to his more famous cousin in 1797.

On a hill above the town is a replica of the medieval tower which was destroyed in World War II. Excellent views in all directions repay the visitor for having made the climb up the hill.

The southern part of the Province of Pisa, while not as spectacular as some of the other parts of Tuscany, is one of the most pleasant and unspoilt areas in the region. With the exception of Volterra, there are no towns of great historic importance, but the rolling green hills are dotted with little villages connected by winding country lanes. There is no specific route to be recommended while viewing this part of Tuscany, the best way is to buy a detailed road map and slowly make your way to Volterra. Villages which merit a short visit (although not a detour) include Montecatini Val di Cecina, Casale Marittima, Castellina Marittima, Casciana Terme, Palaia, Ponsacco, Capannoli and Peccioli.

Montecatini Val di Cecina is a small hilltown which has now become a quiet summer resort. It stands on a hill to the north of the River Cecina with splendid views over the valley and towards

The sixteenth-century bronze doors of the Duomo, Pisa

Volterra. The latter views are particularly impressive at dawn and in the evening, when the last rays of sun pick out the towers of Volterra against a darkening eastern sky. Montecatini itself is basically a medieval town dominated by a high tower, the lower part of which is formed by alternate black and white bands.

Casale Marittima, a sleepy little hilltown, faces over the northern part of the Maremma and developed in the middle ages when malaria drove people off the coast into the nearby hills. Before that, however, the site had been occupied by the Etruscans and several of their tombs have been found near the town. One of these tombs has been dismantled and re-erected in the garden of the archaeological museum in Florence.

Castellina Marittima is a small village 16km (10 miles) inland from Castiglioncello with a medieval fortress and traces of an old defensive wall. The north-south road which passes through the village offers some attractive scenery and in summer offers an interesting alternative to the larger roads nearer the coast which are sometimes jammed solid with traffic.

Roughly half way between Pisa and Volterra, on a hill covered with vines and olives, is **Casciana Terme**. The warm thermal waters of this spa town were known to the Romans for their therapeutic properties. The town was developed commercially in the eighteenth century, and now the thermal baths are open from May to September for the relief of those with various disorders. Just over 2km (1 mile) away, on a slightly higher hill, is the medieval village of **Casciana Alta**. An important polyptych by the early fourteenth-century Sienese artist Lippo Memmi can be seen in the parish Church of Santa Maria Assunta.

Twenty-four kilometres (15 miles) north-east of Casciana Terme, on the road to San Miniato, is the busy little town of **Palaia**. The town developed in the medieval period around a feudal castle. Much of the medieval centre has remained, but new buildings have been added to support thriving furniture and fruit and vegetable businesses. The Abbey of San Martino near the town is a fine example of the thirteenth-century Gothic, being unusual in that most country churches of the same period were in the Romanesque style.

Just outside the small town of Ponsacco, is the fortress-like Medicean Villa of Camugliano which was built by Dukes Alessandro and Cosimo I, both as a residence and as a strongpoint in the event of any revolt by the Pisans. The villa is similar in style to that of other Medicean villas of the period except that a strong fortified tower has been added at each corner. The villa also has more outbuildings than other villas of the period as they were designed to accommodate a substantial number of troops as well as the usual accoutrements of a country residence.

Another fine villa, although this time not a Medicean villa, is the neo-Classical Villa Bourbon del Monte which was built by Felix Baciocchi, Napoleon's brother-in-law. The villa was built over the ruins of an old early medieval fortress in the village of **Capannoli** which had been a feud of the Gherardeschi family.

Just to the south of Capannoli is **Peccioli**, in a fine position on the top of a hill lined with vineyards. Of interest here are the medieval Palazzo Pretorio and the ruins of the fortress erected in the thirteenth century by the warlike Luccan leader Castruccio Castracani.

There are very few towns anywhere in the world with as much historical importance as **Volterra**. The town is built on a spur, high above the confluence of the Rivers Era and Cecina. Stylistically the town has changed little since the late medieval period, when it was last an important city. Before the Florentines gained control of the town in 1360, it had been one of the most important centres in Italy for over 2,000 years.

The first known settlement at Volterra was in the ninth century BC, at the height of the Iron Age. Some of the most advanced examples of Iron Age (Villanovian) artefacts have been found in the area around Volterra. In the eighth century, the Villanovians were over-run by highly educated invaders from Asia Minor, the result of the fusion of the two peoples being the Etruscan civilisation.

Volterra's geographical situation is typical of that favoured by the Etruscans, and the town became one of their most important centres. Even after becoming a Roman *municipium*, the town retained its importance, continuing to strike its own money. When the Roman Empire declined, the town's near-impregnable position and its rich mineral deposits meant that it was relatively untroubled during the Dark Ages and was then one of the first towns to emerge as a strong, free-trading, independent *comune* in the medieval period.

In the fourteenth century, Volterra became involved in the struggle for supremacy in Tuscany, along with Pisa, Siena, Florence, Lucca and San Gimignano. At this point, the town's former strength became its weakness, as the hilltop position limited its capacity for expansion and population increase. As a result of this, Volterra became, like Fiesole and San Gimignano before it, part of the Florentine Republic in 1360, although it was not until 1530 that attempts to regain independence finally came to an end.

The centre of Volterra is Piazza dei Priori, which is completely surrounded by thirteenth-century buildings, all constructed out of the same grey stone. One of the buildings is the Palazzo dei Priori,

Riverfront houses in Pisa

which was built between 1208 and 1254. It is the oldest seat of government in Tuscany, being more than half a century older than Florence's Palazzo Vecchio. The tower of the *palazzo* is pentagonal, which is unusual in Italy.

The second floor of the *palazzo* has been an art gallery since 1905, and the quality of the paintings make it one of the most important in Tuscany. The most important pictures in the gallery are *The Annunciation* by Signorelli, and Ghirlandaio's *Jesus with Saints*. After visiting the gallery, the visitor may also go up the tower, if a custodian is available to act as guide. The top of the tower offers one of the most extensive views in Tuscany. The other building of historical interest in the square is the Palazzo del Podestà which shared the administration of the city in the medieval period.

Behind the Palazzo dei Priori are the Duomo, the Baptistry and the Bishop's Palace. The Bishop's Palace, which is separated from the Duomo by a fourteenth-century cloister, has housed a Museum of Sacred Art since 1936. All the exhibits are from the Duomo and other churches in the diocese of Volterra. The most important exhibit is a gilded bronze crucifix by Giambologna.

In spite of the transfer of many works of art to the museum, the Duomo is still richly decorated with paintings, frescoes and sculp-

Church of Santa Maria della Spina, Pisa

tures. The most outstanding work of art in the church is the pulpit, which was probably erected by a follower of the Pisano family. The exterior of the Duomo was originally Romanesque, but it was altered to the Pisan style in the late thirteenth century. The bell tower, which was added in 1493, was originally higher, but had to be lowered for safety reasons.

The octagonal Baptistry, with its green and white marble will, at first, remind the visitor of the Baptistry in Pistoia; closer inspection, however, reveals it to be smaller and less ornate.

Important though the aforementioned monuments are, the most important site for the visitor to see is the Museo Etrusco Guarnacci. This museum is one of the most important of all the Etruscan museums. Even the visitor who knows nothing about Etruscan civilisation will be fascinated by the variety of carvings on the urns and sacrophagi, and the fine tracery on the mirrors and vases. Although not quite matching the technical level of the Greeks, with whom they shared much mythology, the Etruscans produced art which is far more lively and vigorous than most of that of contemporary Classical Greece.

At the highest point of the town is the fortress. This was formed by linking up two earlier forts, and is one of the most impressive examples of Renaissance military architecture. The fort is used as a prison and is normally only viewable from the outside.

The southern section of the town's medieval wall follows the line of the earlier Etruscan defences. Volterra is unusual in that the most recent of its walls contains the smallest area. The remnants of the 12m (40ft) high, 5m (15ft) wide Etruscan wall circumscribes an area more than three times as big as the medieval town, giving an impression of just how important Volterra once was.

In the middle of the section of wall common to both Etruscans and medievals is the Porta dell 'Arco, the best-preserved Etruscan gateway in Italy. The blocks of stone used in its construction are massive, a fact which is emphasised by the nearby Roman masonry. The three sculpted heads above the gate have been rendered virtually unrecognisable by over 2,000 years of wind and rain, and it is impossible to tell whether they are Etruscan or Roman.

The western extremity of the former Etruscan city is marked by steep cliffs, the Balze, which fall away to the valley below. Erosion takes place continually, and over the centuries two churches and a cemetery have disappeared over the Balze. The nearby Badia, which was damaged by an earthquake in 1846, had to be abandoned in 1861 because of the danger of collapse. Just outside the medieval wall, to the north of the town, is a large, grassy area where excavations have revealed important Roman remains. These consist of the theatre and the baths, along with other buildings of lesser importance. Further to the north, beyond the Etruscan *Porta Diana*, is an area where many Etruscan burial vaults have been found. The treasures which they once contained have been removed, but the tombs themselves may be visited with the permission of the farmers who own the land.

Twenty-four kilometres (15 miles) to the south of Volterra, amid beautiful scenery, is the town of **Larderello**. It is mainly of interest to those whose hobby is industrial history. The hot springs in the area contain boric acid, the extraction and refinement of which began in 1818. From the beginning, the heat of the water drove the industrial plant, and in 1905 the pressure of the springs was harnessed to provide electricity. The modern residential area of Larderello is an example of some of the best post-war Italian architecture.

7

*LIVORNO
AND ITS PROVINCE*

The name **Livorno** first appears in documents of the tenth century, when the castle there became one of the forts defending
Pisa's coastal territories. The town changed hands several times over
the centuries, as the balance of military and financial power shifted.
On the whole, however, the town declined after 1200 until being
redeveloped by the Medici in the sixteenth century to replace the
silted-up port of Pisa. When Florence bought Livorno from Genoa in
1421, Saracen raids and malaria had reduced the town to a village
with little more than 1,000 inhabitants.

To encourage the development of Livorno as a city as well as a
port, Cosimo I introduced what was then a unique constitution for
the town; one which gave rights of settlement to people of all
religions and backgrounds. As a result, the town soon developed
prosperous communities of Jews and other persecuted minorities.
While English communities in Italy were usually formed of Catholic
refugees, when Livorno was developed it was Elizabeth's fallen
favourites, almost all Protestant, who formed the nucleus of the
town's English quarter. The Earl of Leicester's son had his titles
recognised in Livorno by the Holy Roman Emperor, although his
family had been banished and relieved of their titles in England.

The city is unusual for Italy in that it has no medieval monuments.
It is interesting because the centre of the city was designed by
Buontalenti in 1575 in the form of a pentagon. In a way, the design of
the city represents a Renaissance ideal of urban planning.
Buontalenti's pentagonal city can be seen clearly when one looks at
a plan of modern Livorno. The Duomo is at the centre of the
pentagon, the seaward side meets up with the Medicean port, and

two of the corners are dominated by large forts. Livorno's importance as a port and a naval base led to heavy bombardments during World War II which destroyed many of the buildings in the centre.

The focal point of Buontalenti's Livorno is the Duomo, the construction of which was ordered by Ferdinando I in 1594. The original design was by Buontalenti himself but this was adapted by Alessandro Pieroni who carried out the bulk of the work. The portico of the façade is of great interest to historians of architecture as it is an early design by Inigo Jones. The Duomo was devastated by bombs during the last war but has since been rebuilt. Some interesting funeral monuments inside the Duomo survived the bombings; they include that to Count Ginori, the founder of the famous pottery and ceramics firm.

Another church in which Pieroni was involved was the Chiesa dei Greci Uniti. The Grand Ducal galleys were manned mainly by Greeks who lived in a small area of the city to the east of the Duomo. As a reward for their loyalty over many years, Ferdinando I gave them a larger area of the city and provided the money for the building of a Greek Orthodox Church. After damage suffered in World War II, the church was restored but not reconsecrated.

At the top of the pentagon, near the Fortezza Nuova, is an area of the city known as New Venice, because many of the houses were built along two canals as ideal residences for fishermen. In this part of the city is the eighteenth-century Church of Santa Caterina, an octagonal structure with a high dome. The church houses Vasari's *Incoronation of the Virgin*.

Just outside the station, near the Maritime Station, is the Church of San Ferdinando, which dates from the beginning of the eighteenth century. The interior is richly decorated with marble and, despite war damage, it remains one of the most attractive churches in Livorno.

Livorno's most important monuments are to be found on the northern section of the seafront. This corner of the pentagon is protected by the old fort, built by Sangallo in the 1520s over the old medieval castle. The damage suffered during World War II has revealed traces of late Roman fortifications on the site. It was from this fort that Maria de' Medici left Tuscany to become one of the most important Queens of France while, from the Old Basin below the fort, Amerigo Vespucci left Italy to give his name to America.

At the end of the Old Basin, in the middle of the seaward side of the pentagon, is the famous monument of Ferdinando I, usually known as the Monument of the Four Moors because of the chained, bronze Barbarians which decorate the corners of the equestrian statue to the

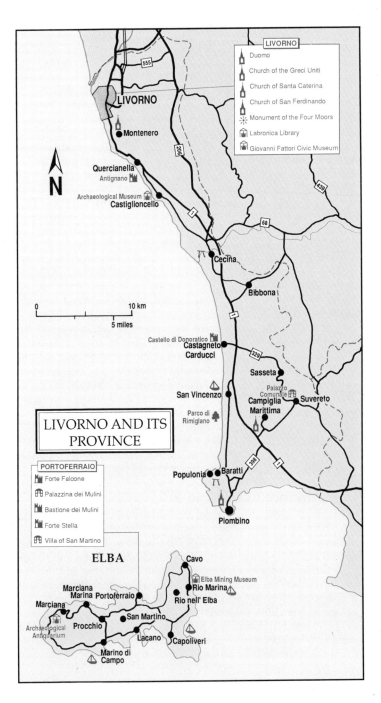

LIVORNO

- Duomo
- Church of the Greci Uniti
- Church of Santa Caterina
- Church of San Ferdinando
- Monument of the Four Moors
- Labronica Library
- Giovanni Fattori Civic Museum

555

LIVORNO

Montenero

206

Quercianella
Antignano

Archaeological Museum
Castiglioncello

439

68

Cecina

Bibbona

N

0   10 km
5 miles

Castello di Donoratico
Castagneto
Carducci

329

Sasseta

San Vincenzo

Palazzo
Comunale
Campiglia   Suvereto
Marittima

LIVORNO AND ITS PROVINCE

Parco di
Rimigliano

398

Populonia   Baratti

PORTOFERRAIO

- Forte Falcone
- Palazzina dei Mulini
- Bastione dei Mulini
- Forte Stella
- Villa of San Martino

Piombino

ELBA

Cavo

Elba Mining Museum

Marciana   Rio Marina
Marina   Portoferraio
Marciana   Rio nell' Elba

Archaeological
Antiquarium   Procchio   San Martino

Lacano   Capoliveri

Marino di
Campo

Grand Duke. The statue was commissioned by Ferdinando I in 1595 and shows him dressed in the robes of the Grand Master of the Order of the Knights of St Stephen. However, the statue itself, which was sculpted by Giovanni Bandini, is far inferior to the superb bronze sculptures by Pietro Tacca which symbolise past naval victories over the Barbarians.

In the new part of the city, only the Park of Villa Fabbricotti will be of any interest to the visitor. At the centre of this large park, in the nineteenth-century villa from which it takes its name, is a library and the city's museum. The Labronica Library contains almost 200,000 volumes including many antique books and manuscripts. The Giovanni Fattori Civic Museum, on the second floor, is named after the city's most famous artist. Most of the museum is devoted to Fattori and his Macchiaioli school, although there is also some fine work by Livorno's other famous artist, Modigliani. Apart from the modern works of art, the museum also has small Roman and Etruscan collections.

One of the best views of the city and the coastline is from **Montenero**, a hill 5km (3 miles) south-east of the city centre. Part way up the hill is the Sanctuary of Montenero which is reached by funicular railway. The church was established by the Jesuits in the fifteenth century, and then amplified at the end of the eighteenth. Inside the church, the rich decoration includes a gilded wooden ceiling and several fine Baroque frescoes. Byron, Shelley, Thorwaldsen and Napoleon III were some of the famous people who lived in the villas around the sanctuary in the last century.

On the coast below Montenero is the small but solid fortress of Antignano. This was built by Cosimo I in 1561 so that the vineyards he had established on the slopes of Montenero would 'not from pirates be protected, but from deer and wild boar'.

The Province of Livorno

Like several of the other Tuscan provinces, the Province of Livorno can be divided into two distinct parts. The first, which is dominated by Livorno itself, consists of a fairly narrow, 90km (55 mile) long strip of land along the coast. Several popular holiday resorts and towns with Etruscan origins constitute the points of interest in this area which is otherwise devoted to agriculture. The more attractive part of the province is that which consists of most of the Tuscan Archipelago islands; Elba, Capraia, Gorgona, Pianosa and Montecristo.

The mainland part of the province is bisected by the SS1 Via Aurelia, from Livorno in the north, all the way to the border with the Province of Grosseto in the south. The first town of any importance after Livorno is **Quercianella**, where a small but popular and well-equipped beach divides the pines from the sea. This stretch of coastline is very attractive, with rocky slopes falling away from the twisting coast road to the sea.

Twenty kilometres (12 miles) after Quercianella is the province's most important seaside resort, **Castiglioncello**. Castiglioncello's access to the sea is by way of several little bays, some of which are sandy and some of which have rocks all the way down to the water's edge. A small museum in the town contains the finds from around 300 Etruscan tombs dating from the third to the first centuries BC which were uncovered when the railway line and the station were built.

Another interesting museum is to be found 13km (8 miles) further on in **Cecina**. Most of the exhibits are Etruscan but there is also a fair collection of Roman antiquities uncovered during recent excavations in the area.

In the next few kilometres, the main road passes turnings on one side to small resorts which are becoming more popular every year, and on the other side to villages which grew up around several medieval castles, such as Bibbona and Castagneto Carducci.

Perched on a hilltop, 5km (3 miles) inland, **Castagneto** was the town where the poet Giosue Carducci spent a part of his youth and set many of his most famous works. Were it not for its literary connections, the town would pass unnoticed by the visitor as it has no important monuments which justify a visit in themselves. However, the town is attractive with many picturesque little alleyways connecting the main streets.

Overlooking the town is the medieval Castello della Gherardesca. The battlements and tower of the castle were restored in the 1930s, partly using stones from the ruined Castello di Donoratico, the remains of which can be seen on a hill 3km (2 miles) to the south-west. Directly underneath the Castello della Gherardesca is the parish church. The visitor who is feeling somewhat indifferent by now towards the dark paintings which fill most of the churches in larger towns, will be pleasantly surprised to find that this church is decorated almost exclusively with polychromatic terracotta statues, set between faded frescoes of saints under a fairly simple wooden roof. After Castagneto do not rejoin the monotonous SS1 'Aurelia' but continue along the twisting SS329 towards Suvereto. The road runs through spectacular wooded scenery, with occasional distant views of the inland hills and valleys, for 8km (5 miles) to Sasseta.

Sasseta is a delightfully picturesque old village, perched on a rocky spur jutting out of the mountainside. As in Castagneto, there are no famous buildings to visit in Sasseta but the village itself is enchanting. Most of the village is inaccessible to cars, the streets having been designed with nothing larger than a mule in mind. However, the visitor can easily pass an hour strolling round the little lanes and alleyways with their colourful windowboxes and tiny vineyards.

San Vincenzo, the next town of note on the coast, is a fairly large resort, reasonably pleasant but somewhat lacking in character. The small harbour, full of pleasure boats, is attractive and there is an extensive beach, the best part of which is to be found to the south of the harbour. At San Vincenzo the Via Aurelia moves inland, cutting off the Piombino Peninsula. Soon after San Vincenzo, a left turn runs up into the hills to **Campiglia Marittima**. At first sight, Campiglia appears to be a tiny village, but once you are inside the medieval walls you find yourself in a tangle of narrow streets winding pictur-esquely around and over each other. At the heart of the town is a splendid, sloping *piazza* surrounded by the principal civic buildings. In mid-May almost every building in the town is decorated with the flag of its quarter for the local festival.

Leave Campiglia on the road for Venturina. After 2km (1 mile) the road is no longer tarmac and descends rapidly through olive groves to Cafaggio. Turn left in Cafaggio and 10km (6 miles) of good road bring you to Suvereto.

The Fosso Reale Canal, Livorno

Colourful pleasure boats moored at Baratti

From a distance, **Suvereto** appears to be a modern town, but there is only a thin fringe of modern buildings. Unlike many medieval Tuscan towns, most of the houses in the old part of the town are only two storeys high. Some of the old houses have small kitchen gardens, while most have the steps which lead up to the standard first floor entrance lined with brightly coloured flowers. The fine, thirteenth-century Palazzo Comunale, with its monumental external staircase, is particularly impressive, as is the Romanesque Church of San Giusto. Another attractive corner of the town is the Cloister of San Francesco, the only remaining part of a thirteenth-century monastery.

The road which leaves San Vincenzo for Piombino runs for the first 5km (3 miles) through the pine woods which dominate the coast here. Beyond the bathing establishments of San Vincenzo itself and the holiday villages which follow on from the town, the woods have been designated as a park, Parco di Rimiglano. A number of footpaths run through the woods to a long, sandy beach which, except for school holidays and weekends in summer, tends to be almost deserted.

An even finer beach is to be found in the Gulf of Baratti, another 5km (3 miles) along the coast. Where the road moves inland slightly, a right hand turn leads to Baratti and Populonia. To get to Baratti itself, follow this road to the end of the bay, but for the beach take the first turn on the right again to a square with two pizzerias, a restaurant and car parking facilities.

The small village of **Baratti**, which consists of little more than a restaurant and a handful of houses, was originally the port through which Populonia, high on the hill above, received its supplies of iron-ore from Elba. It is now the port for a large number of private pleasure boats which make it attractive and cheerful. The area which is now separated from the beach by the road was originally used as the necropolis for Populonia and many important chamber tombs have been excavated in the area. Guides who accompany visitors around the site can be found near the Chapel of San Cerbone. Those visitors who feel they can dispense with a guided tour in order to spend more time on the beach will be pleased to know that a reasonable view of some of the tombs can be had from the road.

Populonia, founded in the ninth century BC, was an important town in both the Etruscan and Roman periods when it was important for the production of iron from the ore mined on Elba. In the Dark Ages the town declined and was for a long time virtually uninhabited. The town developed in the fourteenth century as a rectangular walled settlement.

The greater importance of Populonia in the Etruscan and Roman periods can be judged by the fragments of Roman buildings and traces of the Etruscan defensive wall which lie well outside the limits of the town. Populonia is very attractive but is so small that a visit here will not take up a great deal of time. At number 21 on the main street is a privately owned Etruscan Museum containing objects recovered from tombs in the area. The exhibits include some fine examples of Etruscan vases.

The medieval stronghold at the entrance to the town looks very impressive from the outside with its sturdy square tower, but is something of a disappointment inside. Nothing remains of the interior except the tower, but the view which is to be had from the top more than makes up for the disappointment of the castle itself. On a clear day, Livorno, 70km (40 miles) to the north, is visible. There is also a spectacular view of the Gulf of Baratti with its many small boats.

Piombino was developed as a port by the Romans, and increased in importance with the decline of Populonia. In 1594, the town became the capital of an independent principality, an independence which was maintained until the Napoleonic period and the subsequent annexation by the Grand Duchy of Tuscany.

The old part of the town is pleasant, with several fine churches and houses. Unfortunately, the dominating impression of Piombino is of the massive iron and steel works to the south of the town. However, there is enough of interest in the town to occupy the visitor with time to spare before taking the ferry to Elba.

The Tuscan Archipelago
According to legend, the Tuscan Archipelago was created when the necklace of Venus, the goddess of love, broke and fell into the sea. The main jewel of the necklace, four supporting jewels and several fragments, belong to the Province of Livorno.

Elba
Elba is the centre point of the archipelago and is one of the most beautiful places in Italy. Unlike the more famous islands of Capri and Ischia, it has avoided the heavy commercialisation which tends to spoil the effect of natural beauty in busy periods.

The island was first inhabited by the Ligurians, before the arrival of the Greeks who developed the rich iron-ore deposits from the tenth to the sixth centuries BC. After the sixth century, the production of iron was continued first by the Etruscans, and then by the Romans who erected several fine villas and small towns on the island. In the medieval period, the island belonged first to Pisa and then to the Principality of Piombino.

From 3 May 1814 to 26 February 1815 the island was officially an empire, when it was given to Napoleon as his first place of exile. During his brief rule, many reforms were instigated and the extraction of iron-ore was regulated; he showed himself to be a just and imaginative ruler. In 1815, after the defeat of Napoleon at Waterloo and his exile to St Helena, the Congress of Vienna awarded Elba to Tuscany. Until the growth of the tourist industry over the last 20 years, the island was regarded as little more than a source of iron.

Elba's capital is the fortified town of **Portoferraio**, which stands on a promontory dominating the northern coast of the island. Small towns had existed on the site both in the Roman and the medieval periods, but it was not until 1548, when Cosimo I bought the promontory and a small area of surrounding land, that serious development took place. The citadel was the first of three towns (Livorno was the third) to be developed by Cosimo with a rational urban planning scheme. Under the Medicean Dynasty, Portoferraio was known as *Cosmopolis*.

The most striking aspect of the town is the strength of the fortifications which surround it. The town was designed to withstand assault from both sea and land as, although it was nominally ruled by the Principality of Piombino, the real masters of the island were the Spanish. The landward defences consist of a fortified gateway at sea level, and then four bastions, partly built out of local stone, and partly carved out of the rock face. At the highest point, above the fourth bastion, is the Forte Falcone which is impregnable from any direction.

Walking up through the tunnels and steps which connect the various bastions and the fort, one cannot fail to be impressed by both the unity of the fortifications as a defensive structure, and by the ease with which any section could be isolated if it fell into the hands of an enemy.

After the Forte Falcone, the next section of the defences consists of a strong wall with recesses for defenders, overlooking a steep slope down to the sea. The next bastion is the Bastione dei Mulini, so-called because of the windmills which once stood on the site. Two of the windmills were enlarged and unified to form a large house, the Palazzina dei Mulini, which housed Napoleon and his court during their brief stay on the island.

The Palazzina is open to the public, and displays many rooms as they were during Napoleon's residence, as well as several paintings and caricatures of contemporary figures. The Palazzina's most treasured possession is the Emperor's library of 11,000 volumes. He had brought these from Fontainbleu and then left them as a gift to the *comune* of Portoferraio.

Beyond the Bastione dei Mulini, on the high point at the east end of the town, is the Forte Stella. Its interior has been transformed into private residences, but the battlements and cannon emplacements may still be visited.

Seven kilometres (4 miles) outside Portoferraio is the Villa of San Martino, Napoleon's summer residence. The ground floor of the building consists of servants' quarters, while the first floor comprises the apartment of General Bertrand, the Emperor's bedroom, and the

The seafront of the historic town of Piombino

Emperor's study. In 1851, the villa and its grounds were bought by the Russian Prince Demidoff, husband of Napoleon's niece Mathilde.

Demidoff constructed another, larger villa next to the original one, to house his collection of Napoleonic relics. The relics were unfortunately sold by auction by the prince's heirs in 1880, and the villa now houses the Forese Art Gallery. This gallery contains a fine collection of works, mainly dating from the nineteenth century but with some exhibits dating back to the sixteenth century. The most famous of all the exhibits is Canova's *Galatea*, for which Napoleon's sister Pauline was the model.

After leaving Portoferraio, the first place of interest one encounters when travelling around the island in a clockwise direction is the small spa of **San Giovanni**. More important than the water is the marine mud, which is rich in sulphur and iodine and provides the base for many slimming cures.

Soon after San Giovanni, the road reaches the Punta delle Grotte where the ruins of a once-splendid Roman villa rise out of the gorse. Fragments of mosaic floors can be seen, as can much of the villa's heating system. The locality takes its name from the appearance of some of the villa's rooms, which resemble natural grottoes. The remains of the terraces which fell away to the sea can still be seen in front of the villa.

After Le Grotte, the road descends to the little village of **Magazzini** which, as well as having a sand and shingle beach, also has a small port for pleasure boats. **Bagnaia**, 3km (2 miles) along the coast, is a similar type of village which, until the fairly recent improvements in Elba's road network, was isolated for long periods during the winters. From Bagnaia to the tip of the peninsula, the coastline is mountainous with several small, undeveloped beaches. Some of these are reached by way of minor roads, others can only be reached from the sea.

The main road from Magazzini cuts inland up a steep hill to the ruined fortress of Volterraio, 400m (1,300ft) above sea level. The fort was built by the Pisans in the eleventh century over the site of an Etruscan necropolis, and possible fortress. The rugged ruins of the fort and the splendour of the surrounding scenery offer the sort of views which conjure up thoughts of fairytales and knights in shining armour.

Beyond Volterraio is **Rio nell' Elba**, a picturesque little town which has been continually inhabited since the late Stone Age. Throughout the middle ages and the Renaissance, the town was often attacked by pirates, owing to its wealth which was derived from the area's rich mineral deposits.

Two and a half kilometres (1¹/₂ miles) north of Rio, on Mount Serra, traces of an Etruscan temple can be seen by the roadside. **Cavo**, at the top of the peninsula, is a small resort with a sandy beach and a few small boarding houses. The promontory of Capo Castello, which protects the northern end of Cavo Bay, was once the site of a fine Roman villa. Parts of the mosaic floor of the villa can still be seen, but most of the masonry has been incorporated into more modern buildings.

The most important town on Elba's eastern coast is **Rio Marina**, which, although formerly entirely devoted to mining, is now well-equipped to receive tourists. Rio is the home of Elba's most important sailing club. As a result, there are always many yachts and small boats on the beach and in the bay. They form a contrast with the buildings of the town, which are turned slightly red by the effect of the dust from the iron-ore mines. Rio's town hall houses the Elba Mining Museum, where the visitor can learn more about the 200 minerals which form the island. Fragments of these often brightly-coloured minerals can often be found underfoot while walking in Elba's hills.

As a resort, Rio Marina is less important than **Porto Azzuro**, the next town down the coast. This picturesque town is built around a brilliant blue bay, and has its own ferry link with the mainland. A fine fort, built by the Spanish in 1603, dominates the town, but is not open to visitors as it houses a state prison. Porto Azzuro has several pleasant modern hotels, good beaches, and boats for hire. The boats are best used either to reach some of the otherwise inaccessible smaller beaches or to fish for the mackerel which thrive around Elba.

Capoliveri is the main town of Elba's south-eastern peninsula and is within easy reach of villages and small beaches on both coasts. The small bays at the end of the peninsula are best reached by boat, as many of the tracks which lead to them are the private property of mining companies.

Punta della Calamità (Calamity Point) is so-called because it is said that the magnetic properties of the iron-ore draws boats towards the land, to be dashed to pieces on the rocks. The name is also a pun, as *calamita* means magnet.

Some of Elba's most popular sandy beaches are to be found around the two south-facing bays of Lacona and Stella, separated by the narrow Stella Peninsula. Several fine campsites are situated around Lacona Bay, and the fertile plain behind is well-known for the wine it produces.

After Lacona the road rises steeply into the hills before dropping down to the coast again at Marina di Campo. **Marina di Campo** is the most popular and elegant resort on Elba, having developed principally during the last century with the birth of the tourist industry. Expensive yachts and little fishing smacks mingle colourfully together in front of the town, while waterskiers are almost always to be seen on the calm waters of the bay.

Beyond Marina di Campo, the road stays close to the coastline all the way round the western end of the island, which is dominated by the 1,220m (4,000ft) high Monte Capanne. This end of the island is completely different from the rest being much drier and with very few trees. Despite this, it is one of the more pleasant parts of the island in which to spend a holiday. There was no road here until the late 1960s and, as hardly any of the inhabitants of the small villages could afford a boat, traditions here have very strong roots. Some new houses have been built in recent years and many of the locals let parts of their homes during the summer months. However, even at the height of the season, nowhere gets overcrowded. There are sandy beaches at Fetovaia and Seccheto and a pleasant rocky shore at Chiessi. Twenty-five years ago people here did not think twice about walking 10km (6 miles) each way over the mountains to Marciana to sell their produce and purchase other goods. Exceptional sunsets are often to be seen from this coast road, and on a clear day the outline of Corsica can also be seen in the distance.

Marciana, in the north-west of the island, was the site of a Roman colony in 35BC although it was probably inhabited long before. The nobles of the Principality of Piombino kept residences in Marciana, and a cavern near the town served as the principality's mint. A medieval castle dominates the town, but the oldest building is the twelfth-century Church of San Lorenzo. The most interesting point to visit in this beautiful old town is the Archaeological Antiquarium which contains items relating to the history of the island from the Stone Age to the Roman period.

After Marciana the road rises again to **Poggio Terme**, a small, attractive hilltown. Poggio's water has always been popular as a beverage, but in the last few years the town has been developed as a small spa resort as the curative properties of the waters have been recognised. Poggio is surrounded by woods and vineyards, among which several footpaths wind their way up the mountain. Other mountain footpaths begin from Marciana, but the less energetic visitor may reach the peak of the mountain by a cable-car which leaves from just outside Marciana on the road to Poggio.

A series of hairpin bends take the road back down to the sea at **Marciana Marina**. From Marciana Marina, a small resort and port defended by a twelfth-century Pisan tower, the road runs spectacularly along the coast, past the beautiful bays of Procchio and Biodola, until it cuts across the back of the Monte Poppe Peninsula and descends to Portoferraio. **Procchio** is an excellent base for a holiday on Elba, having a range of hotels, several small but excellent restaurants, and a fine sandy beach which never seems overcrowded.

From Portoferraio a road runs along the top of the peninsula

A sandy beach at Procchio on the Island of Elba

behind Monte Poppe to Capo d'Enfola. Capo d'Enfola is connected to the rest of the peninsula by a thin strip of land, which would often be submerged were it not for the fact that there are only a few inches between high and low tides in the Mediterranean.

The water around Capo d'Enfola is crystal clear and a favourite spot with underwater fishermen. The waters around Elba are ideal for those whose hobby is sub-aqua, as they are not only clear but also well-stocked with fish, coral and sunken wrecks.

While a car is obviously desirable on Elba, most of the towns and villages are connected to Portoferraio by regular and inexpensive bus services. Alternatively, it is possible to hire small mopeds reasonably cheaply. No driving licence is required for mopeds in Italy and anyone over 14 may use them.

Capraia

Capraia is a spectacular island, consisting almost entirely of volcanic rock. A third of the island is closed to the public as it contains a farming penal colony. However, the rest of the island offers pleasant walks and rocky bays to the visitor. The only inhabited centre apart from the penal colony is the village of Capraia, which has limited facilities for receiving visitors. A boat trip around the island, which lasts several hours, is recommended.

Pianosa

The Island of Pianosa is used as a penal colony, and is not open to the public.

Gorgona

The Isle of Gorgona is also largely devoted to a penal colony. The best way to see the islands is to take the daily ferry from Livorno to Elba which calls at the smaller islands on the way, to deliver supplies and mail.

Montecristo

The Isle of Montecristo is a nature reserve with dense vegetation and a variety of wildlife. Special permission is required to land, but for those with access to a small boat, the fishing around the island is excellent.

8

AREZZO AND ITS PROVINCE

T he city of **Arezzo** stands on a hill in the middle of a large plain at the confluence of the Val d' Arno, the Val di Chiana, and the Casentino Valley. The town is also close to the head of the Tiber Valley, and its obvious strategic importance made it a natural centre for habitation from the time of the earliest known civilisations.

The origins of the city are too remote to be clear, but it is known that much later it was one of the twelve most important cities of the Etruscan Federation, and then an important Roman colony. Unfortunately, the destruction wrought by the Barbarians in the Dark Ages removed virtually all traces of the Etruscan and Roman settlements.

In the late medieval period, the city rose to prominence again under a succession of warrior bishops, who fortified the city and extended their authority over the surrounding areas. The city developed along the line of a semi-circle. Traces of the back wall can still be seen, while the wall at the base of the city ran along what is now Via Garibaldi.

The walls were further fortified at the beginning of the fourteenth century but, after the death of Bishop Tarlati in 1328, the city began to decline. Much of the space inside the new circle of walls remained unoccupied until the opening of the railway between Rome and Florence in the 1860s brought about a new upturn in the city's fortunes.

The strength of the city's position allowed it to resist all military attacks by the Florentines and the Sienese. However, in 1384, moral decay led to the sale by the city's Signore of all rights to the *comune* of Florence. Under the Florentines, Arezzo stagnated, despite the fact that men such as Michelangelo, Vasari, Piero della Francesca and the poet Pietro l'Aretino were all born in Arezzo and its Province, as Petrarch had been in the fourteenth century.

At the highest point of the city, in the sixteenth century, Cosimo I had Sangallo construct an impressive fort. Surrounded by a wide open space (now a public park), the fort made the town impregnable to enemies without, and also served to discourage any ideas of rebellion within. The fort is typical of many of those built by Cosimo to consolidate his family's rule but, like many others, it has not been preserved intact. Parts of the fort were dismantled by the French in 1800, as the result of strong Aretine resistance to Jacobinism.

On the other side of the park that surrounds the fort is Arezzo's Duomo. The Duomo is perhaps the purest example of austere Gothic church architecture in Tuscany, with little external decoration to detract from the severe verticals of the pillars. The bell tower at the rear of the church is a nineteenth-century addition.

Inside the church, the visitor should not miss the picture of Mary Magdalen by Piero della Francesca, which is situated near the entrance to the Sacristy. A museum of works of art produced for the Duomo and other churches can be visited in the Sacristy, as can a collection of antique parchments which include an imperial decree by Charlemagne. Other things to note in the Duomo are the funeral monument of Bishop Tarlati, believed to have been designed by Giotto, and the marble setting of the Renaissance organ which was Giorgio Vasari's first architectural commission.

In front of the Duomo is the Palazzo Comunale, built in 1333, and the medieval tower, built in 1337. Both of these buildings have been heavily restored and very little is left which is original, but they enhance the overall effect of the square.

Arezzo is well-supplied with signs indicating the way from one monument to the next. After Piazza del Duomo, the next building to see is the house in which Petrarch was born. The house was badly damaged during World War II and has been heavily restored. It houses a centre for Petrarchan studies, one of the oldest academies in Italy.

Piazza Grande is the finest square in the city, being surrounded by a fine mixture of medieval and Renaissance buildings. The Church of Santa Maria della Pieve was begun at the beginning of the eleventh century, finished in 1330, adapted by Vasari in the sixteenth century and then restored in the nineteenth century.

The façade is a fine example of Romanesque, consisting of five blind archways, surmounted by three rows of loggias which diminish in size, but have increased numbers of openings the higher up the buildings they are. The bell tower, built in a similar style, is known as the Tower with the Hundred Holes, although there are actually only eighty windows. Inside the church, the most important work of

AREZZO AND ITS PROVINCE

art is the polyptych in the Presbytery, which Bishop Tarlati commissioned from Lorenzetti in 1320.

The Palazzetto della Fraternità dei Laici is a beautiful building. The lower part, which was built in the late fourteenth century, is pure Gothic while the upper floors are Renaissance in style. The bell tower was designed in the sixteenth century by Vasari.

Vasari was also responsible for the Palazzo delle Loggie, which dominates the top side of the square. The little shops under the loggia have not changed very much since they were first opened. Several thirteenth-century houses make up most of the rest of the buildings around the square.

More interesting than either the Duomo or Santa Maria della Pieve is the Church of San Francesco at the centre of the city. The church was built in the thirteenth century and altered in the fourteenth. It was originally joined to a large convent, but much of this was demolished when a new central thoroughfare was opened up in the

1860s. The interior of the church has been restored to its primitive simplicity, being decorated almost exclusively by a series of fine frescoes. The frescoes in the Choir by Piero della Francesca are some of the finest in Italy outside the Vatican. The background to many of the religious scenes depicted is a representation of late medieval Arezzo. As Arezzo is built on a hill, the Church of San Francesco also contains another large church, underneath the main chapel. This church is reached by a stairway from the main part.

Vasari's House was designed and frescoed by the artist himself between 1540 and 1548. Apart from Vasari's fine frescoes, the house also contains a collection of excellent Mannerist paintings by other artists of the period. Part of the house contains the Vasari archives where the family documents may be studied, amongst which are letters from Dukes, Popes, and other artists such as Michelangelo.

Palazzo Bruni-Ciocchi is a fine Renaissance town house which now houses the Museum and Gallery of Medieval and Modern Art. The most important works in the gallery are by Luca Signorelli, who was from nearby Cortona. The collection allows the visitor to see how Arezzo as an artistic centre related to and differed from Florence and Siena at various points in time.

The most important work of art in Arezzo is to be found in the Church of San Domenico in the north of the town. San Domenico was built in 1275, but has been much altered over the years. The modern windows let in more light than is usual in many Italian churches, and this allows the visitor to get a good look both at the fragments of fourteenth-century frescoes which decorate the walls, and the magnificent crucifix by Cimabue. This large crucifix, which was painted in the 1260s, was one of the first paintings to give Christ an element of humanity, moving away from the Byzantine tendencies of abstraction and idealisation.

Arezzo's most important traditional festival is the Giostra del Saraceno which takes place on the first Sunday in September every year. A procession in medieval dress, representing the warriors of each of the quarters of the city, parades through the streets to Piazza Grande where the joust takes place. Two horsemen charge towards the effigy of a Saracen in the middle of the *piazza* and score points by striking his shield with their lances. The Saracen rotates after being struck, swinging heavy leather balls and whips. A horseman disarmed by the Saracen loses all his points, while if he is struck by the whips he loses two points. The quarter whose knight wins the joust gains possession of the 'Golden Lance' for the next year.

The Province of Arezzo

The visitor who intends to begin his or her holiday in Arezzo and explore the province before moving on may be surprised to find that time has run out before a tour of this first province has been completed. The Province of Arezzo contains as great a variety of castles, historic towns and beautiful countryside as any province in Italy. Many of the towns have changed very little over the centuries, owing to the difficult terrain which, until fairly recent times, hampered the development of commercial links with large cities such as Florence, Rome and Ravenna.

The most important town in the Province of Arezzo itself is **Cortona**. Cortona was founded by the Etruscans in the fifth century BC as it not only provided a useful trading station between the three major cities of Arezzo, Chiusi and Perugia, but also dominated the routes between them. The town developed rapidly, and the remains of the Etruscan defensive walls suggest that the dimensions of the city were roughly the same at the end of the fourth century BC, when the town allied with the Romans, as they are now.

In the Middle Ages the town shrank to the area immediately around the two central squares, and this was the area which became the administrative centre of the town when its fortunes revived in the tenth and eleventh centuries. Cortona's political tendencies were Ghibelline, and, after a long struggle, the town was defeated by Guelph Arezzo in 1258, and many townsmen were exiled. The exiles returned in 1261, to find much of the town and its defences wrecked. Consequently, a large part of the town which the visitor sees today is the result of the reconstructions which took place in the following period.

From 1325 the town was ruled by the Casali family, who pursued a policy of friendship with the Republic of Siena. When Siena began to be threatened by Florence, the Casali Dynasty fell and, in 1409, Neapolitan troops took possession of the town. Two years later Cortona was sold to the Florentines. Unlike many of the towns that came under Florentine rule, it was not neglected. This was because its distance from Florence and vulnerability to attack gave it considerable strategic importance, and it was important that the loyalty of the inhabitants should be ensured.

Some of the thirteenth-century houses were joined together and given Florentine Renaissance façades at this time. Laws were passed regulating street trading and allocating specific functions to specific areas of the town. The general effect was to create what could almost be described as a middle-class Renaissance town, an atmosphere which can still be felt today.

Arezzo: the colonnades in the Piazza Grande

Two of the town's most historic buildings are to be found in Piazza della Repubblica, the antique centre of the town. Palazzo del Capitano del Popolo is a sixteenth-century transformation of an earlier medieval building, while the Palazzo Comunale was built in the mid-thirteenth century. It was enlarged (the tower was added) in the sixteenth century, and restored somewhat arbitrarily at the end of the nineteenth. Inside the Palazzo Comunale, in the Sala del Consiglio (council chamber), is a large stone fireplace, dating from the sixteenth century. It is possible that the building was originally composed of two separate medieval town houses which were then joined together by a central archway.

Nearby Piazza Signorelli is dominated by Palazzo Pretorio, another medieval building which was given a new façade in the sixteenth century. The *palazzo* was originally the residence of the Casali family, and to this

Etruscan remains can be seen in the walls of many of Cortona's old houses

The Sanctuary of Santa Maria delle Grazie, Cortona

day it remains at the hub of civic life, containing the Etruscan Academy, the Etruscan Museum, the town library and the town archives. The most important exhibit in the museum is the large, elaborately decorated, Etruscan bronze lamp, which was found in a field in 1840.

A little to the west of Piazza Signorelli, opening onto the city walls, is Piazza del Duomo. The Duomo was built in the sixteenth century over the earlier Church of Santa Maria. Some Romanesque traces of the earlier building can still be seen, but mainly the style is that of Sangallo. The inside of the Duomo is light, attractive, and fairly simple, with a finely-carved wooden pulpit.

On the other side of the *piazza*, built right on the side of the hill, is the former Church of Gesú, which now houses the Diocesan Museum. The slope falls away so steeply at this point that the church, which was built at the end of the fifteenth century, is built on two floors. Entering from the *piazza*, you find yourself in what was once the Baptistry, while the nave of the church is on the floor below, and can only be reached by way of a long staircase. The museum contains many fine paintings, including several by Signorelli, and Fra Angelico's famous *Annunciation*.

The Church of Santa Maria Nuova is a fine late Renaissance structure. Situated below the walls at the northern end of the town, the church was largely the work of Vasari. With its symmetrical form and large dome, it is probably the purest example of Renaissance architecture in Cortona.

Another fine church is the Gothic San Francesco. This church was begun in 1245, and the porch and the left flank of the building are wholly original. Much of the rest of the church is the result of sixteenth-century alterations and restorations. The fragmentary frescoes on the inside of the façade were painted by Buffalmacco, who, in addition to his fame as an artist, was well-known for his roguish wit; as a result of which he appears as a character in several of the tales in Boccaccio's *Decameron*.

Perhaps the most beautiful area of the town is the part behind and above the Church of San Francesco. The streets are fairly narrow and very steep, discouraging all but the most determined motorist. When Italian streets are narrow they tend to be poorly lit, but this is not the case in Cortona. The thirteenth- and fourteenth-century houses which line these streets are not the normal tall Italian *palazzi*, but are more like cottages, with masses of brightly coloured flowers hanging outside in window boxes for much of the year. The area also contains two little churches which nestle in amongst the houses and the occasional patch of greenery; the Church of San Nicolò which dates from the fifteenth century, and the Romanesque Church of San Cristoforo.

At the top of the town, dominating the surrounding valleys, is the recently restored Medicean fortress. The fort, which is similar to many others of its period in Tuscany, was built over the ruins of a medieval castle which, in turn, had been built over the highest point of the Etruscan wall. Near the fort and around the slightly lower Montanina Gate, many of the enormous blocks of stone used by the Etruscans for their defensive systems can be seen at the base of the medieval and Renaissance walls.

On the hillside below Cortona, half-way between the town and Camucia, is the Sanctuary of Santa Maria delle Grazie. This was one of the first large churches of the Renaissance to be built well outside the town it was meant to serve. The Sanctuary originally had a fine fourteenth-century wooden crucifix decorating the altar, but this was stolen in 1971.

Not far from the sanctuary are two Etruscan chamber tombs; the Tanella di Pitagoro, which has a circumference of 24m (80ft) and the smaller Tanella Angora.

Half-way between Arezzo and Cortona is **Castiglion Fiorentino**, on the side of a hill, on a bend in the Chiana Valley. The town was fortified by the Romans, and later became Arezzo's stronghold on the frontier with Perugian territory. Before Arezzo passed under the rule of Florence, the town was known as *Castiglion Aretino*.

At the highest point of the town stands the old castle which offers excellent views of the Chiana Valley from the battlements. The castle was originally built in the twelfth century, but has since undergone many modifications. The town's defensive wall has also been modified many times since the medieval period but, along with the castle, it stands as a reminder of the town's original function as a fortress.

If the town's function was orignally to ward off invaders, it would seem that the soldiers' inspiration was drawn directly from God, if the surprisingly high number of churches in the town is anything to go by. Of these, the most important is the Church of San Francesco, built in the second half of the thirteenth century. The basic style of the church is Romanesque but some Gothic influences can be seen. The attractive cloister which adjoins the church was added in the seventeenth century, and is decorated with episodes from the life of St Francis.

Other churches to visit are: the Collegiata of San Giuliano, which was rebuilt on a large scale during the last century; the Abbey, which contains Signorelli's *Deposition of Christ*; the sixteenth-century rectangular Church of Gesú, which contains a fourteenth-century wooden crucifix; and the fine, octagonal Church of the Madonna della Consolazione.

The Palazzo Comunale has been altered too extensively to make it interesting as a building, but it contains the town's art gallery on the first floor. Most of the works in the gallery have been taken from the churches around the town, and it is hard to believe that so much artistic wealth can belong to such a relatively insignificant provincial town.

Just to the south of Castiglion is the Castle of Montecchio. Built in the eleventh century, the castle was given to the English mercenary leader, Sir John Hawkwood, for services rendered to the Florentine Republic in the fourteenth century.

The south-east of the Province of Arezzo contains five interesting little towns which can easily be visited in the same afternoon. **Foiano** is a picturesque town on the crest of a hill. Much of the town dates from the fifteenth and sixteenth centuries, although traces of earlier medieval defences can be seen around the edge of the town. The Churches of San Martino and San Francesco are particularly worth visiting.

The etymology of the town's name reveals a Roman origin, and 3km (2 miles) to the north-east of the centre, the remains of what is believed to have been a Roman bath house have been found at Cisternella. Roman ruins have also been found in the village of **Farneta**, just to the south of Foiano. It is possible that the village and its tenth-century abbey were built directly over a former Roman settlement. Apart from Roman and Etruscan remains, archaeologists have also discovered important fossils, and even the remains of a prehistoric elephant in Farneta.

The town of **Lucignano**, which was originally an Etruscan strong-hold, is interesting as an example of medieval town planning. The town is arranged concentrically around a castle that was rebuilt in the fifteenth century. Examples of finely-worked gold ornaments can be found in the Museo Comunale, which is situated in the fourteenth-century Palazzo Comunale. The Province of Arezzo was once famous for its goldsmiths, and to a certain extent the traditions of the craft have been kept alive in Lucignano. The Churches of San Francesco, and the sixteenth-century Collegiata with its impressive Classical architecture, should not be missed by the visitor.

Marciano della Chiana is another picturesque little village that was once a fortress. Considerable remains of a medieval castle and the wall still exist, including a fortified gate with a tower. The octagonal Chapel of San Vittorio, 3km 2(miles) to the south-east, was designed by Vasari in 1572, to mark the spot where the Florentines defeated the Sienese in 1554.

Sixteenth-century historians attributed the foundation of **Monte San Savino** to Noah. While this may be a little fanciful, it is certain that the town has had a complicated history. The Etruscans and the Romans both built settlements on the site, but after the Romans there is no record of the town until the late medieval period. By the thirteenth century, the town was firmly under the control of Arezzo whose forces razed it to the ground in 1325 for demonstrating Guelph tendencies.

The town was rebuilt after the fall of the Tarlati family in Arezzo. It then passed rapidly through the hands of the Aretines, the Florentines, the Sienese and the Perugians, before becoming part of the Duchy of Tuscany. However, being of little strategic importance, it was given as a feudal fief first to the Del Monte family, and then to the Orsini, as political necessity dictated.

From 1609 to 1640, when the Orsini family died out, San Savino was a principality. After 1640 the area was virtually independent, ruled by brothers of the various Grand Dukes. In 1799 the town paid heavily for putting up spirited resistance to the French, with the virtual extinction of its formerly strong Jewish community, many of whom were burnt at the stake.

As well as the usual interesting churches (Sant Agostino and Santa Chiara should be visited), the town is exceptional for its large number of medieval and Renaissance upper class houses. Palazzo Comunale, Palazzo Tavarnesi, the façade of which is by Sangallo, are the most important *palazzi* to see. One of the finest buildings in the town is the sixteenth-century Loggia dei Mercanti, constructed as a semi-open market venue. The decorative motifs on the pillars were inspired by the coat of arms of the Del Monte family, who not only ruled the town at the time but also had a member of the family on the Papal throne in Rome. Traces of the town's fortifications still survive including the fine Florentine and Roman gates.

The Casentino

The head of the Arno Valley runs in a north-east to south-west direction from the edge of Tuscany to the Aretine Plain. This valley is known as the Casentino, and is one of the greenest and most pleasant areas of Tuscany. The major centre in the Casentino is Bibbiena, but numerous smaller towns and isolated feudal castles also give great interest to a day in these parts.

Many of the small towns and villages are connected by small mountain tracks which often provide pleasant walks. Most of these tracks are marked on the inexpensive maps of the Province of Arezzo produced by the Ente Provinciale per il Turismo. Tracks are marked as Mulattiere or Carreggiabile; the latter are technically suitable for motor vehicles, but unless the vehicle is a Land Rover they are not recommended.

Bibbiena has always been the most important town in the

Casentino. It was originally an Etruscan stronghold, and later Arezzo's defensive bulwark in the north-east. Among the finest buildings in Bibbiena is Palazzo Dovizi, one of the best examples of rustic Renaissance architecture in Tuscany. The *palazzo* was the home of the town's most famous son, Bernardo Dovizi, a humanist and playwright who became secretary to Giovanni dei Medici (Leo X) and was promoted to the rank of Cardinal.

The most interesting of the town's many churches is the Church of the Santissimi Ippolito e Donato which began life at the end of the twelfth century as the chapel to the town's fortress. The church was given a Classical facelift during the Renaissance and it is this style with a few Baroque touches added in the eighteenth century which are most evident. Notable works of art in the church are a *Madonna and Child with Saints* by Bicci di Lorenzo in the apse, and a wooden fourteenth-century crucifix in the right hand transept.

Another fine church can be seen about 2km (1 mile) outside the town along the road towards Querceto. Santa Maria del Sasso also dates from the beginning of the thirteenth century and was largely rebuilt during the Renaissance. The elegant Classical bell tower is particularly fine and was added during the renovation of the church.

From Bibbiena take the SS71 to **Serravalle**, 10km (6 miles) to the north. This pleasant little town stands on top of a wooded ridge between two small rivers. The ruins of a twelfth-century castle and tower are the most conspicuous attractions in the town, but it is mainly visited by those wishing to take tranquil walks in the surrounding countryside.

A similar town, although on a larger scale, is **Badia Prataglia**, 5km (3 miles) to the north-east. The town originated as a Benedictine abbey (*badia*) which was founded in 989 and other buildings were gradually added over the centuries. The Benedictine community was particularly active during the turbulent medieval period, and after supporting the losing side more than once in the various schisms which divided the church, the religious community was supressed in 1397. The morphology of the town is more Swiss than Tuscan as the buildings of the town are scattered over the wooded hillside rather than clustered together in an easily defensible group. The town's position makes it an ideal starting point for mountain walks; there are several summits all within easy reach on well-defined paths and tracks.

Five kilometres (3 miles) to the north-west of Serravalle is the village of **Camaldoli** which, like its neighbours, is a tranquil summer resort. The village itself is attractive enough, but the main reasons why visitors come here are the surrounding Forest of Camaldoli and the famous hermitage 4km ($2^1/_2$ miles) to the north of the town. Originally, Camaldoli was the site of a castle-village belonging to the Counts of Arezzo. In 1012 the castle and the surrounding lands were given to St Romualdo who established the first monastic community on the site. An important part of the monastery was its Foresteria which was built to house visitors who came to spend periods of meditation and debate with the monks. During the Renaissance, the monastery, which had a reputation for liberal thought, became the home for a humanistic academy. This was patronised by Lorenzo dei Medici and presided over by Leon Battista Alberti, the leading intellectual of the period. The Church of Saints Donato and Ilariano, which forms part of the monastery, is decorated with frescoes and paintings by Giorgio Vasari and his school.

At one point, the road leading up to the hermitage passes three large crosses; these once marked the point beyond which no woman was allowed to pass. Nowadays it is only the monks' cells to which women are not allowed entry. The hermitage originally consisted of five simple cells and a central altar. As the number of monks increased it was necessary to increase the number of cells and replace the altar with a church (Chiesa del Salvatore). The church contains some interesting frescoes, particularly those of the visits to the sanctuary by the Holy Roman Emperors, Henry II and Ottone III which took place while St Romualdo was still alive. Next to the church is the simple refectory where, twelve times a year, the monks in the hermitage meet to eat together, although without breaking the vow of silence which they take when entering the hermitage.

Several of the individual cells are of particular historical interest; cell number 13 is known as the Medici cell because its construction was paid for by Maria dei Medici as a penitence imposed by the Medici Pope Leo X for having disguised herself as a man and visited the hermitage; cell number 5 is believed to have been that inhabited by St Romualdo himself, and cell 20 was once inhabited by St Charles Borromeo. The chapel near the cells was originally another cell where Pope Gregory IX was once the inmate. The chapel is the burial place of several of the hermits who have been sanctified.

Eighteen kilometres (11 miles) of winding country lanes bring the visitor westwards to **Pratovecchio**. The birthplace of Renaissance artist Paolo Uccello has an attractive porticoed central square, several of the façades of which are decorated with Dell Arobbian terracottas. Pratovecchio is on the eastern bank of the Arno which at this point is little more than a large stream. Facing the town are two places of interest which can be reached either on foot or by car; the Abbey of San Pietro di Romena and the Castle of San Romena. The abbey is considered to be the finest Romanesque church in the Casentino despite the fact that the original façade was destroyed by an earthquake in 1729 and replaced by a rustic one. The apse of the church is particularly impressive with two tiers of arches below an upper wall broken by two double and one triple mullioned windows.

The ruined Castle of San Romena, where three of the original fourteen towers are still standing, provided one of the episodes made infamous by Dante in his *Inferno (XXX.46-90)*. Under instructions from Conte Guidi who owned the castle, Master Adamo, the estate blacksmith, produced a large quantity of forged Florins and was burnt alive for his pains the following year.

Stia, 3km (2 miles) to the north of the Castle of San Romena, is situated at the confluence of the Arno and the Staggia. It is an interesting little town with a medieval centre clustered around the porticoed Piazza Tanucci, and a more modern, wool-working sector. The parish Church of Santa Maria Assunta is well-worth a visit. The bell tower of the church is a converted medieval fortified tower. The apparently medieval Castello di Palagio was actually built in 1908 in the medieval style.

Another place with Dantesque connections is the tiny hamlet of **Porciano**, on the top of a hill 2km (1 mile) to the north of Stia. It was here, in a now ruined castle belonging to the Conte Guidi, that Dante wrote his famous letter to the Florentines exhorting them to submit to Emperor Arrigo VII and thereby put an end to the Guelph-Ghibelline strife in the city.

Castelcastagnaio stands on a spur between two of the Arno's smaller tributaries. The castle which gives the place its name is in ruins although it is well-worth a visit as the remains of a circular Roman Temple can be seen nearby.

The little hilltown of **Montemignaio** is situated 11km (7 miles) to the south and is notable for the *Virgin and Child with Four Church Elders* by the school of Ghirlandaio (or possibly by the master himself). This can be seen in the eleventh-century Romanesque parish church. The remains of an old castle, situated at the highest point of the town, are also of considerable interest.

Thirteen kilometres (8 miles) to the east of Montemignaio is the ruined tenth-century fortress of Castel San Niccolò which was once one of the Count Guidi's most impregnable strongholds. Below the castle is the small town of Strada which is reached by crossing a medieval bridge. The central Piazza della Fiera, with its medieval grain store, forms an attractive centrepiece to the town.

The plain where the road from Castel San Niccolò meets the

Pontassieve-Poppi road was the scene of the Battle of Campaldino in 1289 which firmly established the dominance of the Guelphs and the Florentines in Tuscany. The nearby church and monastery of Certomondo was erected in 1262 by Count Guidi to celebrate the Battle of Montaperti (near Siena) which had temporarily given the Ghibellines the upper hand.

Poppi, situated on a hillside to the south of the battlefield, is an attractive and tranquil summer resort with several interesting buildings. Palazzo Pretorio was built by the Conte Guidi in the early twelfth century as their principal residence. It remained as such until the last of the Counts was stripped of his title and banished from his lands. This was after the Battle of Anghiari in 1440 when he had fought alongside the Milanese forces. Inside the *palazzo* there is an important library which, amongst its 20,000 manuscripts, can boast 519 dating from the eleventh century, some of which are the only known copies. The *palazzo* also has many fine paintings, a frescoed chapel and a magnificent Renaissance fireplace which dates from 1512.

Legend has it that the little town of **Raggiolo**, 10km (6 miles) to the south-west, was founded at some time during the Dark Ages by a group of Corsican refugees, and even today the people refer to themselves as Corsicans. The town, like most of the other towns in the area, has a ruined medieval castle and it is also particularly well-sited for outings into the Pratomagno Hills.

Seven kilometres (4 miles) south of Bibbiena, at Pieve a Socana, a right turn leads up a rough minor road to the little village of Castel Focognano. Here, the castle which gave the village its name held out for 6 months in the fourteenth century against the powerful forces of Guido Tarlati before being starved into submission.

The church at **Pieve a Socana** is built over an older one which was, in turn, built over the remains of an Etruscan Temple. Amongst the most important of the finds that archaeologists have made on the site in recent years, was a vessel used for collecting the blood of sacrifices.

Take the minor road which runs up to the east from Pieve a Socana towards Chiusi della Verna. The first place of interest along this road is **Chitignano**, on a side-spur of the Alpe di Catenaia. The four-teenth-century Palazzo del Podestà is of interest here, as are the warm springs around the town which are rich in sulphur and iron. Beyond Chitignano the scenery is spectacular with occasional views of the Monastery of La Verna high overhead. At one point the road passes a spring known as the Toad's Spring from where St Francis is said to have removed a toad which was polluting the water. The recently restored castle which dominates the village of Chiusi della

Verna was the home of Count Orlando Cattani who gave the whole of Mount Verna to St Francis.

Mount Verna is a three-peaked dolomitic formation which is visible from almost everywhere in the Casentino and is much visited, both for its great natural beauty and as a place of pilgrimage. In 1217 St Francis and a few companions built the first church on the mountain out of a few trees which they leaned together and it was here that, 7 years later, he received the stigmata while praying. The original wooden church was turned into a stone one by Count Orlando (who is buried there), and it is this which immediately confronts visitors as they enter the gates of the Sanctuary. One of the coats of arms on the façade is that of Eugene IV who placed the convent under the protection of the Florentines in 1431. The bell in the tower to the left of this church was founded in Pisa in 1257. Access to the Sanctuary Museum is also gained from inside this church.

Behind the first church is the Basilica, whose façade was badly damaged during World War II. From the front of the Basilica a long open corridor leads to the Church of the Stigmata. Every day, at 3pm, all the monks form a procession down this corridor on their way to give thanks for the Saint's stigmata. Half way along the corridor is the entrance to a small grotto which was used by Francis himself for his meditations. His stone bed can still be seen in the grotto. A stone slab in the Church of the Stigmata marks the exact spot where the miracle took place.

Thirteen kilometres (8miles) to the south of Chiusi della Verna is the town of **Caprese Michelangelo**. For 300 years there was a dispute between Caprese and Chiusi della Verna as to which had been the birthplace of Michelangelo Buonarotti. When, in 1875, a copy of the original declaration of birth made by Michelangelo's father was found providing irrefutable evidence that he was from Caprese, the town promptly changed its name to Caprese Michelangelo. His father, Lodovico, had been sent to the town by Florence to act as Podestà for a year, and the artist was born in the Palazzo del Podestà. The *palazzo* has now been turned into the Museo Michelangiolesco and a number of plaster casts used by the artist can be seen, together with documentary exhibits to his life and work. The old thirteenth-century castle at the highest point in the town has also been turned into a museum in which more of Michelangelo's plaster casts can be seen along with sculptures by modern artists. Near to the castle walls is the plain, thirteenth-century Church of San Giovanni Battista in which Michelangelo was baptised.

The Val d'Arno

From Florence to Arezzo, most visitors' view of the Val d'Arno will be somewhat limited, as the motorway and the railway are both far more convenient than the ordinary road, which tends to be busy with heavy traffic. The journey is interesting and there are some places which deserve a detour if sufficient time is available.

San Giovanni Valdarno was established by the Florentines in the thirteenth century, as a bulwark against the Aretines. The rectangular historic centre, designed by Arnolfo del Cambio, still stands but is now surrounded by a modern industrial town. Palazzo Pretorio, and the Church of Santa Maria delle Grazie, which contains Masaccio's *Virgin and Child with Four Saints*, are the most important buildings to visit.

Three kilometres (2 miles) to the south of San Giovanni is the Monastery of Montecarlo. This fine Renaissance construction, which is situated on the top of a pleasant green hill, is notable for its elegant cloisters and for the *Annunciation* and five *Scenes From the Life of Mary* which are considered by many to be Fra Angelico's finest works.

Another three kilometres (2 miles) to the south is **Montevarchi**, a busy little town which has retained much of its medieval-Renaissance centre. The Collegiata Church of San Lorenzo and the small museum next to it are worth seeing.

Three kilometres (2 miles) from Montevarchi, on the opposite side of the Arno, is **Terranuova Bracciolini**. The town's strictly rectangular street plan is said to have been planned by Arnolfo del Cambio. Part of the defensive walls erected by the Florentines in the fifteenth century are still standing but the gates and adjoining stretches of wall were blown up during the German retreat in World War II.

Two interesting villages can be seen in the hills above Terranuova. **Loro Ciuffenna** was originally inhabited by the Etruscans and then the Romans and is a characteristic rural medieval village with narrow streets crossed by raised passages between the houses. **Castelfranco di Sopra** was established by the Florentines during the fourteenth century as a defensive stronghold for its south-eastern borders and has changed very little since then.

The Pieve di Galatrona, a simple, Romanesque church 8km (5 miles) to the south of Montevarchi, should be visited for the splendid baptismal font by Luca della Robbia. Nearby, the little village of **Cennina** has a medieval castle that has been fully restored, hosts a series of concerts by Italian and Foreign musicians each summer, and is slowly establishing itself as an important cultural centre.

Pergine Valdarno stands on a small hill just off the main Montevarchi-Arezzo road. This pleasant village retains its medieval atmosphere. It is more easily accessible than some of the other medieval villages in the mountains and includes the remains of a tenth-century castle.

The East

The east of the province is reached by taking the SS73 from Arezzo to Sansepolcro, and then the SS258. The countryside, although varied, is not as interesting as the rest of the province, but several of the towns on the route are worth visiting.

Eleven kilometres (7 miles) from Arezzo, at **Palazzo del Pero**, is a Romanesque church dating from before the turn of the millennium. The church, whose apse is built in terracotta, contains a fine Gothic sculpture of the Virgin Mary.

Another 11km (7 miles) brings the visitor to the junction with the SS221, where a small diversion should be made to visit the medieval hill village of **Monterchi**. Some of the fortifications still remain, but the most important thing to see is Piero della Francesca's *Madonna del Parto*, in the chapel next to the cemetery. In the Etruscan and Roman periods, the village was the site of a temple devoted to Hercules.

Shortly after the junction with the SS221, a side-road to the left leads to the town of **Anghiari**. Anghiari is divided into a modern area on the low ground, and an older part on a hill. The old town dates mainly from the Renaissance, and is built around a central square, but the eastern side of the old town is typically medieval, with picturesque little houses and narrow alleyways. Anghiari contains several interesting churches, but the most important place to visit is the State Museum of the Art and Traditions of the Upper Tiber Valley. This is situated in the fine Renaissance Palazzo Taglieschi.

The largest town in the east of the province is **Sansepolcro**, on the other side of the Tiber. The town is an interesting artistic centre, mainly Renaissance in aspect. At one time the town belonged to the Papacy, but in 1441 it was sold to the Florentines. On the second Sunday of September, the town celebrates its annual festival with the Palio della Balestra, a crossbow tournament held in conjunction with a procession and traditional medieval festivities.

Badia Tedalda, not far from the province's border, is another split-site town. The older part, built on a hill, is a popular site for summer holidays. From Badia Tedalda a side road leads to **Sestino**, which was originally inhabited by the Etruscans, and then became an important Roman outpost. An archaeological museum next to the abbey is opened by the vicar on request. The countryside around Sestino is famous for its truffles.

9

SIENA AND ITS PROVINCE

M ore than any other town, **Siena** can claim to be the most typically Tuscan. It is as beautiful as Florence; the historical centre is as old and as large; and while Florence's immediate surroundings consist mainly of uninteresting suburbs, Siena is surrounded by the beautiful Chianti region.

It is said that the city owes its name to Senio, the son of Romulus. It is certain that the Etruscans had a settlement on the site, which then passed under the control of Rome, during the Republican period. Siena became an important city in the medieval period, and by the 1100s had trading links with many parts of Europe.

Rivalry between Siena and Florence was bitter, and from the twelfth century onwards the two cities were almost always at war until Siena was finally incorporated into the Grand Duchy of Tuscany in 1559. For a long time the Sienese fought as Ghibellines under the banner of the Emperor, while the Florentines fought as Guelphs with Papal sympathies. Paradoxically, it was Siena's greatest victory, at Montaperti in 1260, which brought about the internal divisions that soon reduced it to battling to retain its independence, rather than to dominate Tuscany. After Montaperti, many prominent Sienese were excommunicated, and this served as an excuse for the non-payment of debts to Sienese merchants.

In the sixteenth century, the imperial support that the Medici enjoyed in Florence, and the fact that the Medici and their friends virtually monopolised the Papal tiara, was enough to finally overwhelm Sienese resistance. After a long siege, the city surrendered to Imperial forces and was given to the Medici as an Imperial fief.

Siena is perhaps best-known for its Palio, the bareback horse race around the square which has taken place twice a year since 1659, when it succeeded earlier tournaments. Warriors from each of the city's seventeen zones march in Renaissance costumes and with Renaissance weapons through the city in a highly colourful procession before the race. In the days immediately before the race, six trials are held, to get horses and riders used to the clockwise circuit with its sharp bends. Falls are frequent, and it is very unusual if all the riders survive until the actual race, due to injuries sustained in the trials.

Wooden terraces are set up around the edge of the square by the owners of the buildings. Although places on these terraces are very expensive, they are normally sold out even for the trials. The mass of the public is huddled together in the middle of the square. The race consists of three circuits, after which the Palio is presented, and the winning horse is escorted back to its *contrada* in triumph. Here it takes part in an open-air celebratory banquet with the rest of the *contrada's* inhabitants. Corruption has always played a large part in the Palio, and large amounts of money secretly change hands before the race, creating pacts between *contrade*.

Visiting the city on 2 July or 16 August, when the Palios are held, is a memorable experience, and one best undertaken by train as parking is not easy. Normally the visitor should drive through the outskirts until reaching the city wall, and then turn back and take the first available parking space. Once you are inside the city, almost all roads seem to lead to the central Piazza del Campo, one of the most beautiful squares in Europe.

Piazza del Campo is shaped like a shell, with a beautiful fountain in the middle, and exceptional buildings around the outside. The fountain, Fonte Gaia, is fed by a 25km (15 mile) fourteenth-century aqueduct. It was originally decorated with bas-reliefs by Jacopo della Quercia, but in 1868 these were removed to the Palazzo Pubblico for safety and replaced by copies.

Palazzo Pubblico, the city's seat of government, was built at the beginning of the fourteenth century, and is the most elegant Gothic *palazzo* in Tuscany. The ground floor rooms are still used for the city's administration and are not usually open to the public, although visitors who speak some Italian should not have too much trouble.

The first floor houses the Civic Museum, which is full of many fine works of art. The most famous is Simone Martini's masterpiece the *Maesta*, which has unfortunately suffered greatly from damp over the centuries. Amongst the other famous works are the frescoes that decorate the 'room of peace' by Lorenzetti. The frescoes in this room, celebrating 'Good Government', constitute the largest non-religious medieval pictorial cycle.

On the second floor, a large loggia gives a splendid view of the *piazza*. The museum rooms on this floor are mainly dedicated to Sienese history, but on the loggia itself the remains of Della Quercia's original Fonte Gaia have been reassembled.

A fine courtyard, the Cortile del Podestà, separates the *palazzo* from the Torre del Mangia. The tower is open to the public, and the view from the top makes the 332 steps well-worthwhile.

One of the most impressive former residential *palazzi* in Siena is the Palazzo Chigi-Saraceni on the Via di Città. The *palazzo* dates from the first half of the fifteenth century, is a fine example of Renaissance architecture, and also contains many important works of art. As it houses a musical academy, it is not always possible to visit the *palazzo*. However, current information can be obtained from the Ente Provinciale per il Turismo. This is also situated on the Via di Città in the Merchant's Loggia, which is the best example of the transition between Gothic and Renaissance architecture to be found in Siena.

At the end of Via di Città, Via del Capitano leads directly to Piazza del Duomo where one of Italy's most beautiful churches can be admired. The Duomo was begun in the second half of the twelfth century, and despite many setbacks and changes of plan, was completed by the end of the fourteenth. The lower half of the façade with its statues (these are copies) is the work of Giovanni Pisano and his school, while the later Gothic upper half was an attempt to match the façade of the Duomo in Orvieto.

Inside the Duomo, the visitor, who may be growing weary of trying to remember all the works by the many famous artists, can relax. The majority of the numerous artists who worked in Siena's Duomo are not internationally famous. The only things which the visitor should particularly look out for are the pulpit by Nicola Pisano, which represents probably the highest achievement of the Italian Gothic, and the fourth altar on the left, for which the young Michelangelo sculpted the statues of Saints Gregory, Paul, Peter and Pius.

On the right hand side of the Duomo, a long *piazza* ends with an enormous three-arched façade. This was originally intended to be the façade of what would have been the largest cathedral in the world. Work on the older cathedral was suspended in the 1330s when it was decided that it should become the transept for a larger church. Unfortunately, the financing required for the new church, combined with the disastrous effects of the Black Death in 1348, led to the abandonment of the project in 1355.

Along one side of the 'new' Duomo is the Museo dell' Opera del Duomo. This is a well-set out museum of works which have been moved from the Duomo. Many famous artists are represented here,

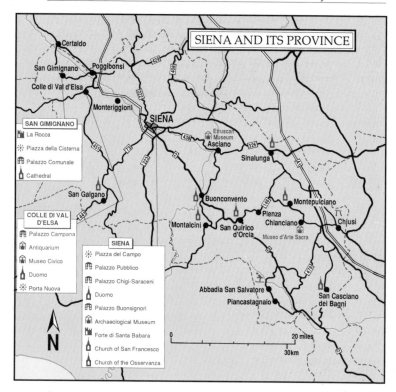

but the most famous work of art is undoubtedly Duccio's *Maestà*, painted between 1308 and 1311.

From the museum it is possible to ascend to a narrow stairway built inside the new Duomo façade. Once you are at the top, some of the finest views in any town in the world open up before you.

In front of the Duomo is the Ospedale di Santa Maria della Scala, which, like many medieval and Renaissance hospitals in Italy, is richly decorated with fine works of art, and contains its own church. Much of the hospital is now open to the public, the porter at the door will be able to give information concerning current arrangements.

If you retrace your steps along Via del Capitano, and then follow Via San Pietro, you soon arrive at the fine early fifteenth-century Palazzo Buonsignori, which houses the city's art gallery. A visit to the gallery is essential for those interested in painting, as it offers examples of the full range of Sienese painting from the thirteenth to the eighteenth centuries.

Siena: the Duomo →

The greatest period for Sienese art was the late medieval period, and the artists to whom special attention should be paid are Guido da Siena, Duccio, Simone Martini, and the Lorenzetti. Other than the Sienese works, the gallery also contains important works by northern Europeans such as Dürer, Altdorfer and Cranach.

The Archaeological Museum was opened in 1956, with the intention of documenting the evolution of civilisation in the area around Siena. Exhibits from the prehistoric to the Etruscan periods are laid out in an attractive and informative manner.

Two smaller museums in Siena are the Museo della Società di Esecutori di Pie Disposizioni, a small private museum devoted to religious relics; and the Museo dell'Accademia dei Fisiocritici, which is run by the University Departments of Zoology and Petrography.

The Forte di Santa Barbara was erected by the Medici in 1590. It is not pentagonal as are most of the Medicean forts, but rectangular, with a bastion at each corner. The walls have been turned into public walkways, while one of the bastions houses a permanent exhibition of prized Italian wines.

Besides the Duomo, Siena has a large number of other interesting churches. At the extreme northern end of the city, just inside the Porta Camollia, is the Chiesa di Fontegiusta. The church, which dates from the first half of the 1480s, is in a sober, Renaissance style highlighted by a fine portal. The portal is surmounted by a marble cornice with bas-reliefs by Urbano da Cortona. The inside of the church is decorated by some fine paintings by lesser known Sienese artists and also by some weapons hung over the main door. According to Sienese legend, the arms were given by Christopher Columbus, who they claim had been a student at the University of Siena. The arms are interesting as museum pieces but there is no evidence to support the legend.

Some of the finest church art in Siena is to be found in the Church of Sant' Agostino at the centre of one of the southern quarters of the city. The most famous of the paintings in the church is Perugino's *Crucifixion with Saints* which adorns the second altar on the right. Il Sodoma, Ambrogio Lorenzetti and Matteo di Giovanni also have works in the church. The church itself dates from 1258 but it was adapted by Vanvitelli in 1755.

Less than 5 minutes walk to the east of Sant' Agostino is another attractive church, that of San Niccolò al Carmine. The adjacent former monastery, which now houses the Faculty of Chemistry of the University of Siena, has a splendid Renaissance cloister which should not be missed.

The Basilica of San Domenico is situated a few hundred metres to the north of the Duomo, over which it has fine views. Built gradually between 1266 and 1465, the Basilica has a particularly attractive cloister. Il Sodoma is again well-represented here while the sculptures at the main altar are by Benedetto da Maiano. Many of the works of art in the Basilica depict scenes from the life of St Catherine of Siena, the fourteenth-century mystic who persuaded Pope Gregory XI to return the seat of the Catholic Church to Rome after it had been transferred to Avignon. Since 1939 Catherine has been joint patron saint of Italy. The house in which Catherine lived is situated in the nearby Vicolo del Tiratoio and was consecrated in 1461. Each room in the house is frescoed with scenes from Catherine's life, while some of her personal effects can also be seen.

The north-eastern quarter of the town is dominated by the church and ex-monastery of San Francesco. The interior of the church is built in the form of an Egyptian cross and is decorated with frescoes by Lorenzetti. A stone stairway leads down from the church to the cloister of the old monastery. The bodies of eighteen members of the Tolomei (one of Siena's leading families) are buried under the steps. The eighteen were invited for a picnic by eighteen members of another leading Sienese family during the fourteenth century and unceremoniously murdered during the meal. The cloisters and the old monastery now belong to the University of Siena.

Nearby is the small Oratorio di San Bernardino, a finely decorated shrine, erected on the spot where the fifteenth-century saint used to preach. The interior of the Oratory is decorated by Il Sodoma and other lesser known artists.

The south-eastern quarter of the city, which is built round the road to Rome, has as its focal point the imposing Basilica of Santa Maria dei Servi. The transept and apse of the church were the first parts to be built and are Gothic in style, while the nave, which was added in the late fifteenth century, is a good example of the High Renaissance style. The artistic high spot of the interior is represented by Lorenzetti's *Rape of the Innocents* which decorates the second altar on the right in the Presbytery.

With the exception of the Duomo, possibly the most impressive of Siena's churches architecturally is the Church of the Osservanza which is crowned by a high dome. The church was built in the late fifteenth century on the site of an old hermitage 3km (2 miles) to the north of the city. Many fine works of art can be seen in the church, particularly some terracotta pieces. A small museum situated to the right of the Sacristry preserves some of the more valuable and fragile works which were originally sited in the Basilica itself.

Two views of Siena's Piazza del Campo, where the famous Palio takes place twice a year

The upper town of Colle di Val d'Elsa

The Province of Siena

The Province of Siena has much to offer the visitor. Whichever direction one takes when leaving the city, there is beautiful country-side. For those who prefer visiting towns and historic sites, the province has a large number of places of great historic and artistic interest.

Visitors based in Siena should not fail to visit San Gimignano and Certaldo, two medieval hilltowns to the north-west. There is an extensive description of Certaldo in Chapter 2. The quickest way to reach them is by taking the toll-free motorway to Poggibonsi, but a far more attractive route is offered by the SS2 as far as **Monteriggioni**. This small village, built by the Sienese in 1203 as a bulwark against the Florentines, was enclosed by a wall with towers between 1213-19. The latter was reinforced half a century later. Since then the village has not changed, and the impression received on approaching is still that described by Dante in the *Inferno*, of giants standing in a circle.

Within the walls the village basically consists of a large square and a central street. The little restaurant in the square is recommended. The best view of Monteriggioni is to be had from the road towards

Colle di Val d'Elsa, particularly in late spring when the surrounding fields are aflame with poppies.

Colle di Val d'Elsa itself is the next town which should be visited. Whereas in many Tuscan towns a new town has grown up around an ancient hilltown to cope with the demands of modern industrialised society, Colle di Val d'Elsa has always been divided into two distinct sections. The upper town was, from the middle ages onwards, the administrative and religious centre, while the lower was first a centre for artisans and then, from the late medieval period onwards, a thriving industrial centre. The upper town has remained virtually unchanged since the late Renaissance, while the lower has continually moved with the times.

The most impressive building in the upper town is undoubtedly Palazzo Campana. The *palazzo*, despite never having been completed, is an excellent example of Mannerist architecture. Situated at the end of Via del Castello, the *palazzo* was built in 1539. The town's Antiquarium is dedicated to relics of the civilisation which thrived in the Elsa Valley from the fourth to the first century BC. Of particular interest are the displays of artefacts recovered from the tombs of local necropoli. Another museum, Museo Civico, is housed in the former Palazzo dei Priori. The museum contains a collection of interesting paintings produced mainly by pupils of leading Renaissance artists.

Colle di Val d'Elsa's Duomo was built at the beginning of the seventeenth century on the site of an earlier Romanesque church. The seven blind archways which form part of the left hand wall were originally part of the façade of the older church. Some of the more important works of art from the Duomo and from other churches in the town can be seen in the Museo dell' Arte Sacra in the former Bishop's Palace (27 Via del Castello). The most impressive part of the fortifications of the old town is the Porta Nuova, a gateway flanked by cylindrical towers, built by Sangallo in the fifteenth century.

After Colle di Val d'Elsa, another 10km (6 miles) of interesting driving brings the visitor to **San Gimignano**. This is known throughout the world as the 'City of the Towers'. When you first see the city in the distance, the justification for this name is immediately apparent, as although only a dozen of what were once over seventy towers still remain, they continue to dominate the city. The practice of building towers grew out of the constant feuds between leading families as they struggled for domination over the medieval towns, or to defend themselves against possible threats. It was not a practice confined to San Gimignano, as many other towns still have one or two towers remaining, and records show that these were once much more numerous.

Usually, when one family or group of families succeeded in establishing themselves as the ruling faction, they ordered the towers of their rivals to be razed to the ground or at least reduced in height. San Gimignano has retained many of its towers and those that have been lost have merely become derelict over the years. This is due to the fact that in 1353 the town council, as a desperate measure to avoid the bloodshed and destruction threatened by a dispute between two of its leading families, sent ambassadors to Florence, asking to be taken under that city's protection. As Florence was then emerging as one of Italy's most important city states with a relatively stable government, this move ensured peace in the city from that date onwards.

The city, which takes its name from a fourth-century Bishop of Modena, stands on a hilltop 330m (1,089ft) above sea level and 250m (820ft) above the River Elsa which courses slowly through the valley below. Virtually the whole of San Gimignano is still contained within the original city wall, which has been maintained in all its splendour through the centuries.

At the central point of the western section is the skeleton of La Rocca, the fortress built by the Florentines in the fourteenth century both to protect and dominate the city. Dismantled by Duke Cosimo I in 1555, the old fort is now a small park where, on hot summer days, the visitor may well decide to spend an hour lying on the grass, either to bask in the sun or to cool off in the shade of the walls. It is also possible to climb on to the walls at this point and enjoy magnificent views, both of San Gimignano itself and of the surrounding countryside. As visitors enter La Rocca they should look to their right at the fascinating sight of the centuries-old tree which has grown into the wall.

If visitors arrive by bus, they will be dropped off in Piazzale Martiri Montemaggio outside the south gate of the city. Those arriving by car are best advised to look for a space along the road which runs along the west side of the city just outside the city wall, and then take the pleasing walk along to the same gate. Passing through this gate, one is immediately on the main street and almost in another world. There are very few vehicles allowed inside the walls and this accentuates the impression that the city has remained unchanged by time.

The shops, which offer all the usual attractions to tourists, restore one to reality although, to be fair, they are not in any way obtrusive. One of the most enjoyable things about wandering through a Tuscan town is browsing through the many wines available in the shops. Sam Gimignano is amongst the most rewarding in this respect as the

The area around San Gimignano produces some excellent wines

area around the city produces an excellent white (Vernaccia) and the local Chianti is also one of the best. Do not rush into buying wine, as the city is not large, and passing by a shop again just before leaving presents no problems. All the wine shops are good, but two are worthy of special note: soon after entering the city a shop on the left is unique in selling wine in beautiful painted bottles; a little further on to the right another shop, entered through an archway, has a terrace behind from which the views are exceptional. Several of the shops sell crossbows; these are not ornaments, but are used for the hunting of wild boar, one of the culinary delights of the area.

Piazza della Cisterna with its ancient well, San Gimignano →

If you continue along the main street, a short rise leads into the first of two adjacent *piazze* which form the heart of the city. The first of these, Piazza della Cisterna, is perhaps the more attractive with its ancient well surrounded by some of the city's oldest buildings which completely encircle the gently sloping square. However, the second square, Piazza del Duomo, which adjoins the north-west corner of the first, contains most of the city's monumental buildings.

The 'old' Governor's Palace, built in 1239, is surmounted by La Rognosa, an impressive 52m (172ft) tower, although this is over-shadowed by the 'new' Governor's Palace (built in 1288) with its 56m (183ft) tower. The tower's battlements, although they blend in well, were only added in 1882. The rest of the building is original and well-worth a visit. The Council Room was frescoed in 1317 with a loose copy of Simone Martini's *Maestà* fresco in Siena's Palazzo Pubblico, which had been completed 2 years earlier. The fresco was then restored in 1467 by Benozzo Gozzoli who added other figures at the edges of the original work.

The Tower Room is also frescoed with scenes representing family life. Apart from the frescoes, which are an intrinsic part of the building, notable works of art by such as Filippino Lippi and Pinturicchio are housed in a small museum along with rare manuscripts and gold ornaments.

Alongside the 'new' Governor's Palace is the Palazzo Comunale. This is particularly outstanding for its courtyard; from a delightful open-sided loggia, reached by ascending the right-angled outside staircase, one can overlook the courtyard (brick-paved around a central well), the town and the surrounding countryside.

The dominating feature of the *piazza*, taking up the whole of the west side, is the Duomo (cathedral). Although the façade, rebuilt several times through the centuries, is not exceptional, the interior, built in 1148 and modified in 1456, is of great interest. The original decoration, executed in the second half of the fourteenth century, was done by local artists of the Sienese school which was the most advanced in Europe at that time. Three groups of Sienese frescoes can be distinguished: *Story of the Life of Christ* by Del Barna, *Story of the Old Testament* by Bartolo di Fredi, and *The Last Judgement* by Taddeo Bartolo.

When the cathedral was enlarged in 1456, leading Renaissance artists were brought in from Florence. *The Martyrdom of Saint Sebastian* by Gozzoli, on the entrance wall, is outstanding, as is Piero Pollaiuolo's *Coronation of the Virgin* in the choir. The latter was painted from a design made by his more famous brother, Antonio. Perhaps most interesting of all, however, are *The Life of Saint Fina* (the local saint) and *The Apparition of Saint Gregory*, as these are believed to be the first important works of Domenico Ghirlandaio. Sculptures in the cathedral include an *Archangel Gabriel* and an *Annunciation* by Jacopo della Quercia.

San Gimignano's second most important church is the Church of Sant' Agostino in the north-eastern corner of the city. The life of St Augustin is represented in a series of seventeen frescoes painted by Gozzoli, while Benedetto da Maiano's statues of Faith, Hope and Charity which decorate the tomb of Saint Bartolo, should also be seen. The visitor should also see the cloisters which, like every corner of San Gimignano, are well-worth exploring.

Even for the visitor without the use of a car, getting to San Gimignano presents no problem as the CIT and Lazzi Express organise regular day trips from Florence which visit Siena first and then San Gimignano. Similar day trips leave from Siena.

From San Gimignano take the road signposted Volterra which, after an initial descent, begins to climb steeply with magnificent views over the town. A turning to the left almost immediately after leaving the town leads up to the early Renaissance Monastery of Monte Oliveto. The attractive fifteenth-century cloister, which is bordered on three sides by porticoes, contains a painting of the Crucifixion which was designed by Gozzoli and painted by one of his pupils. Inside the church, only the Sacristry has retained its original aspect, as the rest was given a Baroque face-lift in the seventeenth century.

When the road reaches its highest point some ruins can be seen in the bottom of the valley to the right. These are the ruins of Castelvecchio di San Gimignano and consist of a fortress built by the Bishops of Volterra and a chapel dedicated to the Irish saint, St Finnian. The road joins the main road from Colle di Val d'Elsa to Volterra at Castel San Gimignano, an old fortified hamlet which still has much of its defensive wall standing.

Five kilometres (3 miles) north of San Gimignano, just off the road to Certaldo, is another splendid church, set at the end of a square lined with cypresses and surrounded by olives and vines. The Pieve di Cellole, a Romanesque church which dates from the first half of the thirteenth century, is constructed out of travertine stone which is particularly suitable for carving. The apse in particular should be viewed closely as it is decorated with carved foliage picked out of the surface of the stone. Etruscan chamber tombs can be seen in the hillside beyond the Pieve di Cellole and this was almost certainly the necropolis for the Etruscan settlement in San Gimignano.

For the visitor with only a short time available, it is possible to visit all the interesting places south of Siena in one long day. However, it is recommended that a more leisurely approach is adopted, with one or more overnight stops along the way.

The SS2 Via Cassia looks like a good straight road on the map, but by the time one reaches Buonconvento, 24km (15 miles) south of Siena, any belief that the Romans only built straight roads has to be drastically revised. **Buonconvento** is a picturesque town that has preserved its fourteenth-century walls virtually intact. The parish church and a small museum nearby contain some interesting works of art.

Eight kilometres (5 miles) east of Buonconvento is one of the most interesting churches in Tuscany. The Monastery of Monte Oliveto Maggiore is the headquarters of the Benedictine monks. A large impressive structure, the monastery contains many important works of art, amongst which the cycle of thirty-six frescoes by Signorelli and il Sodoma which decorates the large cloister is one of the most important of the Renaissance.

The monastic library contains many rare editions and unique manuscripts, while the still-thriving herb garden supplies the monastery's chemist not only with herbal remedies, but also with the ingredients for the world-famous Benedictine liqueurs. The monastery also contains a restaurant to cater for the many visitors.

The town of **Montalcino** stands on a hill on the other side of the SS2, 15km (9 miles) south of Buonconvento. The town became part of the Sienese Republic in 1260 after the Battle of Montaperti. Unrest in the fourteenth century caused the Sienese to fortify the town, and build a fortress, in 1361. The town was so well defended that it was able to withstand sieges by Papal and Imperial forces in 1525 and 1533 respectively.

The visitor with more time to spare should go and see the Abbey of Sant'Antimo, 10km (6 miles) to the south, before returning to the main road. Founded by Charlemagne, the actual church was rebuilt in the thirteenth century. At one point the church and its accompanying monastery (now almost disappeared), controlled large areas of the Province of Siena, until they were suppressed in the fourteenth century by Rome. The church bears more resemblance to French and Northern Italian churches than to most of those in Tuscany.

San Quirico d'Orcia, 16km (10 miles) south of Buonconvento on the Via Cassia, is an attractive medieval hilltown with a well-preserved defensive wall. The Collegiata church is of exceptional beauty, especially its three finely-decorated doorways.

A rough 3km (2 mile) drive or pleasant walk south through attractive countryside brings the visitor to the small, virtually abandoned medieval village of **Vignoni**, where the remains of a fine tower and an interesting church can be seen.

Ten kilometres (6 miles) east of San Quirico is **Pienza**, one of the most interesting towns in Tuscany. During the Medieval period, *Corsignano,* as it was then called, developed into a typical fortified hilltown, roughly rectangular in shape, with a mass of narrow streets divided into quarters by two main roads. In 1458, Enea Silvio Piccolomini, a native of Corsignano, was elected Pope and became Pius II. He believed in the dissemination of Christianity through culture, and one of his most ambitious projects was the rebuilding of *Corsignano* which became Pienza.

From Pienza the visitor should drive due south to rejoin the SS2 at Gallina. Seven kilometres (4 miles) after Gallina a right hand turn leads to the skiing centre of **Monte Amiata**. Since World War II, the village of Abbadia San Salvatore has expanded greatly to provide facilities for the many skiers and walkers who visit the mountain. The village grew up around an eighth-century monastery, which was for a long time the most powerful in Tuscany. The present building dates mainly from the middle ages onwards. The castellated medieval village centre has survived virtually intact and is well-worth a visit.

Piancastagnaio, 5km (3 miles) to the south, is another medieval village which has gradually developed as a mountain holiday centre. The continental climate of Central Italy means that, as well as enjoying a long period of snow, the area also has a good summer, and therefore supports a flourishing flora.

From Piancastagnaio the road gradually makes its way back to the SS2, rejoining it just outside the provincial boundary. From there the visitor should make his or her way east to **San Casciano dei Bagni**. San Casciano is a pleasant village grouped around a castellated villa and an eleventh-century church which contains important primitive frescoes. The village is significant as a thermal centre, having forty-two springs which can provide cures for a variety of different ailments.

Chiusi, 24km (15 miles) to the north, was one of the most important Etruscan cities 2,500 years ago. It remained important during the Roman period, and throughout the middle ages as a trading centre. However, when the Chiana Valley became marshy and unhealthy in the eleventh century, it declined and depopulated rapidly. In the fifteenth century the town was fortified by the Sienese to provide a counterbalance to the nearby Florentine stronghold of Montepulciano. However, the town did not really recover until the last century when the valley was drained and became an important line of communication.

Ten kilometres (6 miles) west of Chiusi is **Chianciano**, one of the most important spa towns in Italy. The therapeutic qualities of the waters were recognised as far back as the Etruscan period, and since then the town has always been a favoured destination of those with liver problems. It has been commercially developed into a popular modern resort during this century and is well-equipped with all kinds of amenities.

Above the modern resort is the old Chianciano, which has retained the appearance and the atmosphere of a medieval hilltown. A small museum, the Museo d'Arte Sacra, contains a small but interesting collection of Florentine and Sienese works of art.

From Chianciano, a highly picturesque route soon brings the visitor to **Montepulciano** which, although inhabited in the Etruscan period, did not begin to flourish until the decline of Chiusi in the late medieval period. In 1234 the Sienese gained control of the town, but in 1390 they were ousted by the Florentines who, with the brief exception of 1495-1511, never lost control of it again.

In the first period of Florentine domination, the central square was redeveloped by Michelozzi, while after 1511, Antonio Sangallo played a large part in the modernisation of the town. Montepulciano is ideal for those who wish to see a perfect example of a fine old town away from the more obvious tourist routes. There are several small hotels and restaurants in the town.

About 3km (2 miles) from Montepulciano, in the valley below, is the Sanctuary of San Biagio. This impressive church fuses the best of the late Florentine Renaissance style with the best of the early Roman Classicism. The church is considered to be the masterpiece of Antonio Sangallo.

In **Sinalunga**, 19km (12 miles) to the north, there are still many old buildings to be seen, despite continuous commercial prosperity through the centuries. Foremost amongst them is the Church of the Collegiata, built in the sixteenth century out of material from a fortress which had stood on the site earlier. Il Sodoma's *Virgin and Child with Four Saints* decorates the altar of the left transept.

Half-way between Sinalunga and Siena is the picturesque medieval hilltown of **Asciano**. The Etruscan Museum contains material recovered from the excavations at Poggiopinci, 7km (4 miles) to the east. The articles come from tombs built between the seventh and fourth centuries BC, and include some fine bas-reliefs with inscriptions. The Museo d'Arte Sacra contains interesting fourteenth- and fifteenth-century Sienese paintings, including a *Virgin and Child* by Ambrogio Lorenzetti. Much of the work in the museum comes from the adjacent eleventh-century Collegiata church, which shows a strong Lombardian influence in its architecture.

For the visitor who likes long drives through beautiful countryside, a visit to the Abbey of San Galgano, to the south-west of Siena, would make a pleasant day out. The abbey is reached by following the tortuous SS73 up and down steep hills and through woods, until the junction with the SS441.

The abbey, which stands at the foot of a hill to the left of the main road, is 3km (2 miles) further on. From the twelfth to the sixteenth centuries, when it began to decline, the monks of San Galgano formed one of the richest, most powerful, and most cultured communities in the south of Tuscany. The monastery, which was one of the finest examples of Cistercian Gothic, was abandoned in the eighteenth century, but has now been taken over by a colony of nuns. Although the abbey and much of the monastery are in ruins, they still offer an awe-inspiring sight.

On the hill above the abbey stands the primitive Chapel of San Galgano, the hermit after whom the abbey was named. This circular chapel contains frescoes by Ambrogio Lorenzetti. The nearby village of **Monticiano** has become a quiet, summertime country resort and offers a couple of small hotels and restaurants.

10

GROSSETO
AND ITS PROVINCE

The city of **Grosseto** lies about half-way down the fertile coastal plain known as the Maremma. In the Middle Ages the city was a fortified village, subservient to Roselle, a much more important town 7km (4 miles) to the east at the edge of the plain. In 935, Roselle was devastated by the Saracens, and Grosseto began to be developed. The new city took on the form of a compact hexagon inside an extremely strong defensive wall, which is still virtually intact.

Politically, the city was a free *comune* until 1336 when Siena managed to gain control. It did not change hands again until 1559, when it was the last Sienese city to capitulate to Florence. At that time malaria was on the increase in the Maremma and for a time the very existence of the town was threatened with the population falling to below 1,000. A concentrated land reclamation scheme at the end of the seventeenth century gave new life to Grosseto, and since then it has been greatly enlarged.

The visitor need not be concerned with the new part of the town as it is of little or no interest. There are, however, a few places in Grosseto which are worth visiting. From the outside, by far the most impressive building in the town is the late thirteenth-century Duomo. The façade of the church, which was added in the middle of the last century, consists of alternate bands of red and white marble, and is probably the most interesting part of the structure. There is little of interest to be seen in the interior which has suffered over the centuries as a result of a series of poor restorations. However, situated above the Sacristy, is the Diocesan Museum of Sacred Art which contains almost all the better works of art from the city's churches. Notable amongst these is a *Last Judgement* from the school

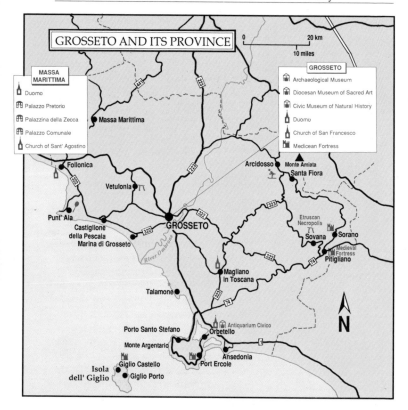

of Guido da Siena.

The city's other two museums are the Civic Museum of Natural History, and the Archaeological Museum. The latter has many relics of great importance dating from the prehistoric, Etruscan and Roman periods. Almost all the exhibits have been found during excavations in the Grosseto area. Of these, the most important are those at Roselle.

Besides the works of art in the Museum of Sacred Art, the most important work in Grosseto is an early crucifix by Duccio in the Church of San Francisco.

The hexagonal city walls survive virtually intact. It is possible to walk all around the top of the walls in less than an hour. A dilapidated Medicean fortress stands at the north-eastern corner of the hexagon, while the other corners all contain public gardens.

Massa Marittima's tiled roofs, the Duomo, and the Tuscan landscape beyond

---

Thirteen kilometres (8 miles) west of Grosseto, on the coast, is **Marina di Grosseto**. This resort, which has a long, wide and sandy beach backed by pines, is growing rapidly in popularity.

The Province of Grosseto

The most important town in the Province of Grosseto is **Massa Marittima**, in the north. Like most of the towns in Tuscany that are situated on hills, this was originally an Etruscan settlement. It began to grow in the middle of the ninth century, when it became a bishopric, in place of the declining city of Populonia. Despite being destroyed by Saracens in 935, the town recovered and most of its important buildings were built around the central square in the medieval period. In the thirteenth century the city doubled in size, with the addition of a new area, which was originally intended to be solely a residential zone.

The hills around the town are rich in minerals, and the wealth which accrued from mining in the medieval period placed the town at the heart of the struggle for territorial expansion between Pisa and Siena. The Sienese gained control in 1335. However, by 1555, when the town became part of the Grand Duchy of Tuscany, the rigours of the Black Death combined with the increasing problem of malaria had brought about a disastrous decline in the town. By 1737 it was virtually a ghost town with only 537 inhabitants. However, the freeing of the coastal plain from malaria and the recommencement of the mining activities in 1830 brought about a reasonable recovery and a degree of prosperity.

A visit to the old (pre-1225) town can be limited almost entirely to the irregularly-shaped central square, as all the important monuments are to be found there. The most imposing of all the buildings is the thirteenth-century Duomo, which gains added dramatic effect from being placed at an angle to the square. Inside the Duomo, particular attention should be given to the sculptures on the baptismal font, the fine arch of San Cerbone in the Crypt, and the *Madonna delle Grazie* in the left-hand transept, which is possibly by Duccio.

To the right of the Duomo is the severe but impressive thirteenth-century Palazzo Pretorio which now houses the town's administration, and a recently-formed museum, which amongst other major exhibits contains Ambrogio Lorenzetti's *Maestà*. Behind the *palazzo* is the Palazzina della Zecca, which was once the town's mint.

Next but one to the Palazzo Pretorio is the fortress-like Palazzo Comunale, which was formed in the fourteenth century by joining together three medieval tower houses. The ceiling of the Gabinetto del Sindaco on the first floor is decorated with a sixteenth-century cycle of frescoes. Facing the Palazzo Comunale is the Loggia del Comune which, although built in the medieval period, was almost completely restructured during restoration work in the 1870s.

Direct communication with the post-1225 'new town' is by a flight of steps which passes through two thicknesses of defensive wall. The 'new town' is attractive, but its original purpose as a residential area means that only the Church of Sant'Agostino, which dates from the early fourteenth century, should be given particular attention.

Between the two parts of the town is a Fortezza dei Senesi, which the Sienese built in the fourteenth century to dominate both parts. The fortress has now been transformed into a hospital. Just inside the new town, not far from the fort, is the former armoury which now houses an archaeological museum.

The Province of Grosseto is one of the largest in Tuscany and, being mainly rural, needs to be visited in several stages. However, one route which takes in much of the best of the province is the coast road. It would be a pity not to visit the interior, but a day or even two days on the coast is a must for any visitor.

The first coastal town in the province is **Follonica**, an industrial resort with a fine sandy beach, and some interesting nineteenth-century architecture. The Parish Church of San Leopoldo is the foremost amongst these buildings, while the town library houses a collection of wooden models relating to the industrial practices of the last century.

Shortly after Follonica, a side road leads along a peninsula to the ruggedly beautiful **Punt'Ala**, with its two medieval towers. A luxury holiday residence, a golf course and campsites have been developed here over the last few years.

Castiglione della Pescaia is originally believed to have been an Etruscan port, but now, although there is a small picturesque fishing fleet, the town's major industry is tourism. The beach is long and slopes gently up to pine trees for much of its length. Behind the new town is a small attractive hilltown, closed inside a formidable defensive wall with towers.

When the coast road reaches Marina di Grosseto it turns inland to Grosseto, and does not return to the coast until after the Maremma National Park. Most of this park, which consists of beautiful countryside with ruins of several medieval castles, is a protected nature reserve, and special permission is required to visit it. However, the sandy beach at the northern end of the park may be reached along a narrow road from the small town of Alberese. The road is normally open to traffic on Wednesdays and at weekends. It has fine views over the Monti dell' Uccellina to the south and of fields with prized Maremman cattle and wild horses on the northern side of the road. The beach has no buildings of any kind to spoil its rugged beauty and the only concession to the tourists are the picnic tables and litter bins amongst the pines.

At the southern extremity of the park, a side road leaves the main road for **Talamone**. This attractive fishing village was once an important Etruscan, then Roman port. In the Middle Ages, the Sienese intended to develop a new port there to rival Pisa and Genoa, an impractical project owing to the vast distance and the difficult terrain between Siena and Talamone.

Eight kilometres (5 miles) further down the coast a side road runs off along a narrow strip of land to Monte Argentario. This beautiful mountain was once an island, but sand deposits eventually formed two narrow strips of land which link it to the mainland. A further link with the mainland is provided by a dyke which links the island to the Orbetello Peninsula. Following the road anticlockwise around the island, the first place of importance is **Porto Santo Stefano**, which was founded in the late fifteenth century by fishermen. Fishing is still the major activity in the town, but tourism is growing steadily in importance, particularly as the town is the ferry port for the islands

The picturesque fishing village of Talamone

of Giglio and Giannutri.

The coast road offers considerable natural beauty and, for the most part, has a fairly good surface, although parts are rough and tortuous. The second largest centre is **Port' Ercole** which has more antique origins than Porto Santo Stefano, having been developed by the Romans. Modern holiday facilities are overlooked by a Spanish fortress, and by the parish church where Caravaggio is buried.

The beautiful Isola dell'Giglio is the second largest of the Tuscan islands, and was possibly the first to be inhabited. It passed through many hands, including those of Redbeard (the pirate), before becoming part of the Grand Duchy of Tuscany in 1558. Much of the coast can only be reached by boat, but in the three inhabited centres a rational development of tourist facilities has taken place which increases rather than spoils one's appreciation of the island's natural beauty.

Giglio Porto and Campese were both originally fishing villages

The fifteenth-century fishing village of Porto San Stefano

The beautiful Monte Argentario, which was once an island

with some defences against pirates. They have now expanded to cater for the increased flow of tourists. However, **Giglio Castello**, high on the hill above, is a typical medieval hilltown with a maze of alleyways clustered around a castle.

The rocky island of Giannutri is the most southerly island of the Tuscan Archipelago, and one whose only economic resource lies in the tourist industry. Two shingle beaches cater for some tourists, but most of the visitors are there for the sub-aqua possibilities that the island offers. At the north of the island are important remains of a first-century Roman villa. These consist of out-houses, a large water tank, a landing point, servants' quarters, a bath house, and the remains of the villa itself. Traces of several mosaics can be seen among the ruins.

The antique town of **Orbetello** is situated at the end of the mainland peninsula connected to Monte Argentario by the dyke. There are still considerable remains of the town's Etruscan walls, together with most of the sixteenth-century Spanish fortifications, which are a fine example of military architecture. The Duomo was built in 1376 and enlarged in the seventeenth century. Of the original building, the most important feature is the central Gothic façade which has taken on a weathered, golden look over the centuries.

Important Greek, Roman and Etruscan items found in the area are housed in the Antiquarium Civico. Among the exhibits are important vases decorated with mythological scenes.

At the mainland end of the southernmost strip of land connecting Monte Argentario to the coastal plain are the important ruins of two towns. The first of these towns, *Cosa*, was an important Roman *municipium*, but was devastated by the Visigoths in the fourth century. Later, a new town, *Ansedonia*, grew up on the site, but this was devastated in turn by the Sienese in 1330. More recently, a modern tourist village has been developed by the sea.

The Roman city was situated on top of the hill, and one can still walk in its streets amongst the remains. At the centre of the city, the forum is clearly distinguishable, and around it, the basilica, the senate house, two temples and the market. At the highest point are the remains of the acropolis and the capitol. Other less important buildings, and the fine view of Monte Argentario and Giannutri, make a visit to *Cosa* well-worthwhile.

Should the visitor be based in Grosseto, after following the coast road he or she would be advised to return to the city by one of the minor inland roads which passes through Magliano in Toscana. Situated on the top of a hill almost completely covered in olives, **Magliano** was originally an Etruscan town. In the tenth century, a fortress was built over the Etruscan and Roman ruins, and a typical medieval hilltown grew up around it. The southern section of the town's wall dates from the thirteenth century, while the rest was rebuilt by the Sienese in the fifteenth century. Only a small part of the walls has become derelict, and for the most part they are very impressive. As in many Tuscan towns, the most interesting monuments are the churches; San Martino, San Giovanni Battista, and the Church of the Annunziata should not be missed.

Twenty-nine kilometres (18 miles) north of Grosseto is another seemingly typical medieval hilltown. Close inspection, however, reveals that extremely large blocks of stone form part of many buildings, showing that it was once an Etruscan town. The town in question is **Vetulonia**, which was once one of the twelve major cities of the Etruscan Federation.

The most important visit to make in the town itself is to the Antiquarium, where a representative selection of previous finds, together with new discoveries, are set out to document the evolution of Etruscan civilisation. A large area around the town was used by the Etruscans as a necropolis, and many important tombs are located there. New archaeological excavations are constantly being undertaken in the area, and important finds are still being made.

Three towns worth visiting are grouped together on the eastern side of the province, 80km (50 miles) from Grosseto. Of these the largest is **Pitigliano**, which stands on a spur of rock between the Rivers Lente and Meleta. Nowadays the area in front of the spur is also built up, but this is divided from the medieval town by a formidable fortress built in 1554 by Sangallo the Younger.

The general aspect of the town is medieval, with houses built right on the edge of the spur-like battlements. However, the town's main monuments date from the Renaissance period when Pitigliano took over the administrative role which had formerly been performed by Sovana. From the fifteenth century until the middle of this century, the town housed a flourishing Jewish community, who sought refuge from Papal persecution.

The town is very picturesque and the visitor will enjoy looking around it. Two things should be mentioned, as otherwise they are easily missed: the section of Etruscan city wall below the Capisotto Gateway, and the ruins of the Synagogue and Jewish bakery which are situated immediately behind the cathedral.

Eight kilometres (5 miles) from Pitigliano is the region's former capital, the partially abandoned **Sovana**. The town came to prominence in the Middle Ages, after Gregory VII, who was born there, became Pope. However, in the fourteenth century many of the inhabitants left for Pitigliano which was less vulnerable to Sienese attacks. Malaria hastened the decline of the town and, despite various efforts at repopulation, it has never recovered; many buildings are in ruins or in an advanced state of decay. However, the town is extremely evocative and virtually tourist-free, making it an interesting and unusual place to visit.

About 2km (1 mile) from the town is the Etruscan necropolis (ask at the Taverna Etrusca in Piazza Pretorio for permission to visit). Several important tombs can be seen, including the Tomba Ildebranda, which is built in the form of a temple.

The third town in the area, **Sorana**, was also originally an Etruscan settlement. Like Sovana, it has suffered from neglect over the centuries, but most of the medieval buildings and the town walls are still intact. The most impressive buildings are those constituting the Rocca, which dominates the town; the rest of the town is picturesque and easily explored on foot.

Forty kilometres (25 miles) east of Grosseto is **Arcidosso**, a picturesque medieval town which has recently expanded to cater for summertime walkers and winter sports fanatics. The Abbey of Lamulas, and the village of Montelaterone, 3km (2 miles) and 4km ($2^1/_2$ miles) to the north-west respectively, are nearby destinations for walkers. Another interesting destination is **Monte Labbro**, where one can visit the ruins of a church established by David Lazzaretti, who presented himself in the 1870s as the second coming of Christ. To the east is **Monte Amiata** with its winter sports facilities and rich summertime vegetation.

Another similar town is **Santa Fiora**, which is situated a few kilometres south of Arcidosso. Apart from its role as host to summer and winter holidaymakers, the town should also be visited for its abbey and the fortified Palazzo Comunale, which is the most characteristic of the many medieval buildings.

11

SAN MARINO AND THE HISTORIC HILLTOWNS

The borders of Tuscany are to a large extent natural boundaries but the Etruscans, who gave the region its name, spread beyond these geographical limits. The present chapter is, therefore, the first of two in which Tuscany is seen as the land of the Etruscans rather than as the present day, geo-political entity.

Lying in a gentle curve, which more or less follows the eastern side of the Tuscan triangle, are seven of Italy's most historic and beautiful hilltowns. Each one of these is within easy reach of the main Tuscan centres, and each is well-worth visiting. The most interesting of these towns is **San Marino**, which, surrounded by its tiny republic, is a living museum of medieval Italy.

To get from Florence to San Marino, follow the route described for Florence to Ravenna in Chapter 12 as far as Faenza and then take the SS16 southwards to the outskirts of Rimini, from where a fast dual carriageway leads to the foot of Monte Titano. Alternatively, take the train to Bologna and from there to Rimini. There are regular bus services from Rimini to San Marino.

About 1,700 years ago, a young Dalmatian stonecutter arrived on the Italian coast looking for work. Such was his piety that the Bishop of Rimini made him a Deacon, and when the Christians were forced to flee from the persecutions of Emperor Diocletian, the young Dalmatian was chosen to lead a group of pilgrims in search of safety. On reaching the three-peaked Monte Titano, Marinus stopped on a small plateau just below the peaks and used his skills to build a chapel. Little is known of the community over the next few centuries. However, when the position was fortified against the Barbarians and became a *comune* in the tenth century, the inhabitants elected St

Marinus as their patron saint.

The liberal statutes which form San Marino's constitution were in existence as early as the 1250s, with the principal aim of preserving liberty and freedom. The area around the town that makes up the Republic was gradually purchased from the neighbouring states, while the three peaks were successively fortified and linked by the town's wall as a defensive precaution. Close alliances were avoided, as was excessive Papal domination. In this way, while the other Italian city states were gradually merging to eventually form a united Italy, San Marino retained its identity as an independent city state run as a republic.

For at least the last 800 years, San Marino has been governed by two Consuls, or Captains Regent, who hold office together for 6 months at a time, either from April or from October. Any of the citizens of the Republic can be nominated as Consuls by the Grand Council, and any agricultural worker could suddenly find himself elevated to a position from which he must meet other world leaders on equal terms. Strict rules govern the conduct of the Consuls, which discourage them from attempting to extend their tenure of office.

In the past, the San Marinesi often fought as mercenaries, and volunteers from the Republic fought for Italy in both World Wars. The Republic itself has four voluntary military corps, which now serve mainly ceremonial functions. The Fortress Guard were originally the artillery; the Milizia, in which all San Marinesi aged from 16 to 55 may enlist, was the infantry; the Noble Guard has the duty of protecting the Consuls and the Grand Council; while the fourth corps is the Crossbow Division, which every year on 3 September, San Marino's day, compete for the San Marinus Pallium, after marching through the town with full insignia. To save on the defence budget, the Fortress Guard are still equipped with English front-loading rifles made in 1860, while the Milizia carry muskets made in 1891.

Visitors are advised to leave their cars in Borgo Maggiore below the old town, and then take a very short cable car journey to San Marino itself. Parking in the old town is limited and the traffic wardens are efficient.

The first things to be seen in San Marino are the three interlocking circles of medieval defensive walls. These are very well-preserved and offer pleasant walks, particularly along the stretch linking the three castles. The first of the castles, known in the local dialect as the Guaita (watch tower), is a pentagonal building with a double circle of fortified walls. Until 1970, some of the cells in the tower were used as prison cells although the maximum term which can be served in a San Marino prison is 6 months.

The second castle, known as the Cesta (derived from a Latin word signifying a place where sacred relics are held), dates from the thirteenth century and is built on the highest of the three peaks. The castle was abandoned and reduced to a ruin before being restored in the 1920s. It now contains the Museo della Cesta (Museum of Historic Arms and Armaments). This has examples of all the various types of arms which have been used by the San Marinesi since the medieval period. On a clear day the visitor can see the mountains in Yugoslavia on the other side of the Adriatic.

The third castle, the Montale, is further away from the town than the other two and was not originally within the city walls. It originally served to block the way to the town to the forces of the Malatesta in Rimini and of the Castello di Fiorentino on the next hilltop. The destruction of the latter in 1479, and the decline of the former, led to the castle falling into disuse until it was restored in the 1930s.

The town's Basilica is a splendid example of neo-Classical architecture which dates from the middle of the last century. Unfortunately, the previous Basilica, which was demolished to make way for it, was one of the finest examples of the Romanesque in Italy. Next to the Basilica is the small, sixteenth-century Church of San Pietro, the apse of which is formed by the bare rock of the mountain. Two niches hewn out of the apse are said to have been the beds of Saints Marinus and Leo.

The oldest church in the Republic is the Church of San Francesco which was founded in 1361, built by stone masons from Northern Italy and frescoed at the beginning of the following century. The monastery next to the church originally housed San Marino's university and is now the home of a small museum and art gallery containing some fine paintings.

The seat of San Marino's government is built at one end of the central Piazza della Libertá. The *piazza* is one of the most attractive in Italy; one long side is completely open with views over the Apennines and the two ends are occupied by imposing public buildings.

The greater importance of the Palazzo del Governo is emphasised by the subtle architectural contrasts between it and the Palazzo delle Poste which faces it from the site of the old Domus Magna Comunis. Both façades are broken by three arches; those of the Palazzo dell Poste are rounded, whereas those of the Palazzo del Governo are pointed, indicating that those who pass through do so for spiritually higher purposes. Both buildings have three windows on the first floor, each with a balcony in the centre; that of the Palazzo del

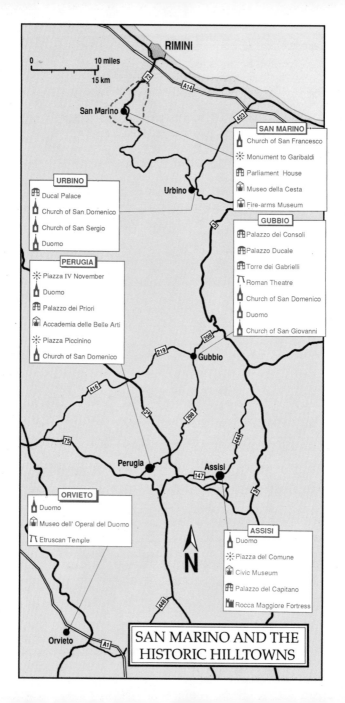

RIMINI

0   10 miles
     15 km

San Marino

72

A14

423

SAN MARINO
- Church of San Francesco
- Monument to Garibaldi
- Parliament House
- Museo della Cesta
- Fire-arms Museum

Urbino

URBINO
- Ducal Palace
- Church of San Domenico
- Church of San Sergio
- Duomo

5

GUBBIO
- Palazzo dei Consoli
- Palazzo Ducale
- Torre dei Gabrielli
- Roman Theatre
- Church of San Domenico
- Duomo
- Church of San Giovanni

PERUGIA
- Piazza IV November
- Duomo
- Palazzo dei Priori
- Accademia delle Belle Arti
- Piazza Piccinino
- Church of San Domenico

298

219

Gubbio

416

3

298

75

441

Perugia   Assisi

147

3

ORVIETO
- Duomo
- Museo dell' Operal del Duomo
- Etruscan Temple

ASSISI
- Duomo
- Piazza del Comune
- Civic Museum
- Palazzo del Capitano
- Rocca Maggiore Fortress

N

443

Orvieto   A1

SAN MARINO AND THE
HISTORIC HILLTOWNS

Castle tower at San Marino

Governo forms a focal point, while the central window of the Palazzo delle Poste is smaller than those which flank it. This appears to diminish the importance of any one standing there facing a crowd in the *piazza*. The statue of Garibaldi, in a small public garden not far from the central square, was the first to be erected to him in the whole of Italy.

Below the northern end of the town and connected to it by a *funivia* (funicular railway) is the suburb of Borgo Maggiore.This grew up around the site of the thirteenth-century market which has been held every Wednesday since then. Two museums of interest in the Borgo are the Philatelic Museum and the Fire-arms Museum.

The Philatelic Museum contains examples of all the postal stamps and coins issued by San Marino, and of all the stamps issued by each of the members of the Universal Postal Union since 1920. A section of the museum is given over to an exhibition documenting Garibaldi's connection with San Marino.

About 50km (30 miles) south of San Marino is one of Italy's most attractive and interesting cities. **Urbino**, which is built on two hills, has a degree of architectural unity and a cultural heritage which few other cities can match.

The city can be reached either via San Marino or by following the SS73 from Arezzo to San Sepolcro and then the SS73b across the Alpe della Luna (Moon Alps). Taking this spectacular mountain route, the visitor passes through another attractive town a few kilometres before reaching Urbino. The town is **Urbania** which took its present name when its government was brought under the direct control of the Church in 1636 by Pope Urban VIII. The Palazzo Ducale of the

Montefeltro in the town was given its present look during a Renaissance rebuilding programme undertaken by the enlightened Dukes of Montefeltro in the previous century. The basically simple lines of the palace, which contains the municipal art gallery and museums, are enhanced by two cylindrical towers and a hanging loggia.

Several of the town's churches contain important works of art but without doubt the most important of these is the Gothic portal which was added to the twelfth-century Church of San Francesco by the then 20-year-old Lorenzo Ghiberti in 1398. Evidence of the talent which was later to produce the *Doors of Paradise* in Florence can clearly be seen.

Although Urbino first came to prominence as a Roman *municipium*, it attained its real importance thanks to the development which took place after 1135, when the city was granted to the Montefeltros as an imperial fief. Under the first nine Montefeltro dukes, the city gradually became more influential, overshadowing the neighbouring small duchies, and creating a more logical urban structure than many other cities of the time. However, it was the tenth duke, Federico da Montefeltro, who with great political and military ability, allied to a wide but discriminating patronage of the arts, made the city one of the most important in Italy.

Under Federico (1444-82) and his son Guidobaldo (1482-1508) the Urbinese dominions were greatly extended, the Palazzo Ducale was built, and the leading men of letters gathered in the city. Baldassare Castiglione's *Il Cortegiano*, the most representative work of Italian Renaissance literature, is based on the learned discussions which took place at the court of Urbino.

After 1631, when the Montefeltro family and their successors, the Della Rovere, had died out, the city dropped out of the limelight. There was a further period of glory at the beginning of the eighteenth century, when the patronage of the Urbinese Pope Clement XI and his nephew Cardinal Albani brought the town to life again. Some structural changes were made in the Napoleonic period, but both these and later developments have been done with taste and with due respect for the unique character of the city.

The first place to visit in Urbino is without doubt the Palazzo Ducale, which Castiglione described as a city within a city. The palace covers most of the summit of one of the two hills, and its light, open and elegant aspect marks it out as different from all other Italian palaces of the period. The change from the normal, fortress-like construction shows how strongly humanistic thought had gained a hold over all aspects of the city's life.

Inside the palace are two museums; the Galleria Nazionale delle

Marche, and the Museo Lapidario. The former contains by far the most important art collection of the region, with paintings by Paolo Uccello, Piero della Francesca, Signorelli, Titian, and the city's most famous son, Raphael, amongst others. The Museo Lapidario on the ground floor was formed in 1756, and contains a large number of vases, busts and other lapidary objects.

Unlike many Italian cities, the most impressive church is not the Duomo, but the Church of San Domenico, which is built over a primitive frescoed chapel. Other churches worth visiting are San Sergio, Sant' Agostino, and Santa Chiara, which was adapted by the Della Rovere in the seventeenth century to house the family mausoleum. San Bernardino's church, outside the city to the south, was built in the late fifteenth century by Federico as the Montefeltro mausoleum, although by that time the last male Montefeltro had already been born.

Many visitors come to Urbino to visit Casa Santi, where Raphael was born. This typical house, which is built around a small courtyard, contains information on and mementoes of the artist's life.

Seventy kilometres (40 miles) south of Urbino is another interesting city, this time at the foot of Monte Ingino. The origins of **Gubbio** belong to the remote past, but it became important in the second century BC when it became a Roman *civitas*. The most conspicuous reminder of the Roman period is the impressive semi-circular open-air theatre in the north of the town.

Much building was done by the Romans, but the city was not fortified and, with the decline of the Empire, it was largely abandoned in favour of more secure places. In 917 almost all the Roman city was razed to the ground by the Hungarians, and the Gubbio of today is the result of the redevelopment which took place after that.

To reach Gubbio from Florence take the A1 motorway southwards as far as the intersection for Perugia and then the Perugia link road for just under 30km (20 miles) to the Tuorlo turn-off. From Tuorlo take the scenic SS416 through the hills to Umbertide and then the SS219 along the Assino Valley to Gubbio.

Umbertide is situated on the East bank of the upper Tiber Valley and is an important centre for the production of pottery. A small art gallery is housed in the thirteenth-century Palazzo Comunale which also contains the original fourteenth-century statutes governing the town. High above the town, on the way to Gubbio, is **Civitella Ranieri**, one of the best-preserved castellated villages in the area.

In Gubbio itself, which is reached after another 24km (15 miles), a new cathedral and a *palatium communis* were built in the highest part of the city in the twelfth century. The city grew around these two

Opposite: The Palio della Balestra, performed in Gubbio on the last Sunday in May (top); the Festa dei Ceri, performed on 15 May in Gubbio (bottom)

buildings, and a defensive wall was erected. Many new buildings were also erected to fill up the spaces inside the walls, although this was never quite achieved.

From 1384 Gubbio was ruled by Urbino, and the most important monument from this Montefeltro period is the Palazzo Ducale, built in 1470. This completely incorporates the old *palatium communis*, whose function as seat of government had already been partially superseded by the large Palazzo dei Consoli, built in the mid-fourteenth century.

A slow but continual decline in population meant that most of the sixteenth- and seventeenth-century changes in the town consisted of the joining up of two or more medieval houses to form larger dwellings. In the eighteenth century, however, several new civic buildings were erected by the city's ecclesiastical rulers, including the theatre, the seminary and the hospital. From then onwards the city remained unchanged until after World War II, when new residential areas began to spread southwards in a hydra-like growth. The new part of the city is interesting, and can be ignored by the visitor.

Any visit to Gubbio should start in the fourteenth-century Palazzo dei Consoli. Inside the impressive grey stone building is the Archaeological Museum which has seven stone tablets bearing pre-Roman inscriptions on the organisation of the city. There is also a small art gallery on the upper floor, which contains mainly local pictures from the thirteenth to the eighteenth centuries; and a stone fountain in the council room which is probably older than the building itself.

Palazzo Ducale is notable mainly for its architecture, particularly the fine Renaissance courtyard which divides the *palazzo* in two. Next to the Palazzo Ducale is the cathedral, which was completed in 1188. This is typically medieval, with a fine rose window over a simple façade. Gubbio also boasts several other impressive churches.

Perugia, widely known as a centre of culture and learning, occupies one of the earliest inhabited sites in Italy. People have lived on this hill since prehistoric times, and the city was developed by the Umbrans before being swallowed up by Etruscan expansion in the sixth century BC. One of the twelve major cities of the Etruscan

Confederation, Perugia consistently opposed Rome until being overrun in 295BC.

Under the Romans, the city continued to thrive until being sacked and burned by Octavian's troops at the end of the civil war in 40BC. After it was rebuilt, Perugia was governed by the Bishops until 548 when, being overrun by the Goths, it was again destroyed. In the eleventh century the city began to thrive again as a free *comune*. Strong ties were developed with the Papacy, and many of the surrounding towns were forced into subjection. The city's grip over these dominions was weakened by internal rivalries in the four-teenth century, but it did not lose its independence until 1540, when it was incorporated into the Papal States.

At this time, the houses of the ruling family were demolished and a fortress erected on their site by Antonio da Sangallo, but this was destroyed in its turn during the 1848 Revolution.

The city is reached relatively easily from Florence as a motorway link connects the city with the A1. There are also fairly frequent direct trains and several others which can be joined by taking the Florence-Rome line to Terontola and changing there.

The centre of Perugia is formed by the large Piazza IV Novembre, at the heart of which is a fountain. This fountain was erected in 1278, when an aqueduct was constructed to bring water to the city from a mountain several kilometres away. The marble and bronze sculp-tures which decorate the fountain are the work of Nicola and Giovanni Pisano.

The Duomo has occupied one side of the *piazza* since the ninth century, although the bulk of the present building was constructed between 1147 and 1490. The outside is simple, with little or no decoration, although the interior, which is formed of three naves of equal height, is well-stocked with fine paintings. Behind the cathe-dral are two fine cloisters, a Dominican library and the Museo del Duomo, which has as its most important exhibit a painting by Luca Signorelli.

The large Palazzo dei Priori originally consisted of a much smaller building entered from the flight of external steps which can still be seen. It was gradually enlarged, incorporating several surrounding buildings, and given the Gothic façade which unifies the whole.

On the third floor of the *palazzo* is the Umbrian National Art Gal-lery. This contains not only works by all the main Umbrian artists, but also examples of other schools and a section dealing with the history of Perugia. The finest paintings are those by Duccio, Fra Angelico, Il Perugino and Piero della Francesca.

More paintings can be seen in the Accademia delle Belle Arti, situated in Piazza San Francesco. This contains a rich collection of works from the nineteenth and twentieth centuries. There is also a section containing plaster casts which have been used at the modelling stage of sculptures, including some by Canova and Michelangelo.

Next to the Palazzo dei Priori is the Collegio del Cambio, originally the seat of the Bankers' Guild. Inside, in the main hall, is a statue of Justice by Benedetto da Maiano, and a series of frescoes by Il Perugino dating from around 1500.

Piazza Piccinino is another interesting spot, with a fine early sixteenth-century church, Chiesa della Compagnia della Morte, built in the form of a Greek cross. In front of the church is an Etruscan well; 5m (15ft) across and more than 30m (100ft) deep.

In a small chapel next to the Church of San Severo, visitors can enjoy frescoes which are the product of the combined talents of Raphael and Il Perugino. Raphael began with the top section and, after his sudden death, the work was continued by his former teacher.

The tall octagonal Church of Sant' Ercolano, which nestles against the city wall, stands on the spot where Bishop Sant' Ercolano was beheaded by the Goths. Inside, the decoration consists of a harmonious Baroque over the original Gothic. The altar is formed of a Roman sarcophagus.

Giovanni Pisano was the architect for the Church of San Domenico, which is the largest in the city. Shoddy workmanship by a group of seventeenth-century painters and decorators severely damaged the delicate Gothic decoration, and this was replaced by pedantic and uninspired Baroque embellishments. Some interesting works of art are to be seen in the side chapels.

Next to the church is the former Monastery of San Domenico, where the Umbrian Archives and the Umbrian Archaeological Museum are housed around a fine Renaissance cloister. The museum contains important Neolithic, Etruscan and Roman objects.

Another impressive church and monastery is the Basilica of San Pietro, the bulk of which was built in the tenth century. The monastery has a beautiful cloister, while the church contains an altar by Mino da Fiesole and paintings by Il Perugino, Reni and Vasari.

Under the former fortress which was destroyed in 1848, a medieval street, buried when the fort was built, has been excavated. The street, which can be followed by the visitor, is almost entirely underground. Another fine medieval street is Via Maestà delle Volte, which takes its name from the thirteenth-century fresco *Maestà* in the Church of the Oratorio delle Volte. Beyond the bottom

Perugia: Via Acquedotto

Perugia: the Duomo San Lorenzo, its doorway and exterior pulpit (right)

Perugia: the Piazza IV Novembre

of this street, to one side of the Italian University for Foreign Students, is one of the finest Etruscan archways still in existence; it is surmounted by Doric embellishments. By passing through the arch and ascending again towards the centre, the visitor will find another fine archway, this time Roman, and dating from the third century BC.

Another gateway worth looking at is the thirteenth-century Porta Sant'Angelo, an excellent example of a medieval gateway in the form of a fortified tower.

Assisi, less than half-an-hour's drive from Perugia, is famous above all for St Francis of Assisi. The Basilica of St Francis stands at the extreme west of the town. It comprises two large churches, one above the other, against the slope of the hill. The lower Basilica contains the body of the saint which was transferred there in 1230, 4 years after his death. Frescoes by Cimabue, Giotto, Simone Martini and Pietro Lorenzetti make this one of the worlds most artistically important churches. The upper Basilica was largely built by English priests who headed the Order after 1239 and the refined Gothic interior bears more than a passing resemblance to some of the English cathedrals. The main decoration is provided by Giotto's magnificent series of frescoes on the life of the saint.

There are many other points of interest in a town where much of the original charm has been maintained, despite recent rapid and often uncontrolled expansion.

The city is built on the southern side of a hill at the foot of Mount Subasio. Although many relics of the Roman period can still be seen, little is known about Assisi's early history. The Roman city was built on a series of terraces to counteract the steep slope, an urban plan which was carried over into the medieval period.

The site of the Roman amphitheatre is clearly visible in the east of the city, even though it is occupied by medieval buildings, while traces of the Roman theatre can be seen near the Duomo. The Duomo itself, although attractive, has seen too many restorations to be of interest to the purist, although the crypt (which belonged to an earlier church on the site) contains a third century AD sarcophagus, and eleventh-century frescoes.

For the Romans, the city's chief place of worship was the Temple of Minerva, the Corinthian façade of which still stands in Piazza del Comune. The building behind the façade was first a monastic hospice, then the prison, and from 1539 a church. The Temple originally stood on a plinth above the square, but over the centuries the street level has been raised considerably. Excavations of the Roman city are taking place beneath the square, and entrance to these can be gained from No 2 Via Portica. Roman and Etruscan relics are collected in the Romanesque crypt of the adjacent ex-church of San Nicola, now the Civic Museum.

Other important buildings in the Piazza del Comune are the thirteenth-century Palazzo del Capitano, and the 1337 Palazzo dei Priori, which now houses the Town Hall and also a rich art gallery. Many of the paintings are detached frescoes which have been saved from old churches.

Dominating the city is the impressive Rocca Maggiore Fortress; built in 1367, it is one of the best-preserved fortresses of the period.

Seventy kilometres (40 miles) south-west of Assisi, on the flat top of a former volcano, is **Orvieto**. The site has been inhabited since the Iron Age and supported a flourishing Etruscan community, until being destroyed by the Romans in 264BC. After this the Romans took little interest in the site, and it was not until the Byzantine period that the town began to grow again, becoming a bishopric in the eighth century.

In 1157 Pope Hadrian IV (the only English Pope) recognised Orvieto as a free *comune*, and the town began to extend its domination over the surrounding area, reaching its zenith towards the end of the thirteenth century when most of the buildings were erected. Afterwards, internal strife and the Black Death weakened Orvieto so much that in 1354 it was absorbed by the Papal States. Several Popes stayed there, including Clement VII who took refuge there after the Sack of Rome.

Although few new building projects were undertaken during the Renaissance, many existing constructions were given facelifts, with typical fifteenth-century façades being imposed. This accounts for the town's Renaissance aspect. The only recent developments have been in the valley near the railway, which is far enough away to have no effect at all on the real Orvieto.

The town is easily reached from Florence as the hilltop on which it stands is situated just off the A1 motorway, 170km (105 miles) to the south of Florence. It is also easily reached by train as many of the Florence-Rome trains stop at the station. The station is situated at the foot of the hill on which the town stands; although it looks very close, those tempted to walk up should be warned that it is further than it seems.

The central point of the town is Piazza Duomo, where many of the most important buildings are situated. The group of medieval cottages on the north side almost all sell the local white wine, which is excellent. On the other side of the Duomo is the group of Papal palaces. These were built for the Popes who visited Orvieto in the

Assisi: the Church of St Francis

thirteenth century, and contain the Museo dell'Opera del Duomo, seat of some excellent works of art. In front of the Duomo is the Palazzo dell'Opera del Duomo, which houses the archaeological section of the museum, and offers a fine view of the façade of the Duomo from the upper floor windows. The adjoining *palazzo* contains urns and vases recovered from the nearby Etruscan necropoli.

Construction of the Duomo itself began in 1290, and the result is one of the finest examples of the Gothic in Italy. The façade, which took over 200 years to build, is outstanding both for its form and for

Assisi: Church of Santa Maria Maggiore

Assisi: detail of the colourful ceiling in the Church of St Francis

its colourful and harmonious decoration. Inside, some Romanesque influence may be detected in the nave, but the transept is pure Gothic. Many fine works of art decorate the interior, but none finer than the frescoes by Fra Angelico and Luca Signorelli which decorate the New Chapel at the end of the South Transept.

At the eastern end of the town are the remains of the fourteenth-century papal fortress, which is now a public garden, and behind it the famous Pozzo di San Patrizio. This 'well' down the face of the rock contains two interlocking spiral staircases which were used for trade and communication with the outside world during wartime, all other entries to the town being blocked up. This well was built in the sixteenth century by Antonio da Sangallo. Once having seen these principal sights, the visitor should spend some time walking around the town; it deserves to be seen as a whole.

Just outside the town, near the Pozzo di San Patrizio, are the remains of an Etruscan temple dating from the fourth century BC. The temple, which consisted of three large chambers behind two rows of columns, was excavated at the end of the last century. To the north-west of the town are the Etruscan necropoli, where the tombs are partially dug out of the rock and then covered with large blocks of stone.

To reach Tarquinia either continue along the Via Aurelia for 30km (20 miles) after crossing the Tuscany-Lazio border or follow the SS2 from Siena as far as the southern end of Lake Bolsena and then head west, over the hills towards the coast. The first of these routes has little of interest between the Tuscan border and Tarquinia but the second offers an abundance of attractive scenery and interesting small towns. Of these towns on the route the most interesting of all is **Tuscania** on the top of the ridge between the Rivers Marta and Capecchio, 20km (10 miles) south of Lake Bolsena.

Although today Tuscania is a quiet rural town, it was once an important and powerful Etruscan city which later continued to flourish under the Romans. The Romanesque Church of San Pietro stands on top of a hill which was once the site of an acropolis while many other remains are visible to the visitor. In the thirteenth century Tuscania was a free city state but the inevitable internal strife weakened the city to the point where it became a feudal fief.

In the fifteenth century, after an unsuccessful rebellion against papal domination, the name of the city was changed to *Toscanella* (Little Tuscania) as a punishment, the original name being restored in 1911. The Papal forces demolished the city's fort and defensive structures and more destruction was wrought by the troops of the French King Charles VIII in 1495. The rebuilding which then took place gave the town a Renaissance aspect which it retains to this day, despite the damage inflicted by an earthquake in 1971.

The earliest parts of the Church of San Pietro (mainly the rear) dates from the ninth century having been erected at the time Charlemagne gave Tuscania to the Pope. The rose window in the façade is a particularly fine example of the Lombardian style, although the actual window is a reconstruction of the original which was destroyed during the 1971 earthquake. The twenty-eight columns which support the church over the crypt were originally part of Roman buildings in the town.

The other important monument in the town is the Church of Santa Maria Maggiore which, like that of San Pietro, is built over the remains of a large Roman building. Of particular interest inside the church is the baptismal font. Due to a privilege granted by Pope Alexander III in the twelfth century, this was for several centuries the only place where babies could be baptised in the town. The hills to the north of the town are covered with Etruscan necropoli where a programme of archaeological excavations has been in place for the last 40 years, throwing much new light on Etruscan civilisation.

The original **Tarquinia** was situated on the top of a hill 3km (2 miles) from the sea in a position which, like those of most of the main Etruscan cities, was virtually impregnable in its day. It is said that the city was founded by Tarconte, the brother of the Etruscan leader Tirreno (who gave his name to the Tyrrhenian Sea) in the thirteenth century BC. However, archaeological excavations have not produced any evidence of inhabitation before the ninth century BC.

It is believed that at some time in the sixth or seventh century BC the Etruscans of Tarquinia, led by Lucio Tarquinio, conquered Rome and established the Tarquini Dynasty which lasted until 510BC. For 80 years in the fourth century BC, Tarquinia was at war with Rome before finally being overwhelmed. In the Dark Ages the ravages of malaria and the incursions of the Barbarians virtually wiped out the city and the remainder of the population moved to a nearby hill where the bulk of the present town is situated.

During the time of Lucio Tarquinio some of the leading Greek artists came to Tarquinia and this led to a far greater documentation of Etruscan life than occurred in other centres and to the construction of some of the finest of the decorated Etruscan tombs.

The town itself is very attractive and is essentially medieval in character. The 3km (2 mile) long defensive wall is virtually intact, as are eighteen of the old defensive towers. The bases of another twenty towers can also be seen. The centre of the town is Piazza Cavour which is dominated by Palazzo Vitelleschi; the latter demonstrates

Detail of the Duomo's carved friezes and colonnades

←Orvieto, the Duomo façade which took over 200 years to build

the architectural transition period between the Gothic and the Renaissance. The Tarquinian Cardinal who was responsible for the construction of the *palazzo* was put to death in Castel Sant' Angelo in Rome in 1440 after which it was used as an occasional residence by several Popes.

Since 1924 the *palazzo* has been the seat of the Museo Nazionale Tarquiniese which is the most important of all the museums dedicated to the Etruscans. The exhibits are too extensive and varied to list in full but mention must be made of the magnificent Tomba del Triclinio (fourth century BC). This is one of several Etruscan tombs which have been reconstructed within the museum. The end wall is decorated by a banqueting scene, the side walls by scenes of dancing and music, and the entrance wall by paintings of foliage. The Etruscan necropoli themselves can be visited to the east of the city although only a limited number of the tombs are open to the public at any one time.

Tarquinia has a number of fine churches, particularly Santa Maria di Castello. The construction of this Romanesque church was initiated in 1121 and the bulk of the external decoration carried out by craftsmen from Lombardy. The marble baptismal font in the centre nave is believed to have been made out of a Roman sarcophagus.

On the shore to the south of the town are the remains of the old Roman port of *Gravisca* which, after being restored several times over the centuries, was finally destroyed during the German retreat in World War II. Nearby is the old Porto di Tarquinia which is completely silted up; the port and the old town were abandoned at around the same time. Excavations during the last 20 years have begun to uncover the secrets of the old town.

12

BOLOGNA, RAVENNA AND RIMINI

Bologna

Although previously the site of primitive settlements, it was not until the arrival of the Etruscans in the sixth century BC that the first real town was built. The Etruscan name, *Felsina*, was replaced by *Bonomia* when the site became a Roman *municipium* four centuries later. With the decline of the Roman Empire and the passing of Byzantine domination, the city passed through several hands. Although officially a Papal possession from 756 onwards, it was continually disputed by the Pope and the Holy Roman Emperor. In 1114, however, the will of the people prevailed and the city proclaimed itself a free *comune*, which was officially recognised by the Emperor in 1183.

This is the period when Bologna was at its most important; it was the first city in Italy to abolish serfdom, and in 1088 the first European university was founded there. The prosperity of the period is also shown by the number of important buildings which date from the time of the *comune*.

Towards the end of the thirteenth century the *comune* collapsed as a result of the struggle between Guelphs and Ghibellines. After being ruled over by a succession of *signori* (lords), it was the property of the Papacy from 1506 to 1859, with the exception of the Napoleonic period.

Situated as it is, where the southern end of the Val Padana meets the Apennines, the city is almost unavoidable if the visitor is to do any more than localised travelling in Italy. It has become a key point in the Italian communication systems; both the main motorways and the most important railway line pass through the city. For the visitor

Bologna: the doorway to the Duomo

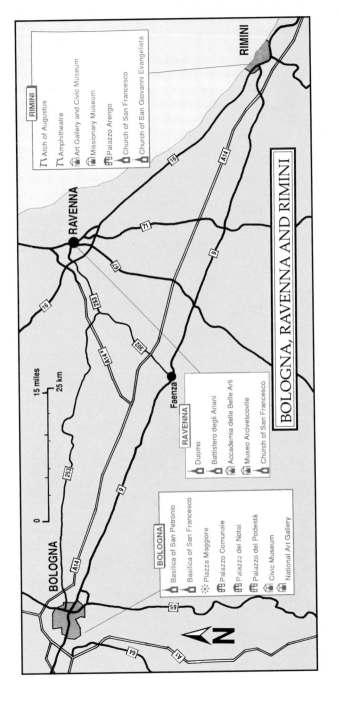

BOLOGNA, RAVENNA AND RIMINI

BOLOGNA
- Basilica of San Petronio
- Basilica of San Francesco
- Piazza Maggiore
- Palazzo Comunale
- Palazzo dei Notai
- Palazzo del Podestà
- Civic Museum
- National Art Gallery

RAVENNA
- Duomo
- Battistero degli Ariani
- Accademia delle Belle Arti
- Museo Arcivescovile
- Church of San Francesco

RIMINI
- Arch of Augustus
- Amphitheatre
- Art Gallery and Civic Museum
- Missionary Museum
- Palazzo Arengo
- Church of San Francesco
- Church of San Giovanni Evangelista

15 miles
25 km

0

N

BOLOGNA
Faenza
RAVENNA
RIMINI

A14
A1
64
59
253
253
9
302
16
A14
67
71
9
A14
16

who comes to Italy by air, it is certainly well-worth considering one of the frequent charter flights to Bologna's G. Marconi airport, and spending at least a couple of days in the city before moving on.

There are three ways in which the visitor can travel from Florence to Bologna: the direct modern railway line, the A1 motorway, the old railway over the Apennines, and the SS66 over the Futa Pass. The direct railway line from Florence is by far the quickest way, particularly if one travels by *Rapido*. However, much of the journey consists of tunnels through the Apennines and the journey is almost entirely uninteresting.

The A1 route also has several tunnels but most of the route is reasonably scenic. It is, however, a horrible stretch of road to drive on, particularly from Monday to Saturday when it is full of juggernauts which are irritatingly slow on the ascents and dangerously fast on the descents.

Before the new railway was built, all trains for Bologna travelled via Pistoia where it is now necessary to change in order to take the old line to Bologna. From Pistoia the line climbs up into the mountains through several short tunnels and over numerous bridges and viaducts with magnificent views of the mountains and back over Pistoia, before a 2.5km ($1^1/_2$ miles) tunnel takes it under the crest.

※ The main place of interest along this line, if the visitor wishes to break the journey, is Porretta Terme, a pleasant mountain spa town in the Reno Valley. Beyond Porretta the line descends gently but continually for 40km (25 miles) before rejoining the main line just before Bologna.

The first part of the SS66 takes the visitor as far as the Medicean Villa of Cafaggiolo — this is described in the excursion to the Mugello (Chapter 2). Soon after Cafaggiolo the road begins to climb ever more steeply with hairpin bends as it becomes the Futa Pass. This is not the route to take if you are in a hurry or if the weather is bad. However, in fine weather and with plenty of time to enjoy the views, it is by far the best way of making the journey.

Most visitors will arrive in **Bologna** either at the bus depot or at the railway station. Both of these are situated on the old city wall, to either side of Porta Galliera, one of the original thirteenth-century gateways. From here, Via dell'Indipendenza leads directly to Piazza Maggiore, the centre of the city.

Before going into the centre, spare a few minutes to look at the station itself, the scene of the 1980 Fascist bombing which killed over ※ 80 people. The station has been reconstructed exactly as it was, except that a zigzag pane of glass, reaching the full height of the building, marks the point where the wall of the waiting room was blown away. It forms a permanent memorial to those who died.

Piazza Maggiore marks the centre of the city, and is surrounded by its most important buildings. The Palazzo Comunale was originally a private house until it was taken over by the *comune* in 1287. From then on it underwent almost continual extension and embellishment for the next 300 hundred years, being unified with a fine façade in the sixteenth century. Inside the *palazzo*, a fine staircase, built by Bramante, leads up to rooms which were decorated to receive popes and emperors and which now house the art collections of the *comune*.

In front of the *palazzo* is the fine sixteenth-century statue of Neptune, the figure for which was made by Giambologna. Water is sprayed out of the fountain through ninety jets.

The Basilica of San Petronio, which dominates the southern side of the *piazza*, was begun in 1390, to celebrate the city's patron saint. The original plans, which would have made it the largest church in the world, were never fully executed, but it is still one of the largest. Jacopo della Quercia was responsible for the central door (1425-38) and the rest of the marble lower façade was completed in the middle of the following century. Many richly decorated chapels line the sides of the nave; in the seventh of these, the funeral monuments of Elisa Bonaparte and her husband can be seen. Near the eleventh chapel, a small museum contains the original plans for the church, along with rare manuscripts and religious relics. The bells in the tower, which was built at the end of the fifteenth century, are still the originals.

Next to the church, the southern side of the *piazza* is completed by the fourteenth-century Palazzo dei Notai, which once housed the Guild of Notaries. Facing this *palazzo* is the Palazzo del Podestà, built in the thirteenth century and partially adapted at the end of the fifteenth. The Renaissance façade was never completed, as the ruling Bentivoglio family was expelled and the work suspended. However, on the lower part, more than three thousand sculpted rosettes can be seen on the marble pillars.

Next to the Palazzo del Podestà is the Palazzo di Re Enzo, where King Enzo, son of the Emperor Frederick II, was kept prisoner for 23 years after being captured in battle, being released only by death in 1272.

Ravenna

Legend has it that the city of Ravenna was founded seven generations before the fall of Troy. The earliest inhabitants to leave any traces were the Umbrians, who later made way for the Etruscans. The city's splendour dates from the late Imperial and Byzantine periods.

Bologna: the Palazzo del' Archigimassio — ceiling of the cloisters

Bologna has 50km (30 miles) of colonnades: good examples are those in Piazza Maggiore (above), and Via del' Indipendenza (right)

At the beginning of the fifth century, the Emperor Onorio transferred the capital of the Western Roman Empire from Milan to Ravenna, for safety reasons. From being a provincial town and small port (the Adriatic then covered much of what is now a coastal plain), the city developed rapidly into a fitting seat for emperors.

Much new building was undertaken, and the finest masters of mosaic were called in to see to the decoration. In 476 the King of the Barbarians became King of Italy, but was driven out of Ravenna 17 years later by the Ostrogoths of Theodoric. Under Theodoric and the Ostrogoths, not only were the fine religious buildings which had been erected by the Byzantines respected, but other important buildings were added.

In 540, the Byzantine general Belisarius retook the city, and for a while it flourished again, until enthusiasm diminished with the realisation that Justinian's dream of creating a strong, united empire was doomed to failure because of political fragmentation and the power of the Barbarians in the west.

The receding shoreline, which rendered useless the large port of Classe, 5km (3 miles) from Ravenna, and the rise of Bologna as a cultural centre in the medieval period, finally relegated the city to its original position of a quiet, provincial town. Only with the Unification of Italy did it begin to make a recovery.

The visitor travelling from Florence to Ravenna has three alternatives. The simplest way is to take the train for Bologna and then travel from there to Ravenna which makes the journey around $2^1/_2$ hours but which has little to recommend it other than speed. Travelling by motorway involves going up the A1 to Bologna and then along the A14 towards Rimini until the motorway link for Ravenna just after Imola.

The third and most interesting alternative is to take the normal roads over the mountains. Getting onto the Via Faentina in Florence is made very complicated because of the one way system, so the best way is to leave the city on the Via Bolognese and then cut across.

About 2km (1 mile) after the start of the Via Bolognese, in Piazza della Libertà, a small right hand turn signposted Fiesole takes you down a steep hill to meet up with the Via Faentina. Turn left here towards Borgo San Lorenzo. After about 3km (2 miles) the road begins to climb steeply up to the little village of **Olmo** which has a good *pizzeria*. Beyond Olmo the road descends steadily down a wooded valley until it reaches the Sieve Valley just before Borgo San Lorenzo.

From Borgo San Lorenzo follow the signs for Marradi, Brisighella and Faenza. The road climbs steadily through olives, vines and chestnuts until the Casaglia Pass on the Apennine Ridge. From here there is a steady descent to **Marradi**, a busy little town 5km (3 miles) before the regional boundary. The town is a pleasant place from which to start a number of mountain walks.

Brisighella, 24km (15 miles) further on, is a very attractive late medieval hillside town dominated by several imposing monumental buildings. The town was already important in Roman times and it is said that the Church of San Giovanni in Ottavo, $2^1/_2$km ($1^1/_2$ miles) back towards Marradi, was built on the site of a pagan temple at the request of Gallia Placidia, the sister of the Emperor Onorio.

Three chalky outcrops, each capped by an important building, overlook the town. The medieval fortress, which has tall and squat cylindrical towers, stands on the central outcrop and houses an interesting museum of local customs and traditions. A large seventeenth-century church stands on the westernmost outcrop while the easternmost one bears the town's clock tower, which dates from the end of the thirteenth century.

In the town itself, the neo-Classical town hall is impressive while the nearby Val Lamone Museum contains interesting relics of the period when Ravenna was the capital of the western Roman Empire. The town has for centuries been notable as a spa and its waters are believed to be beneficial for inflammatory disorders of the respiratory tract.

Thirteen kilometres (8 miles) beyond Brisighella, on the coastal plain, is **Faenza**. This was founded by the Romans in 180BC at the point where the road from Florence to Ravenna crossed the Via Emilia. The main monumental buildings of the town are grouped around the two adjacent *piazze*; Piazza della Libertà and Piazza del Popolo. The Florentine influence of Giuliano da Maiano can clearly be seen in the construction of the Renaissance cathedral, while the open loggias of the former Palazzo del Podestà provide the perfect Classical balance for the colonnaded porticoes of the *piazza*.

Faenza is justly famous for its ceramics industry and, with over fifty pottery workshops in the city, it is not surprising that the city's most important museum is dedicated to ceramics. The main part of the International Ceramics Museum is given over to a display of local productions from the Roman period to the present day. Other sections, however, contain exhibits from all the other Italian centres of production as well as major centres from other countries. The museum also has a fine collection of modern paintings by artists such as Picasso, Chagall and Matisse.

Finally, 18km (11 miles) to the East of Faenza, is **Ravenna**. Those visitors who think they do not like mosaics should visit the city as the

Colourful mosaic on the ceiling of the Archives, Ravenna

Ravenna: Mausoleum of Gallia Placidia with its fifth-century mosaic ceiling

The Tempio Malatestiano, Rimini

quantity and quality of the mosaics there will make them change their minds. The Basilica of San Vitale offers the finest examples. Octagonal in form, work was begun in 526 and the Basilica was consecrated 21 years later. Almost the whole of the story of the Bible is condensed into the mosaics, as well as a representation of Justinian and his court endowing the church, which can be seen in the apse. In a former monastery which adjoins the Basilica is the Museo Nazionale, which contains a collection of Roman and early Christian relics, including coins and marble inscriptions.

Another fine octagonal building, of which the bottom 3m (10ft) have been hidden by successive rises in the street level, is the Baptistry of the Ortodossi o Neoniano; its dome is decorated with richly coloured mosaics.

The Basilica of Sant'Apollinare Nuovo was built under Theodoric, and given its name when the bones of the city's patron saint were moved there. Amongst the many mosaics, the finest is the procession of the Martyrs and the Virgins.

The Church of San Francesco, although altered many times, was first built in the fourth century. The only original part is the crypt, the mosaic floor of which is usually underwater, owing to the gradual sinking of the city. Next to the church and dependent on it, is a temple-like tomb containing the grave of Dante, who died in exile in Ravenna. The poet's remains were hidden for over 250 years by the Franciscans, after Leo X ruled that they should be removed to Florence. The temple was built when they were found again in the eighteenth century, although the city of Florence still claims it has a right to the bones of its most famous son.

The sister of Emperor Onorio is commemorated by the Gallia Placidia Mausoleum; a small cruciform building with a plain exterior but a fine mosaic interior. Gallia ruled as Regent after her brother's death, and may have died in Ravenna in 450.

There are several other places of interest in Ravenna which the visitor should endeavour to see. The Baroque cathedral was built in 1734 on the site of an earlier church of which some of the marble elements are incorporated. Other fragments of the old cathedral can be seen in the adjacent Museo Arcivescovile, including a carved ivory lectern which originally belonged to Saint Maximilian.

The Battistero degli Ariani is a late fifth-century church with a fine mosaic of the Baptism of Christ. The Basilica of Santa Maria in Porto is a sixteenth-century church (although the façade was added 200 years later). Of particular interest inside the church are the delicately carved choir stalls, and a marble bas-relief known as the Greek Madonna.

Next to Santa Maria in Porto, the old monastery to which it originally belonged now houses the Ravenna Accademia delle Belle Arti (Academy of Fine Arts), the Civic Art Gallery and an Ornithological Museum with over 2,000 different species of bird and a specialist library. The restored cloisters and garden loggias of the monastery are fine examples of Renaissance architecture.

The fifteenth-century Rocca Brancaleone fortress, which was built by the Venetians in the fifteenth century, houses a children's playground and an open-air theatre where opera and ballet can be seen each summer.

Just beyond the fortress, on the other side of the railway lines, is the severely Classical sixth-century Mausoleum of the Emperor Theodoric which is built on the spot where he was struck down by lightning.

Five kilometres (3 miles) from Ravenna, but still part of the urban bus network, is the Basilica of Sant' Apollinare in Classe. The impressive exterior was once covered in marble, until this was taken away to decorate a new church in Rimini. Inside, the mosaics on the floor have almost worn away, but those on the walls and ceilings are the equal of those anywhere in the world. Most outstanding of all is that in the apse, which represents Sant' Apollinare himself standing in the midst of nature, green fields, rocky outcrops and animals.

The whole of the coastline near Ravenna consists of fine sandy beach and a long line of lively resorts stretching from Casal Borsetti in the north to Lido del Savio in the south. The beaches are separated from the resorts by a continuous band of pine woods which have fortunately been preserved to stop the towns from encroaching too much. The resorts themselves, although mainly modern, are far less extensively developed than many on the Adriatic Coast. However, this does not prevent them from offering an extensive range of sports and entertainment facilities.

Rimini

Thanks to its development over the last 150 years into one of the world's most flourishing holiday resorts, Rimini is now one of the better-known Italian resorts. There is a large amount of commercialisation, but for the visitor who is looking for warm sea and almost guaranteed sunshine, with every possible facility on hand, the town is ideal. However, unlike many European holiday resorts, Rimini also has something to offer the more active visitor.

As well as a myriad of sports and leisure opportunities, the old medieval/Renaissance town of Rimini is waiting to be visited. This old part of the town, standing behind the new suburb of Marina, which is entirely dedicated to the tourist industry, contains important Roman monuments as well as buildings of a later date.

Rimini was first established as a settlement during the Iron Age, and after several centuries of Umbrian and Etruscan culture it passed under Roman rule in 268BC. The town quickly became an important port, and two of the main Roman roads, the Via Emilia and the Via Flavia, ended there. The Roman Amphitheatre is in ruins but two other monuments are still virtually intact. One of these is the magnificent Arch of Augustus, built as the southern gate of the city, and dedicated to the Emperor in 27BC. The top of the arch is surmounted by battlements which were added in the medieval period.

Augustus was also responsible for the construction of the five-arched bridge, known as the Ponte Tiberio (Tiberius' Bridge) because it was finished during the reign of his successor. The fifth arch was cut in 552, to repel the invading Byzantines.

From the end of the twelfth century until 1503, when Cesare Borgia siezed the city, Rimini was ruled by the Malatesta family. They were immortalised by Dante in the *Inferno*, in which Paolo Malatesta and his brother's wife Francesca represent those who are condemned to hell for the sin of lust. After the Borgian period and a short occupation by Venetians, the town was ruled quietly by the church until the Risorgimento (Unification), and since then has been devoted almost entirely to the tourist industry.

It is possible for the visitor to take part in almost any kind of sport in Rimini, from horseriding to hang-gliding, from tennis to ten pin bowling. There are also regular excursions on the Adriatic to Venice and Yugoslavia.

Tips for Travellers

Accommodation

Hotel reservations cannot be made through ENIT (Italian Tourist) Offices. They do, however, hold lists of organizations who can book hotels, (normally 4 or 5 star) in all major tourist areas. The tourist offices (EPT) in the provincial capitals, the local tourist agencies (Aziende Autonome di Cura, Soggiorno e Turismo — AACST) in larger towns and villages, and the Pro Loco offices in smaller centres hold more comprehensive lists of hotels. Most of the larger offices (the notable exception being Grosseto) will supply the lists on written request.

Camping

Camping forms a major part of the Italian tourist industry. The tourist offices will supply details of local sites. Alternatively, the Italian Camping Federation publishes two lists covering the whole country. The first of these is a comprehensive list with details of all the country's sites which costs around £10 (US $17). The second is a more abbreviated list which is issued free. Either list may be obtained from:

Centro Internazionale Prenotazioni
Federcampeggio
Casella Postale 23
50041 Calenzano
Firenze
☎ 055 882391

Mountain Refuges

Most of the mountain huts (*rifugi*) are owned by the CAI (Club Alpino Italiano). The huts offer cheap overnight accommodation with basic facilities and simple meals for

passing walkers. Details from:
Club Alpino Italiano
Via Foscolo 3
Milano
☎ 02 802554 or 8057519

Youth Hostels

The Italian Youth Hostel Association has over fifty youth
hostels in Italy, full details of which can be found in the
International Youth Hostel Federation handbook. They
are of a high standard and have good facilities. Many
have family rooms but these must be booked in advance.
It is also important to book in advance for hostels in
major centres during busy periods to avoid disappointment.

Notable hostels include:
Florence A superb villa with 400 beds, about 280 of
which are in four-bedded rooms. It has good food, a bar
with a lively atmosphere and is set in beautiful surroundings. It was once Mussolini's villa.
Massa This is in a nice position, 200m (220yd) from the
coast. About half of it is taken up by conventional
dormitories with eight and ten beds but there is also a
suite of family rooms, each with a self-contained wash-
room.
Bologna This is conveniently placed, a short bus ride
from the heart of the city.
Ravenna A modern building with good facilities in six-
bedded rooms. There is a cafeteria, disco and bar and
there are also family suites.
Cortona This is a converted monastery. The rooms are
conventional dormitories with eight, ten or twelve beds.
The washrooms are excellent and the food is superb.

Further information is available from:
Associazione Italiana Alberghi per la Gioventú
Via Cavour 44 (terzo piano)
00184 Roma
☎ 06 462342 or 06 4741256

Climate

The temperatures are generally milder along the coast than in the interior. Average January temperatures are: Florence 4.7°C, Arezzo 4°C, Pisa 6.1°C and Portoferraio (Elba) 9.3°C. The hottest month is July when average temperatures are Florence: 24.6°C, Arezzo 24.2°C and Pisa 23.5°C while in the mountains they can be as low as Abetone 16.1°C.

Weather Information: Florence

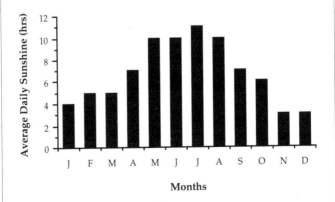

Credit Cards

All major credit cards (Access, American Express, Visa etc.) are taken at most large restaurants, hotels and shops. Eurocheques and travellers cheques are also accepted. The notable exceptions are filling stations, which tend to only accept money or fuel coupons.

Banks are normally open between 8.30am-12.30pm and 3-4pm, Monday to Friday only.

Currency Regulations

The Italian monetary unit is the Lira (plural Lire). No traveller may import or export more than 400,000 Lire in hard currency although this restriction should be lifted by 1992. It is advisable to check the current situation. The present regulations also restrict the re-exportation of unused travellers cheques to 1 million Lire unless a customs V2 form has been completed on entry.

Customs Regulations

Normal EEC Customs regulations apply. The Italian age limit for the import of duty-free alcohol and tobacco is 17 (this is largely a technicality as supermarket prices in Italy tend to be lower than duty-free prices for alcohol).

Normal personal equipment — cameras, jewellery etc — can be taken into the country, but professional photographers need an AFA Carnet for the importation of their equipment.

Entry into Italy
No visa is required for stays of less than 3 months for holders of passports from Britain, Canada, Ireland or the United States. A valid passport is required.

Electricity

The voltage is 220v ac, 50 Hertz (cycles/sec). Four different types of plug are commonly used — two with two pins and two with three pins in a line. Plugs can be bought easily for less than 1,000 Lire each. While carrying an adaptor is recommended, purchasing a handful of plugs on arrival is normally the best solution.

Health Care

British and Irish travellers have a right to claim health services in Italy by virtue of EEC regulations. Form E111 — available from the Department of Social Security — should be obtained to avoid complications. For minor problems it is advisable to use the extensive private sector as the problem will have probably resolved itself before you manage to see a doctor in the public health service.

American and Canadian tourists will need to check the validity of their personal health insurance to ensure they are adequately covered.

If drugs are prescribed by a doctor and these are dispensed at a pharmacy (*farmacia*), a minimal local tax is payable which will not be reimbursed.

Those wishing to walk in lonely mountain areas should purchase *siero anti vipera* before beginning their walk. This is a vaccine to be taken after snakebites. The vaccine is available over the counter in Italian chemists.

Emergency Services
For Fire, Police and Ambulance, ring 113.
For immediate attention at airports, railway stations (large) and hospitals, look for the sign PRONTO SOCCORSO.

Holidays and Festivals

Italy has the following national holidays:
New Years Day
Epiphany (6 January)
Easter Monday
Liberation Day (25 April)
Labour Day (1 May)
Assumption Day (15 August)
All Saints Day (1 November)
Immaculate Conception (8 December)
Christmas Day
St Stephen (26 December)
In addition, some town's celebrate the patron saint's day. In Florence and several other towns covered in this book the patron saint is St John the Baptist (24 June). Major festivals are included in the information on each town in the Further Information section.

Maps

The Touring Club Italiano's 1:200,000 Carta Automobilistica della Toscana is a very good map of the whole region. Most of the local tourist offices issue free maps of individual provinces and town plans for the major cities.

Police Registration

A hangover from the late 1970s, when terrorism was a major problem, is that all tourists must register with the police within 3 days of entering the country. If you stay at a hotel, campsite etc, this registration will be carried out for you.

Post and Telephone Services

Stamps (*francobolli*) are sold at both post offices and tobacconists. Post offices are normally open from 8.30am-2pm, some in large towns remain open until 7 or 8pm. Tobacconists are normally open from 8.30am until 8pm with a break between 1 and 3.30pm.

Phones in phone booths occasionally take coins — 100 and 200 Lire — but these, and all older phones, take *gettoni* (200 Lire tokens). The latter are available at tobacconists, bars and some news stands. Some bars have *telefoni a scatti* which record the number of units of each call; this avoids the need to be continually feeding in small change. This is more convenient but the bar price usually includes a surcharge and the meter cannot usually be seen from the phone. In larger towns look for the SIP 'shop' where you can phone from a soundproof booth with a meter inside it. It is also increasingly possible to purchase magnetic phone cards although this still appears to be limited to larger towns.
Dial codes from Italy are:

Great Britain 0044
Canada   001
USA   001

Remember to leave out the first zero of your home country number — eg to dial the Italian Tourist Office in London (071 4081254) from Italy dial (00 44 71 4081254)

Photography

All types of film are widely available in Italy. In almost all museums and churches it is forbidden to use tripods or flash so it is well-worth purchasing a 1000 ASA film when planning to visit important cultural centres, although in summer any film faster than 200 ASA will make outdoor photography difficult. It is forbidden to take photographs in the museums, galleries and churches of Florence.

Travel

By Air

Bologna, Pisa and Rimini all have international airports, while there is talk of a large new airport being constructed just outside Florence. The existing airport at Florence is for domestic flights only, although it is possible to buy a through ticket, changing at Milan or Rome. Many airlines offer discounts to full-time students (with a valid identity card) and anyone under 26.

By Rail

Regular services connect Florence to Bologna with most major European cities.

A range of greatly reduced tickets are available to those under 26 on international journeys, while tourists whose normal place of residence is outside Italy may purchase a *biglietto turistico libera circolazione*. This ticket allows unlimited travel on the Italian rail network, and does not require a supplement for travel on the *Rapido* (see below). Italian National Tourist Offices (see Useful Addresses in the Further Information section) will provide details of where tickets may be purchased. Other reductions for 3 day returns, circular journeys, party and family tickets are also available. Children under 4 not occupying a seat travel free, while children under 12 receive a 50 per cent reduction on all journeys. The Italian rail network is notoriously difficult and prone to strikes but it is very comprehensive and almost all towns of any size can be reached by rail.

Italian trains have the following specifications:
Super-Rapido (Trans Europa Express). Very fast, luxury class only, supplements are payable and seat booking is obligatory.
Rapido. Fast, inter-city trains. Some are first class only. Supplement charged (about 30 per cent of standard fare, children pay full supplement). On some trains seat booking is obligatory.
Espresso. Long-distance trains between cities, stopping only at major stations.

Diretto. Trains stopping at most reasonable-sized towns. Look at timetables carefully as there is often little difference between *Espresso* and *Diretto*.
Locale. Stopping at all stations.

A useful but rather expensive French motorail service operates between Boulogne (or Paris) and Milan.

By Road
Coaches and Buses
Italy has an extensive long-distance coach system and reliable local bus services. Most major cities offer specific bus tours.

Cars
It is best to go over the Alps, as passing through the South of France adds a considerable amount to the journey and the roads are very crowded in summer.

Recommended Routes:
1 Boulogne/Calais, Rheims, Lausanne, Great Saint Bernard, Milan, A1 Autostrada.
2 Boulogne, Paris, Bourg en Bresse, Mont Blanc, Milan, A1 Autostrada.
3 Ostende, Munich, Innsbruck, Brenner, Milan, A1 Autostrada.

Fuel
By British standards, diesel in Italy is very cheap, while petrol (gasoline) and oil are very expensive. LPG is also reasonably priced and fairly widely available on the continent. Petrol (gasoline) coupons may be purchased from ACI (Automobile Club Italiano) offices at major border crossings on production of a vehicle registration document. These give tourists a discount of around 10 per cent on pump prices, and also contain five 2,000 Lire *autostrada* tokens (which will take you most of the way to Milan). Purchase of the booklet also entitles the tourist to call on the free ACI breakdown service, as well as free car hire for up to 10 days if the vehicle is off the road and being repaired for more than 12 hours.

Driving Restrictions

All Italian motorways are toll-roads with tickets usually dispensed automatically on entry, and payment made on exit. At the time of writing, speed limits on Italian motorways vary, depending on the day of the week and whether it happens to be a particularly important saint's day. Current speed limits on various types of road are normally displayed at all road border crossings. In urban areas there is almost always a speed limit of 50kph (30mph).

Parking facilities in the larger towns are generally inadequate and it is usually quicker to park well out of the centre and proceed on foot or by public transport than to attempt to find a space in the centre. Parking fines are generally insignificant but, if your vehicle is towed away, it is very expensive to get it back.

Mopeds

No driving licence is required for mopeds in Italy and anyone over 14 may use them.

Driving Documents and Requirements

All vehicle documents; registration, insurance, driving licence (and Italian translation — available from national motoring organisations or the Italian State Tourist Authorities) must be carried at all times with on-the-spot penalties for offenders. With traditional green British driving licences it is necessary to carry an Italian translation (available free of charge from the AA and the RAC); this is advisable with all licences. It is now compulsory for front seat passengers to wear seatbelts at all times. All children under 5 must be strapped into a child car seat. In theory, all vehicles must be fitted with a left-hand-side wing mirror, although this is not generally enforced.

Car Hire

Car hire is available at airports, large stations and in most large towns. The major international firms are represented throughout Italy, supplemented by local concerns. Most British and American travel agents selling flights or package holidays to Italy will be able to offer competitive terms for car hire.

Ferries
Ferries for the islands of the Tuscan Archipelago are run by the following companies:
Maregiglio Societa di Navigazione
Isola del Giglio (GR)
☎ 0564 809309 for Giglio

Toremar — Toscana Regionale Marittima

Livorno — Scali del Corso 5
☎ 0586 22772

Piombino (LI)
Piazzale Premuda 13-14
☎ 0565 31100

Porto Santo Stefano (GR)
Piazzale Candi
☎ 0564 814615.
For Elba, Giglio, Capraia, Gorgona, Pianosa.

Navarma Lines
Portoferraio (LI)
Viale Elba 4
☎ 0565 918101

The Italian Language

Italian is a straightforward language in which words are written as they are pronounced and each letter has only one sound (except for the letters e, o, c and g which have two each).
The basic pronunciation rules are as follows:

c before *e* or *i* is pronounced *ch* (as in cheese) eg. *vicino* (near) veecheeno
elsewhere *c* is pronounced as in cat eg. *camera* (bedroom)
ch is pronounced *k* eg. *perchè* (why/because) pairkay
e is pronounced either as in *hen* or as the *a* in *day* eg *ecco* (here) echo or *che* (what) kay

g before *e* and *i* is pronounced *j* eg. *Germania* (Germany) jairmarnia

elsewhere *g* is hard eg *grosso* (big)

gh is pronounced *ly* eg. *aglio* (garlic) alyoe

gn is pronounced *nye* as at the beginning of new eg. *gnomo* (gnome) nye-omo

h is silent eg. *ha* (has) a

sc before *e* and *i* is pronounced *sh* eg. *fascismo* (fascism) fasheezmoe

elsewhere *sc* is pronounced *sk* eg. *tasca* (pocket) taska

z and *zz* are pronounced *ts* or *ds* (*dz*) although this tends to vary according to the local dialect. eg. *mezza* (half) medza

Useful Phrases

Si — Yes (see)

No — No

Per favore or *Per piacere* — Please

Grazie — Thank you (gratseeay)

Prego — Don't mention it (pray-go)

Va Bene — All right (va bayney)

Buongiorno — Good morning (bwon-jorno)

Buona Sera — Good afternoon/Good evening (bwona saira)

Buona Notte — Good night (bwona nottay)

Dové? — Where is? (doughve)

Quando? — When? (kwandough)

Che Cosa? — What? (kay koza)

Quanto? — How much? (kwantoe)

Quanto Costa? — How much does it cost? (kwantoe kosta)

Parla Inglese? — Do you speak English? (parla in-glay-say)

Non Capisco — I don't understand (known capee-sko)

Posso Avere? — Can I have? (posso av-ay-ray)

Vorrei — I would like (vorray)

Mi Scusi — Excuse me (me skuzee)

aperto — open (a-pair-toe)

chiuso — closed (queue-zoe)

caldo — hot (cal-doe)

freddo — cold (fray-doe)
grande — large (gran-day)
piccolo — small (pronounced as the musical instrument)
buono — good (bwon-oh)
cattivo — bad (ca-teevoe)
cambio — currency exchange (cam-bee-oh)

Numbers
zero — 0
uno — 1
due — 2
tre — 3
quattro — 4
cinque — 5
sei — 6
sette — 7
otto — 8
nove — 9
dieci — 10
venti — 20
trenta — 30
quaranta — 40
cinquanta — 50
sessanta — 60
settanta — 70
ottanta — 80
novanta — 90
cento — 100
due cento — 200
mille — 1000
duemila — 2000
tremila — 3000
primo — first
secondo — second
terzo — third

In the Hotel
una camera — a room
due, tre camere — two, three rooms
con bagno — with bathroom (cone banyoe)
con doccia — with shower (cone dot-chee-ah)

giorni — days (jor-knee)
una settimana — a week (oona set-tim-arna)
la colazione — breakfast (col-lats-ee-oh-nay)
la cena — evening meal (latchaynah)

Motoring
Accendere i Fari in Galleria — Use Headlights in Tunnel
Tenere la Destra (*Sinistra*) — Keep Right (Left)
Divieto di Transito — No Entry
Divieto di Sosta (or *Sosta Vietata*) — No Parking
Avanti — Walk (at pedestrian crossings)
Entrata — Entrance
Uscita — Exit
Lavori in Corso — Roadworks in Progress
Pericolo — Danger
Rallentare — Slow Down
Polizia Stradale — Highway Police
Senso Unico — One Way Street
Senso Vietato — No Entry
Divieto di Sorpasso — No Overtaking
Sosta Autorizzato — Parking Allowed (followed by times)
Vicolo Cieco — No Through Road
Zona Pedonale — Pedestrian Zone

In the Restaurant
Il conto — The bill
La lista — The menu
Vino Bianco — White wine
Vino Rosso — Red wine (often referred to as Vino Nero)
Vino della casa — House wine, order this by the *litro* or
mezzo litro (litre or half litre)
Servizio Compreso — Service charge included
Acqua gassata — Fizzy mineral water
Acqua minerale non gassata — Still mineral water

FURTHER INFORMATION

This information is arranged alphabetically by city or major town, while the smaller towns are listed under their respective provinces which follow immediately after information on the provincial capitals. The address of the local tourist information office precedes the information on the cities. The tourist offices are usually called Ente Provinciale per il Turismo, Azienda Soggiorno e Turismo, or Azienda di Promozione Turistica. The quality of service available from these tourist offices may be variable although the vast majority are very helpful. Museum opening times may change slightly from year to year but will be substantially as stated below.

Arezzo

Ente Provinciale per il Turismo
Piazza Risorgimento 116
☎ 0575 20839

Museums
Museo Archeologico Mecenate
Via Margaritone 10
Open: Monday-Saturday (except Wednesday), 10.30am-3pm, Sunday, 9am-12noon.

Galleria a Museo Medioevale e Moderno
Via San Lorentino 8

Open: Tuesday-Saturday, 9.30am-3.30pm, Sunday, 9am-1pm.

Museo di Casa Vasari
Via Settembre 55
Open: Monday-Saturday. No fixed time, knock at the door.

Museo Diocesano di Arte Sacra
Piazza del Duomo
Open: Monday-Saturday, 10am-12 noon and 1-5pm.

Theatres
Teatro Petrarca
Via Guido Monaco 12

Politeama Universale
Via Lorentino d'Arezzo

Arena Eden (Open-air)
Junction of Via Niccolo Aretino and Via Antonio Guadagnoli.

Traditional and Regular Festivals
April-May, National and International Art Exhibition.
End of August, international competition for male voice choirs.
First Sunday in September, Joust of the Saracen in medieval dress.
September, religious festival.
First Sunday of every month, antiques market in Piazza Grande.

Province of Arezzo

Abbazia di Farneta
A small museum housed in the abbey.

Anghiari
September 10, Medieval Mystery and Miracle plays. Last Sunday in July, poetry reading contest.

Bibbiena
Last day of Carnival (Shrove Tuesday) Festival of Traditional Dances and songs.

Caprese Michelangelo
Michelangelo Museum
Aziendi di Promozione Turistica
Piazza del Comune 12
06081 Assisi
☎ 075 812534

Cortona
Museums
Museo dell' Accademia Etrusca in Palazzo Pretorio
Open: 9am-12noon and 3-6pm.
Museo Diocesano, Chiesa del Gesù, Piazza del Duomo
Open: 9am-1pm and 3-7pm.

Traditional or Regular Festivals
August 15, Beef-steak Festival, celebration of food and local folklore.
Summer, open-air theatre, cultural manifestations and art displays.
End of August-September, antique furniture fair.

Lucignano
Museo Comunale, in Palazzo Comunale
Last two Sundays in May, procession of floats decorated on allegorical themes.

Monte San Savino
Third Sunday in September, Suckling Pig Festival with folklore celebrations.

Montevarchi
Museo Paleontologico
Via del Museo
February, Carnival, fancy dress processions.

Poppi
July and August, historic and artistic exhibitions in the Guidi Castle.

San Giovanni Valdarno
Museo della Basilica
Piazza Masaccio
Every 2 years, Premio Masaccio, Art Competition.
February, Carnival, Medieval music concerts.

Sansepolcro
Communal Art Gallery
Palazzo Comunale
Open; Monday-Saturday, 8am-2pm and 4-6pm.
Second Sunday in September, Crossbow tournament.

Terranuova Bracciolini
House-Museum of the Humanist Poggio Bracciolini.

Assisi

Azienda Autonoma di Turismo
Piazza del Comune 12

Museums
Tesoro della Basilica di San Francesco
Open: April-October, Tuesday-Sunday, 9am-12.30pm and 2.30-6pm.

Museo della Basilica di Santa Maria degli Angeli
Piazza Porziuncola

Open: April-September, Thursday-Tuesday, 9am-12.30pm and 2.30-6pm.

Museo e Archivio Capitolare
Cattedrale San Rufino
Piazza San Rufino
Open: 8am-12noon and 2pm-sunset.

Pinacoteca Comunale (Art Gallery)
Piazzo del Comune
Open: (except Monday), Summer, 9am-12.30pm and 4-7pm; Winter, 9am-12 noon and 3-6pm; Sunday, 9am-12.30pm.

Foro Romano
Via Portica
Open: except Monday, Summer, 9am-12.30pm and 4-7pm; Winter, 9am-12noon and 3-6pm; Sunday, 9am-12.30pm.

Galleria d'Arte Contemporanea
Citadella Cristiana
Via Ancajani
Open: Monday-Friday, 10.30am-1pm and 4.30-6.30pm.

Galleria del Cantico
Santuario San Damiano
Open: April-September, 2-6.30pm; October-March, 2-4.30pm.

Theatres
Teatro Comunale
Piazzetta Verdi

Auditorio della Cittadella Cristiana
Via Ancajani

Teatrino delle Rose
Via Santa Maria delle Rose

Teatro Istitute Patrono d'Italia
Piazzale Poriuncola
Santa Maria degli Angeli

Sports Facilities
A large sports centre with an outdoor swimming pool is situated just to the east of the city.

Events
April 15, Peace Celebration. Olive branches are sent to all the main cities in the world.

Easter week, processions and celebrations of the Easter Story.

End of April/beginning of May, International Antiques Market.

Beginning of May, Calendimaggio, medieval music, theatre and processions.

Ascension day, celebrations on Mount Subasio.
June 22, Feast of the Holy Vow, celebrating Saint Clare saving the city from the Saracens.

June 24, Corpus Christi, procession.

July 1, Procession through streets carpeted with flowers for the eight day of Corpus Domini.

July 2-31, Music festival.

August 1-2, Festival of Forgiveness.

August 11, St Rufino's Day (Patron Saint), Palio della Balestra, Medieval tournament.

August 12, Festival of St Clare, Patron Saint of Television.

September, Antique Music Festival.

September 16, Canticle of the Creatures Festival.

October 3-4, Festival of St Francis.

October, Congress of Franciscan Studies.

December 24-January 6, Concerts of Christmas Music.

Bologna

Azienda di Promozione Turistica

Via Marconi 45
40122 Bologna
☎ 051 237413

Museums
Biblioteca e Museo Carducci
Piazza Carducci 5
Open: Tuesday-Sunday, 9am-12
noon.

Pinacoteca Nazionale
Via Belle Arti 56
Open: Tuesday-Saturday, 9am-
2pm, Sunday, 9am-1pm.

Collezioni Comunali d'Arte
Palazzo Comunale
Open: Monday and Wednesday-
Saturday, 9am-2pm, Sunday, 9am-
12.30pm.

Galleria Comunale di Arte
Moderna
Piazza della Costituzione 3
Open: Wednesday-Monday, 10am-
8pm.

Galleria d'Arte e Museo d'Arte
Industriale Davia Bargellini
Strada Maggiore 44
Open: Monday and Wednesday-
Saturday, 9am-2pm, Sunday, 9am-
12.30pm.

Museo Civico, Risorgimentale e
Archaeologico
Portico del Pavaglione 8
Open: Tuesday-Saturday, 9am-
2pm, Sunday, 9am-12.30pm.

Museo di San Domenico
Basilica di San Domenico
Piazza San Domenico

Museo di San Petronio
Basilica di San Perronio
Piazza Maggiore

Museo di Santo Stefano
Basilica di Santo Stefano
Via Santo Stefano 24

Theatres
Teatro Bibiena
13 Via San Vitale

Teatro Comunale
1 Largo Respighi

Teatro Cooperativa Il Cerchio
4 Via Acri

Teatro delle Celebrazioni
236 Via Saragozza

Teatro Duse
7 Via Castellata

Teatro Evento Societa
53 Via Pratello

Gruppo Teatrale Radneui
16 Via Pratello

Teatro La Soffitta
41 Via D'Azeglio

Teatro Nuova Edizione
1 Via Moline

Teatro Ridotto
255 Via Elm Lepido

Teatro San Leonardo
63 Via San Vitale

Teatro Tenda Bologna
Via Stalingrado

Teatro Testoni
2 Via Tiarina

Skiing in the Province of Bologna
Information from:
Azienda Autonoma di Turismo
Piazza Marconi
Lizzano in Belvedere
(Bologna)
☎ 0534 51052

Azienda Autonoma di Turismo
Via Marconi 28
Vidiciatico
(Bologna)
☎ 0534 53159

Florence

Ente Provinciale per il Turismo
Via Manzoni 16
Firenze
☎ 055 2478141

British Consulate
Lungarno Corsini 2

Museums and Buildings of Interest
Museums in Florence normally
open 9am-1pm or 2pm and 3 or 4-
7pm Tuesday-Saturday and 9am-
1pm Sunday. However, this can
vary amongst the smaller museums.

There is free admission to all
national museums and galleries in
Florence for those aged 60 and
over, if they show their passport.

Alberto della Ragione Collection
Piazza della Signoria 5

Archaeological Museum
Via della Colonna 36

Bardini Museum and Corsi Gallery
Piazza de' Mozzi

Bargello
Via del Proconsolo 4

Botanical Museum and Gardens
Via della Pira 4

Brancacci Chapel
Church of Santa Maria del Carmine

Casa Buonarroti
Via Ghibellina 70

Cenacolo di Ghirlandaio
Ognissanti Church
Borgo Ognissanti

Cenacolo of San Salvi
Via San Salvi 16

Cenacolo of Sant' Apollonia
Via XXVII Aprile 1

Cenacolo of the Conservatory of
Foligno
Via Faenza 42

Cenacolo of Santo Spirito
Piazza Santa Spirito 29

Certosa of Galluzzo
Galluzzo

Cloister of the Scalzo
Via Cavour 42

Cloisters of Santa Maria Novella
Piazza Santa Maria Novella

Excavations of Santa Reparata
Entrance inside Duomo

Gallery of the Hospital of the
Innocents
Piazza SS Annunziata 12

Giotto's Tower
Piazza del Duomo

Horne Museum
Via dei Benci 6

Medici Chapels
Piazza Madonna (behind San
Lorenzo)

Medici Riccardi Palace
Via Cavour 1
Closed on Wednesday.

Mineralogy and Lithology Museum
Via La Pira 4

Museum of Anthropology and
Ethnology
Via Proconsolo 12

Museum of Florence 'Com'era'
Via Oriuolo 4

Museum of Geology and
Palaeontology
Via La Pira 4

Museum of San Marco
Piazza San Marco 1

Museum of the Bigallo
Piazza San Giovanni 1

Museum of the Florentine House
Palazzo Davanzati
Via Porta Rossa 13

Museum of the History of Science
Piazza dei Giudici 1

Museum of the Opera del Duomo
Piazza Duomo 9

Museum of the Opera of Santa
Croce
Piazza Santa Croce

Opificio delle Pietre Dure
Via degli Alfani 78

Palazzo Vecchio
Piazza della Signoria

Perugino Fresco
Chiesa dei Pazzi
Borgo Pinti 58

Pitti Palace
Piazza Pitti
    Palatine Gallery
    Monumental Apartments
    Gallery of Modern Art
    Silver Museum
    Contini-Bonacossi Donation
    Porcelain Museum
    Museum of Carriages

Prehistory Museum
Via Sant'Egidio 21

Stibbert Museum
Via Stibbert 26

Zoological Museum of the
'Specola'
Via Romana 17

Theatres
Teatro Affratellamento
Via G. Orsini 73

Teatro Affrico
Via M. Fanti 20

Teatro Amicizia
Via il Prato 73

Teatro Apollo
Via Nazionale 41/r

Teatro Colonna
Via G. Orsini 32

Teatro Comunale
Via Corso Italia 12

Teatro dell'Oriuolo
Via dell'Oriuolo 31

Teatro della Pergola
Via della Pergola 12

Teatro Humor Side
Via Vittorio Emanuele 303

Teatro Niccolini
Via Ricasoli 3

Teatro Rondo di Bacco
Piazza Pitti 1

Teatro Sangallo
Via Sangallo 45/r

Teatro Tenda Citta di Firenze
Lungarno Aldo Moro

Teatro Verdi
Via Ghibellina 99

Films in English are shown at the
Cinema Astro, Piazza San Simone
every day except Monday.

Sports Facilities
Club Assi Giglio Rosso
Viale Michelangiolo 61
Tennis and Athletics.

Centro Sportivo Fiorentino
Via Bardazzi 15
Gymnasium, Sauna and covered
Swimming Pool.

Circolo Tennis alle Cascine
Viale Visarno 1
Tennis and Open-air Pool.

Piazzale Michelangiolo
Viale Michelangiolo 61
Tennis and Rollerskating.

Il Poggetto
Via M. Mercati 24/b
Bowls, Tennis, Rollerskating and
Open-air Pool.

Tennis Club Rifredi
Via Facibeni
Tennis.

Ugolino
Grassina, 7km (4 miles) south of
Florence
Golf, Tennis and Swimming Pool.

Societa Canottieri Firenze
Lungarno dei Medici 8
Rowing.

Montefreddi
SS della Futa, Via Bolognese
Horse-riding.

Centro Ippico Toscano
Via de'Vespucci 5/a
Horse-riding.

Piscina Costoli
Viale Paoli
Covered and Open-air Pools.

Amici del Nuoto
Via del Romito 38
Covered Swimming Pool.

Tropos
Via Orcagna 20/a
Covered Swimming Pool.

Bellariva
Lungarno Colombo 6
Open-air Pool.

Le Pavoniere
Via degli Olmi
Cascine.
Open-air Pool.

Boxing Club
Via G. da Montorsoli 8.

Motovelodromo Club Sportivo
Firenze
Via Fosso Macinante, 13
Motorcycling.

Rari Nantes Florentia
Lungarno Ferrucci 24
Swimming, Diving and Water Polo.

Associazione Aeronautica Militare
Via I da Diacceto 1-3/b
Parachuting.

Circolo Scherma Firenze
Via Fiume 5
Fencing.

Tiro a Segno Nazionale
Piazzale delle Cascine 6
Shooting.

Bicycles can be hired in the
Cascine:
Summer, Tuesday-Friday, 3.30-
7.30pm, Saturday and Sunday,
9.30am-12.30pm and 3.30-7.30pm;
winter, Saturday and Sunday,
9.30am-12.30pm and 2-4pm.

Parks and Gardens
Boboli Gardens
Behind Palazzo Pitti
Open: Summer, 9am-7pm; Winter,
9am-5.30pm.

Giardino dell'Orticultura
Junction of Via Vittorio Emanuele
II and Via XX Settembre

Villa Medicea di Castello
Via del Castello
Sesto Fiorentino
Open: summer, 9.30am-6.30pm;
winter, 9.30am-4.30pm.

Province of Florence

Carmignano
Palio di San Michele. Donkey race
and procession of decorated floats.

Castelfiorentino
Galleria d'Arte
Church of Santa Verdiana

Cerreto Guidi
February, Carnival with allegorical
processions and floats throughout
the month.

August, Annual Festival with
sports day.

End of August, Palio del Cerro,
horse race between the Quarters,
with procession in Renaissance
dress.

Early September, Children's
Tournament.

Certaldo
House of Boccaccio
Via Boccaccio

Empoli
Museo della Collegiata
Piazza San Giovanni

Fiesole
Archaeological Museum and
Archaeological Area
Via Partigiani 1

The Bandini Museum
Via Dupre 1

Missionary Ethnographic Museum
Church of St Francis
Via San Francesco

Grassina
Good Friday, Historical reconstruction of the day's events.

Greve in Chianti
April, Bric-a-brac fair.

May, flower show.

June, Gorse Fair.

September, Chianti wine fair.

Impruneta
September 13, Festival of St Luke.

Marradi
July-August, Marradi Summer Fair
and Festival of Gastronomy.

August 11-12th, Festival of San
Lorenzo.

August 25, Festival of the Birds.

Last week in October, Chestnut
Festival and folklore shows.

Montespertoli
February, Carnival.
End of March, Gastronomic
Festival.
End of May, Chianti Wine Fair.
June, Tuscan Folklore Festival.
Late August, Gastronomic Festival.
Beginning of September, Gastro-
nomic Festival.

Palzzuolo sul Senio
July and August, Folklore Festival
with concerts and sports.
August 15, Donkey derby (*palio dei
ciuchi*).
Mid-October, Chestnut Festival.

Panzano
April, Folklore Festival.

Poggio a Caiano
September, Festival of Gastronomy and Music.

Pontassieve (Santa Brigida)
Early September, Wine Festival.

Prato
Museums
Galleria Comunale
Palazzo Pretorio
Piazza del Comune

Museo dell'Opera del Duomo
Palazzo Vescovile
Piazza Duomo 49

Museo di Arte Murale
Church of San Domenico
Piazza San Domenico 8

Textile Museum
Viale della Repubblica 9

Festivals
Easter Sunday, May Day, Ascension Day, Christmas Day, The presentation of the Holy Girdle from Donatello's Pulpit
Early September, Fiera di Prato, large pageant in historical costume, and the Gara della Palla Grossa, a Renaissance ball game.
Boxing Day, Festival of St Stephen (Prato's patron saint)

Regello
Early December, Olive-oil Festival with folk events.

San Donato in Poggio
June 24. St John the Baptist's Day
Donkey derby (*palio dei ciuchi*)
Vintage car procession
Craft fair

San Godenzo
End of June, Pecorino Cheese fair with folklore attractions.

San Mauro a Signa
February, Carnival, folklore with allegorical processions.

San Polo
Beginning of May, International Iris Show and folk events.

San Quirico di Vernio
Late February, Polenta Gastronomic Festival.

Scarperia
End of August-beginning of September, Traditional Fair with Medieval pageant.

Vinci
Museums
Museo Da Vinci, in the castle.
House of Leonardo, Anchiano.

Festivals
15 April, Leonardo's Birthday.

Sesto Fiorentino
Museo della Porcellana di Doccia
Via Pratese 31.

Vicchio
Museo di Palazzo Comunale
Palazzo Pretorio

Giotto's House
Vespignano

Grosseto

Ente Provinciale per il Turismo
Via Monterosa 206
Grosseto
☎ 0564 22534

Museums
Museo Archaeologico Comunale
Via Mazzini 34
Open: 9am-12 noon and 4-7pm.

Museo Civico di Storia Naturale
Via Mazzini (next to Theatre)
Open: 4.30-7pm closed Tuesday
and Friday.

Museo Diocesano di Arte Sacra
Piazzetta del Campanile 3
Closed on Tuesday.

Province of Grosseto

Burano
World Wildlife Fund Oasis
Open: September-May, Thursday
and Sunday, 10am-1pm.

Massa Marittima
Museo del Risorgimento
6 Piazza Cavour

Museo Archaeologico
Palazzo delle Armi
Corso Diaz
Open: April-October, Monday-
Saturday, 10am-12 noon and 4-
6pm, Sunday 10am-12 noon.

Museo di Mineralogia
1 Viale Martiri di Niccioleta
3rd Sunday in May, Balestro del
Girifalco, Crossbow tournament.

Orbetello
Antiquarium Civico
Via Ricasoli 26
Open: Summer, Sunday-Friday,
8am-1pm and 4-6pm. Winter,
Sunday-Friday, 10am-1pm and
2.30-6pm.

Orbetello (Lagoon of) World
Wildlife Fund Oasis
Open: October-April, Thursday
and Sunday, 10am-1pm.

Porto Santo Stefano
15 August, Palio Santo Stefano,
Rowing race at sea, preceded by
procession in medieval dress.

Punt' Ala
Golf course and other sports
facilities.

Saturnia
Antiquarium
Villa Ciacci
Ring the bell to be admitted.

Vetulonia
Antiquarium

Gubbio

Azienda di Promozione Turistica
Piazza Oderisi 5/6
Gubbio
☎ 075 9273693

Museums
Museo e Pinacoteca Comunale and
Archaeological Museum
Palazzo dei Consoli
Open: October-March, 9am-1pm
and 3pm-5pm; April-September,
9am-12 noon and 3.30-6pm

Museo di San Francesco
Piazza 40 Martiri

Museo del Duomo
Via Ducale

Sports Facilities
Swimming Pool
San Biagio
Open: October-June, Monday-
Friday, 6-8pm, Saturday, 2.30-
7.30pm, Sunday, 2-7.30pm; July-
September, daily, 8am-1pm and 2-
8pm

Tennis Courts
San Biagio
Open: 8am-7pm.

Gymnasium
Liceo Classico
Via Carducci

Multi-sport Stadium
San Biagio
Open: 8am-5pm.

Stadio della Gioventù Beniamino
Ubaldi
San Biagio
Open: summer, 7am-7pm; winter
8am-5pm.
Outdoor sports.

Skating Rink
Teatro Romano
Bowls Centre
San Biagio

Traditional Festivals
15 May, Wax Candle Festival,
traditional procession and
celebration of Gubbio's patron
saint.

Last Sunday in May, Palio della
Balestra, crossbow tournament
with procession in medieval
costume.

14 August, Palio dei Quartieri,
crossbow tournament between
representatives of the city's
quarters.

July/August, classical dramas in
the Old Roman Theatre.

December, Albero di Natale
(Christmas Tree), illumination of
Mount Ingino.

Good Friday, procession of the
Dead Christ. Recreation of the
procession with Christ's body,
accompanied by sixteenth-century
religious hymns.

Livorno

Ente Provinciale per il Turismo
Piazza Cavour 6

Livorno
☎ 0586 33111

Museums
Museo Civico 'G. Fattori'
Villa Fabbricotti
Piazza Matteoli 19
Open: mornings, Tuesday-Sunday,
10am-1pm, afternoons (summer),
Thursday and Saturday 4.30-
7.30pm, (winter), 4-7pm.

Museo Progressivo di Arte
Contemporanea
Villa Maria
Via Redi 22
Open: mornings, Tuesday-Sunday,
10am-1pm, afternoons (summer),
Thursday and Sunday, 4.30-
7.30pm, (winter), 4-7pm.

Museo Provinciale di Storia
Naturale
Via Roma 234
☎ 802294
Open; Tuesday-Sunday, appoint-
ment only.

Museo Risorgimentale delle Armi
Porta San Marco
Piazza XI Maggio
Open: Thursday and Saturday,
8.30am-12.30pm and 4-6pm,
Sunday, 10am-1pm.

Parks
Opening times: summer, 10am-
8pm; winter, 10am-5pm.

Zoo
Viale Carducci

Parco di Villa Fabbricotti
Entrance from Piazza Matteoli and
Via della Libertà.

Parco di Villa Maria
Via Redi 22.

Parco di Villa Mimbelli
Via San Jacopo in Acquaviva.

Parco della Fortezza Nuova
Scala delle Pietre.

Parco di Villa Mauro-Gordato
Via di Monterotondo 36.

Parco di Villa Morazzana
Via di Colline 68 or Via Curiel 68.

Theatres
Goldoni
Via Mayer 51.

La Goldonetta
Via Mayer 51.

Cinema-Teatro La Gran Guardia
Via Grande 121.

Cinema-Teatro I Quattro Mori
Piazza Pietro Tacca.

Cinema-Teatro Grande
Piazza Grande.

Sports Facilities
Stadio Comunale
Piazzale Montello
Football and Athletics.

Ippodromo F. Caprili, Ardenza
Viale Italia.
Horse racing.

Piscina (swimming pool)
Comunale Coperta (covered)
6 lane, 25m
Via dei Pensieri

Piscina Olimpica Scoperta (open-air) 9 lane, 50m

Via dei Pensieri

Piscina Centro Nuoto
Via Lamarmora 19

Palazzo dello Sport
Via Allende

Basketball, Tennis, Volley-ball,
Boxing, Gymnastics.

Palazzetto dello Sport
Via Allende
Basketball, Volley-ball, Boxing,
Gymnastics.

Palazzetto della Scherma
Via Allende
Fencing.

Campo Sportivo Scolastico
Via dei Pensieri
Athletics.

Campo Comunale
Via dei Pensieri
Rugby, Baseball.

Centro Sportivo Sorgenti
Villaggio Sorgenti
Via Orlando
Football, Basketball, Speed Skating.

Centro Sportivo Giovanile
Viale Risorgimento 87
Football, Basketball, Volley-ball.

Tennis Club Livorno
Via delle Case Rosse 38

Junior Club Tennis
Via dei Pensieri 48

Tennis Livorno
Via San Lega 6

Tennis Courts
Via Roma 59
Villaggio Emilio Stagno

Complesso Sportivo Gymnasium
Viale Carducci

Via delle Sedie 16
Parco Sportivo di Via Micali

Events
Early May, Regatta.

June, Evening horse-races (racecourse).
Coppa Barontini boat race (ten oars) between areas of the city.

Coppa dei Risiatori boat race held out at sea.

July, horse-racing every Thursday and Sunday evening.

Mid-July, outdoor theatrical season.
Palio Marinaro, boat race.

August, horse-racing every Thursday and Sunday evening.
Open air theatre.

Mid-September Coppa Liburna Rally (part of Italian Rally Championship).

November and December, horse-racing usually on Sundays.

December, Lyric Season at La Gran Guardia Theatre.

Province of Livorno

Azienda Autonoma di Soggiorno e Turismo

San Vincenzo

(Livorno)

Campiglia Marittima
May Festival

Castiglioncello
Museum, for admission apply to Tourist Information Office, Via della Pineta 6.
Early June, Fish Festival.
July, International Dance Festival.
September, Literary Festival.

Cecina
Museo Civico 'Antiquarium',

Piazza Carducci.
February, Open cycle race.
Late April, Leisure Festival.
Mid-July, Antique Festival.
Mid-September, Cecina Festival; sports, traditional events.
Mid-October, October Fair.

Elba
Consorzio Servizi Albergatori
(Tourist Accommodation)
Viale Italia 20
57037 Portoferraio
(Elba)
☎ 0565 915555

Marciana

Museum 'Antiquario Comunale'
Portoferraio
Casa di Napoleone
Open: Summer, Wednesday-Monday, 9am-1pm and 3-6pm;
Winter, 9am-2pm.

Villa Napoleonica di San Martino, and Pinacoteca Demidoff
Open: Summer, Tuesday-Sunday, 9am-1pm and 3-6pm.

Events
May, Elba Rally.

August, Boat race.
September, 100km (60 miles) road race (for athletes). Literary Festival.

Procchio
Antiquarium

Rio Marina
Museo Minerario Elbano (minerals) near Palazzo Comunale.

Futorto
1 May Artichoke Festival.

Piombino
Last Sunday in July, Fish Festival.

Populonia
Museum
21 Main Street
Enquire at adjoining farm.

San Vincenzo
Last three Sundays before Lent,
Carnival.
May, professional cycle race.

Sasseta
October, Thrush and Chestnut
Festival.

Suvereto
Beginning of September, Wild Boar
Festival.

Lucca

Ente Provinciale per il Turismo
Piazza Guidiccioni 2
Lucca
☎ 0583 87245

Gardens
Botanical Gardens
Via del Giardino Botanico 14
Open: October-April, weekdays
9am-12noon; May-September,
Tuesday-Sunday 9.30am-12.30pm
and 4pm-7pm.

Garden of Villa Buonvisi
Via Elisa
Open: 9am-1.30pm.
☎ 0583 41449

Museums
Capitoline and Diocesan Library
and Archives
Palazzo Vescovile
Lucca
Open: Monday-Saturday 9.30am-
12.30pm.
☎ 0583 43722

Comunal Historical Archives
Piazzale San Donato
Open: Monday-Saturday 9am-1pm.
☎ 0583 55929

Eighteenth and Nineteenth-century
Customs (Permanent Exhibition)
Palazzo Controni-Pfanner
Via degli Asili 33
Open: April-September 10am-5pm. In
winter enquire at Comune. Closed
Mondays.
☎ 0583 41449

House of Puccini
Corte San Lorenzo 9
Via di Poggio
Open: October-March, 10am-4pm,
April-September 10am-6pm. Closed
Mondays.
☎ 0583 584028

Lucca State Archives
Piazza Guidiccioni 8
Open: Saturday 8am-1pm.
☎ 0583 56098

Museo Nazionale di Villa Guinigi
Via della Quarconia
Open: Summer, Tuesday-Sunday,
9.30am-1pm and 3-6pm; Winter,
Tuesday-Saturday, 9.30am-4pm,
Sunday, 9am-1pm.

Palazzo Mansi
Via Galli Tassi
Open: May-October, 9.30am-4pm;
November-April, Tuesday-Saturday,
9am-2pm, Sunday, 9am-1pm. Closed
Monday and Bank Holidays.

Palazzo Ducale
Piazza Napoleone
Pinacoteca Nazionale e Museo di
Palazzo Mansi
Via Galli Tassi
Open: Tuesday-Saturday 9am-7pm,
Sunday 9am-1pm.
☎ 0583 55570

Torre Guinigi (Tower)
Palazzo Guinigi
Via Sant'Andrea
Open: October-March 10am-4pm,
April-September 9am-7pm.

Theatre
Teatro del Giglio
Piazza Giglio

Province of Lucca

Additional Tourist Agencies:
AARV
Viale Carducci 10
Viareggio
☎ 0584 46382

AARV
Piazza Umberto 1
Lido di Camaiore
☎ 0584 64397

AARV
Via Donizetti 14
Marina di Pietrasanta
☎ 0584 20331

AARV
Piazza Marconi 1
Forte dei Marmi
☎ 0584 80091

AASC
Via Umberto I 139
Bagni di Lucca
☎ 0583 87946

PRO LOCO
Piazza Angelio
Barga
☎ 0583 73499

PRO LOCO
Rocca Ariostesca
Castelnuovo di Garfagnana
☎ 0583 62268

Barga
Theatre
Teatro dei Differenti
Piazza del Teatro 5

Museum
Museo Storico
Open: 10am-12noon and 3-6pm,
Call at PRO LOCO office.

Camigliano
Villa Torrigiani
Villa open April-November 5, 9am-
12noon and 2-6.30pm. Gardens
open all year.
☎ 0583 928008

Camporgiano
Archaeology and Renaissance
Ceramics Museum
Open: June-September 9am-12noon
and 3-6pm, October-May 9am-
12noon.

Castevecchio Pascoli
Pascoli's House
Open: summer 10am-1pm and 4-
7.30pm, winter 10am-1pm and 2-
4.30pm
☎ 0583 766147

Celle di Pescaglia
Puccini's House
Open: weekends 3-7pm

Colognora
Chestnut Museum
Open: Monday-Saturday 9am-7pm
☎ 0583 358012

Correglia-Antelminelli
Museum of Emigration and Plaster
Figures
Palazzo Vanni
Open: winter Monday-Friday
10am-1pm, summer weekdays
10am-1pm, Sunday 10am-1pm and
4-7pm.
☎ 0583 78082

Marina di Pietrasanta
Theatre
La Versiliana
Viale Morin-Fumetto

Montecarlo
Theatre
Teatro dei Rassicurati
Via Carmignani

Pietrasanta
Permanent exhibition of local crafts
Viale Marconi 5
Open: October-May 9.30am-
12.30pm and 3-6.30pm. June-
September 9.30am-12.30pm and 4-
8.30pm. June-September 9.30am-
12.30pm and 4-8pm.
☎ 0584 733363

Museo Archaeologico Versiliese
Palazzo Moroni
Piazza del Duomo
Open: winter, Tuesday and Friday
9am-12.30pm, Saturday 3-6pm,
Sunday 9am-12noon. Summer,
Tuesday and Friday 9am-12noon,
Thursday, Saturday and Sunday 4-
7.30pm.

San Pellegrino in Alpe
Country Museum
Via del Voltone 1
Open: July-September 8.30am-1pm
and 3-8pm.
☎ 0583 665068

Torre del Lago
Villa Puccini Museum
Open: April-September 9am-
12noon and 3-7pm. October-March
9am-12noon and 2.30-5pm.
☎ 0584 341445

Viareggio
Theatre
Teatro del Torre del Lago Puccini
Piazza Puccini

February: one of the biggest
carnivals in Italy.

Massa

Ente Provinciale per il Turismo
Piazza 2 Giugno 14
54033 Carrara
☎ 0585 70668

Museums
Ethnological Museum of the
Apuan Alps
Madonna degli Uliveti
☎ 0585 251330 for appointment.

Museo d'Arte Sacra
Duomo
☎ 0585 42643 for appointment.

Museum of the Malaspina Castle
Via Rocca
Open: daily (except Monday), 9am-
12 noon and 4-7pm.

Theatres
Cinema Teatro Guglielmi
1 Via E. Chiesa
Teatro Grifalco
Via Casola, Marina di Massa.

Province of
Massa-Carrara

Aulla
Lunigiana Natural History
Museum
Open: Tuesday-Sunday 9am-
12noon and 4-7pm (2-5pm in
winter).
☎ 0187 402374

Carrara
Museums
Civic Marble Museum
Viale XX Settembre

Open: 9.30am-12.30pm and 3.30-6.30pm (closed Saturday afternoon and Sunday)
☎ 0585 840561

Gallery of the Accademia di Belle Arti
1 Via Roma

Theatres
Teatro Cinematografico Marconi
Piazza Farini

Teatro Comune di Carrara
Piazza Battisti

Casola Lunigiana
Museum of the Upper Valley of the Aulella
Open: Tuesday-Sunday, 9am-12noon and 4-7pm (2-5pm in winter)
☎ 0585 90361

Luni **(Province of La Spezia)**
Archaeological Site and Museum
Open: winter, Tuesday-Sunday 9am-12noon and 2-5pm. Summer, Tuesday-Sunday 9am-12noon and 4-7pm.
☎ 0187 66811

Pontremoli
Museo del Comune, Castello del Piagnaro
Open: winter, Tuesday-Sunday 9am-12noon and 2-5pm. Summer, Tuesday-Sunday 9am-12noon and 4-7pm.
☎ 0187 831439

Villafranca Lunigiana
Ethnographical Museum
Via Borgo (in an old water mill)
Open: Tuesday-Sunday 9am-1pm and 3-6pm.

Orvieto

Azienda di Promozione Turistica
Piazza Duomo 24
☎ 0763 41772

Museums
Museo dell'Opera del Duomo
Palazzo Papale
Piazza del Duomo
Open: mornings, Tuesday-Sunday 9.30am-12.30pm. Afternoons, November-February 2.30-4pm; July and August 3-6pm. Other months 2.30-5pm.
☎ 0763 42477

Opera del Duomo Archaeological Museum
Palazzo dell'Opera del Duomo
Piazza del Duomo

Fondazione Museo Claudio Faina
29 Piazza del Duomo
Open: October-March, Tuesday-Sunday 9am-1pm and 2.30-4.30pm. April-September, Tuesday-Sunday 9am-1pm and 3.30-6pm.
☎ 0763 41216

Pozzo di San Patrizio
Open: October-March 8am-6pm. April-September 9am-7pm.
☎ 0763 43768

Etruscan Necropoli
Open: 8.30am-dusk all year.
☎ 0763 43611

Theatre
Teatro Comunale
Corso Cavour

Festivals
Pentecost, Festa della Palombella. Reconstruction of the descent of the Holy Spirit to Mary and the Apostles.

Corpus Domini, religious procession, preceded by a procession in Medieval costume.

14 August (evening), Festival of the Ascension of the Virgin. Procession in Medieval dress with a statue of the Virgin Mary at the head.

Perugia

Azienda di Promozione Turistica
Via Mazzini 21
☎ 075 23227

Museums
Museo del Duomo
Cathedral
Piazza 4 November
Open: 9am-12noon and 3.30-6pm.
☎ 075 21581

Umbrian National Art Gallery
Palazzo dei Priori
Piazza 4 November
Open: Tuesday-Saturday 9am-2pm.
Sunday 9am-1pm.
☎ 075 20316

Gallery of the Accademia delle Belle Arti
Piazza San Francesco
Open: Monday and Thursday 10am-12noon.
☎ 075 29106

Umbrian Archaeological Museum
Piazza San Domenico
Open: Tuesday-Saturday, 9am-2pm and Sunday 9am-1pm
☎ 075 21398

Natural Science Museum
Open: Tuesday-Saturday 8.30am-1.30pm and Sunday 9am-1pm.
☎ 075 25205

Theatres
Teatro Fonte Maggiore
36 Via Sant' Agata

Teatro la Turrenetta
10 Via Sole

Pisa

Ente Provinciale per il Turismo
Lungarno Mediceo 42
☎ 050 542344

Museums
Domus Galilaeana
Via Santa Maria 26
Open: Monday-Saturday, 9am-12 noon and 3-6pm.

Domus Mazziniana
Via Mazzini 71
Open: Monday-Friday, 9am-12 noon and 3-8pm, Saturday 9am-12 noon.

Museo dell'Opera del Duomo
Piazza Arcivescovado
Open: winter 9am-5pm, summer 9am-7pm.
☎ 050 560547

Museo di Mineralogia e Petrografia
Via Santa Maria 53

Museo di Paleontologia
Via Santa Maria 53

Museo di Zoologia e Anatomia Comparata
Via Santa Maria 53
(For admission to the above three museums, ring the bell and ask permission.)

Museo Nazionale di San Matteo
Lungarno Mediceo.
Open: winter, Tuesday-Sunday, 9.30am-4pm; summer, Tuesday-Saturday, 9am-1pm and 3-6pm, Sunday, 9am-1pm.

Theatres
Teatro Rossi
Piazza San Nicola.

Teatro Verdi
Via Palestro.

Traditional Festivals
Gioco del Ponte
Tournament on Bridge

17 June, Regata di San Ranieri, Boat race.

Province of Pisa

Calci
Museo di Storia Naturale
1 Via Roma

Cascina
Cooperativa Teatro delle Pulci
48 Corso Matteotti

Certosa di Pisa
Certosa.
Open: May-October, Tuesday-Saturday,
3-6pm, Sunday, 2-6.45pm; November-April, Tuesday-Saturday, 2-5pm, Sunday,1.30-4.15pm.

Pontedera
Piccolo Teatro di Pontedera
22 Via Manzoni

San Giuliano Terme
Teatro Crear e Bello
36 Via Leopardi

San Miniato
Museo Diocesano
Prato del Duomo
Open: Tuesday-Sunday, 10am-12.30pm and 3.30-7pm.
Istitute del Dramma Popolare, 40 Via Conti.

Santa Croce sull' Arno
Teatro Comunale G. Verdi
Via Verdi

Volterra
Museums
Museo e Biblioteca Guarnacci
11 Via Don Minzoni
Open: April-September, Monday-Saturday, 9am-1pm and 3-6pm, Sunday,9.30am-1pm;
October-March, Monday-Saturday, 9.30am-1pm and 2.30-4.30pm, Sunday, 9.30am-1pm.

Museo Diocesano di Arte Sacra
1 Via Roma
Open: 16 March-14 November, Monday-Saturday, 9am-12.30pm and 3-6pm, Sunday, 9-12 noon and 3-6pm; 15 November-15 March, Monday-Saturday, 10am-1pm, Sunday, 10am-12 noon.

Art Gallery
Palazzo dei Priori
Open: March-October, Monday-Saturday, 10am-1pm and 3-6pm, Sunday, 9am-1pm and 3-6pm; November-February, Monday-Saturday, 10am-1pm and 3-6pm, Sunday, 9am-1pm and 3-5pm.

Theatre
Teatro Gruppo Internazionale
L'Avventura
22 Via Minzoni

Pistoia

Ente Provinciale per il Turismo
Corso Gramsci 110
☎ 0573 34326

Museums
Museo Capitolare
Piazza del Duomo

Open: Monday-Saturday, 9am-12 noon and 3.30-7pm.

Museo Civico
Via Curatone e Montanara 63
Open: Tuesday-Saturday, 9.30am-12.30pm, Sunday, 10am-1pm.

Museo Diocesano
Palazzo Vescovile
Via Puccini
For entrance ask Custodian.

Theatre
Teatro Comunale Manzoni
121 Corso Gramsci.

Zoo
La Verginiana
Open: all year.

Festival
9 March Giostra dell'Orso
Bear Joust.

Province of Pistoia

Abetone
Azienda Autonoma di Soggiorno e Turismo
Piazzale dei Piramidi
Abetone
☎ 0573 60231

Collodi
Villa Garzoni Gardens.
Open: daily, 8am-8pm.
Pinocchio's Park and The Kingdom of Toys.

Cutigliano
Wide range of leisure facilities to cater for skiers in winter and walkers in summer.

Information:
Azienda Autonoma di Soggiorno e Turismo
Via Tigri

Cutigliano
☎ 0573 68029

Gavinana
Museo Ferrucciano
Open: daily, 9am-12 noon and 4-7pm.

Montecatini Terme
Azienda Autonoma di Cura e Soggiorno
Viale Verdi 66a
Montecatini Terme
☎ 0572 70109

Museum
Accademia d'Arte
Viale Diaz
Open: Tuesday-Sunday 4-7.30pm.

Theatre
Teatro Giardino Verdi
45 Viale Verdi

Information on the Thermal Cures
Direzione delle Terme
Palazzina Regia
41 Viale Verdi.

Pescia
Museo Comune di Pescia
9 Piazza Obizzi
Open: Monday, Wednesday, and Friday,
4-7pm.

Piteglio
Theatre
Teatro Comune di Piteglio
Via delle Corti
Popiglio

San Marcello Pistoiese
Wide range of leisure facilities to cater for skiers in winter and walkers in summer.

Information:
Azienda Autonoma di Soggiorno e Turismo

Via Marconi
San Marcello Pistoiese
☎ 0573 630145

Ravenna

Azienda di Promozione Turistica
Via Salara 8/12
48100 Ravenna
☎ 0544 35404

Azienda Autonomia di Soggiorno e
Turismo
Viale Matteotti 29
Abbadia San Salvatore
☎ 0577 778608

Azienda Autonomia di Cura
Via G. Sabatini
Chianciano Terme
☎ 0578 63538

Museums
Archiepiscopal Museum
Duomo
Church opening times.

Museo Nazionale di Ravenna
Via San Vitale

Musical Instruments Museum
Km 163,000 SS Adriatica

Accademia delle Belle Arti
Via Roma

Theatres
Teatro Alighieri
5 Via Garibaldi

Compagnia Teatro del Drago
71 Via Maggiore

Teatro Comunale Rasi
39 Via Roma

Teatro Estivo Comunale Rocca
Brancaleone
Via Rocca Brancaleone

Teatro Mariani
9 Via Ponte Marino

Teatro Municipio di Ravenna
4 Piazza Garibaldi

Around Ravenna
Faenza
International Ceramics Museum
Piazzale R. Pasi

Civic Art Gallery
Via Santa Maria dell'Angelo

Local information office
IAT
Piazza del Popolo
☎ 0546 25231

Brisighella
Val Lamone Museum and Graphics
Museum
Via degli Asini

Local information office
IAT
Piazza Stazione
48013 Brisighella

June-July Medieval Festival

Rimini

Azienda Autonoma di Soggiorno
Piazzale Indipendenza 3

Museums
Art Gallery and Civic Museum
Palazzo Gambalunga

Rimini Primitive Arts Museum
Piazza Cavour

Missionary Museum
Col di Covignano

Theatre
Teatro Novelli
3 Via Cappellini

In summer many cinemas show films in English and German.

Festivals
Late April, Annual Rimini-San Marino race.

Late May, Sailing Regatta, Rimini-Corfu-Rimini.

7 June-11 September, Malatesta Music Festival.

Sports Facilities
Athletics
Palazzetto dello Sport
Via Flaminia 28
Open: 7.30am-10pm.

Basketball
Palazzetto dello Sport
Via Flaminia 28
Open: 7.30am-10pm.

Boxing
Palazzetto dello Sport
Via Flaminia 28
Open: 7.30am-10pm.

Bodybuilding
Palazzetto dello Sport
Via Flaminia 28
Open: 7.30am-10pm.

Gymnastics
Palazzetto dello Sport
Via Flaminia 28
Open: 7.30am-10pm.

Swimming
Palazzetto dello Sport
Via Flaminia 28
Open: 7.30am-10pm.

Garden Sporting Centre
7 Via Euterpe
Open: Monday-Sunday, 9am-12 noon and Wednesday, 7-10.30pm, Sunday, 3-7pm.

Polisportiva Lungomare
Piazzale Kennedy
Open: Afternoons.

Parachuting
Stadio Romeo Neri
Piazza del Popolo

Aeroclub
Aeroporto Civile Miramare

Rollerskating
Palazzetto dello Sport
Open: 7.30am-10pm.

Garden Sporting Centre
Open: Friday, Saturday, and Sunday, 10.30-12 midnight.

Centro Polisportivo Regina Pacis
Viale Aleardi
Open: 7am-12 pm.

Palestra Casa del Popolo
Via Brava 18
Open: 7am-12 pm

Centro Sportivo Arci
Via Marconi
Open: 7am-12 pm

UISP Circondariale
2 Via dei Warthema
Open: 7am-12 pm

Fishing
Lago Riviera
Via Celli 2
Open: 7am-12 noon and 1pm-12 pm

Squash
Squash Inn
Superstrada San Marino Km 7
Cerasolo di Coriano
Open; 5pm-12 pm

Tennis
Garden Sporting Centre
Open: Monday-Saturday, 8am-12pm Sunday, 8am-10pm.

ASC Tennis Rimini
9 Lungomare A. Tintori
Open: 8am-12pm.

Polisportiva Lungomare
Piazzale Kennedy
Open: daily.

Dopolavoro Ferroviario
Via Roma 70
Open: 7am-12pm

Impianto Sportivo Salesiano
Viale Regina Elena
Open: 9am-7pm.

Lago Riviera
Via Celli 2
Open: 7am-12 noon and 1pm-12pm

Centro Polisportivo Regina Pacis
Viale Aleardi
Open: 7am-12 pm

Centro Sportivo Arci
Via Marconi
Open: 7am-12pm

Palestra Casa del Popolo
Via Brava 18
Open: daily.

Table Tennis
Garden Sporting Centre
Open: daily, 8am-12pm.

Impianto Sportivo Salesiani
Open: daily, 8am-12pm.

Stand V. Moretti
387 Via Santa Giustina
Open: Tuesday-Sunday, 9am-dusk.

Archery
Garden Sporting Centre
Open: Monday-Saturday, 8am-9pm, Sunday, 8am-1pm and 3-8pm.

Sailing
Circolo Velico Riminese
145 Via destra del Porta

Open: Tuesday-Friday, 4-6.30pm,
Saturday-Sunday, 9am-12.30pm
and 4-7.30pm.

Club Nautico Rimini
Piazzale Boscovich 12
Open: 7am-12pm.

San Marino

Ufficio di Stato per il Turismo
Palazzo del Turismo
☎ 0549 993299

Museums
Opening times:
December-February 9am-12.30pm
and 2.30-5.30pm.
March and October 8.30am-12.30pm and 2.30-6pm.
April 8.30am-12.30pm and 2.30-6.30pm.
May-15 June 8.30am-12.30pm and 2.30-7pm.
15 June-15th September 8am-8pm.
November 9am-12.30pm and 2.30-5.30pm.

Museo Pinacoteca di San Francesco
Via A. Orafo

Museo Pinacoteca di Stato
Palazzo Valloni, Via Carducci

Museo delle Armi Bianche
Torre detta Cesta

Museo delle Armi Moderne
Palazzo Manzoni

Museo Postale, Filatelico-Numismatico
(Borgo Maggiore)
Piazza Belzoppi

Museo delle Armi da Fuoco
(Borgo Maggiore)

Mostra-Mercato dell'Artigianato
Piazzale Giangi

Museo Santa Chiara
158 Via Carducci

Theatres
Teatro Concordia
Via Teatro (Borgo Maggiore)

Teatro Nuovo
Piazza Nuova
Dogana

Teatro Titano
Via Teatro (Borgo Maggiore)

Festivals
5 February, Anniversary of the
Liberation of the Republic from the
Papal forces in 1739.

25 March, Assembly of the Heads
of Families.

April and October, Instalment of
New Consuls with traditional
processions and ceremonies.

3 September, Anniversary of the
Foundation of the Republic with
Palio dei Balestrieri Crossbow
Tournament.

The Republic has a new swimming
pool, and facilities for tennis and
bowls. Fishermen are also catered
for.

Siena

Ente Provinciale per il Turismo di
Siena
Via de Montanini 92
☎ 0577 47051

Hotel Reservation Agency
Cooperativa Siena Hotels
Promotion
Piazza San Domenico
☎ 0577 288084

Museums and Other Places of Interest
Museo Civico and Monumental
rooms
Palazzo Comunale, Piazza del
Campo
Open: April-September, 8.45am-12
noon and 2.30-6.30pm; October-
March, 9am-2pm.

Opera Metropolitana
Piazza del Duomo
Open: 15 March-15 October, 9am-
1pm and 2.30-6pm (7pm on
Sunday); 16 October-14 March,
9.30am-1pm and 2.30-4.30pm
(closed Sunday afternoon).

Libreria Piccolomini
In Duomo
Open: May-September, Monday-
Saturday, 9am-7pm, Sunday, 9am-
6pm; October-April, Monday-
Saturday, 9am-7pm.

Museo Archaeologico Etrusco
8 Via della Sapienza
Open: Monday, Tuesday, Thursday, Friday, and Saturday, 9am-
2pm, Sunday, 9am-1pm.

Santuario e Casa di Santa Caterina
Costa di Sant'Antonio
Open: 8am-12 noon and 3.30-6pm.

Oratorio di San Bernardino
Piazza San Francesco
Apply for admission to the
custodian.

Museo della Societa Esecutori Pie
Disposizioni in Siena
71 Via Roma
Open: Monday-Saturday, 9am-12
noon.

Accademia dei Fisiocritici
Piazza Sant' Agostino 4
Museum of Palaeontology,
Mineralogy and Zoology.

Open: Sunday and 2 July, 15 and 16
August, 9.30am-12.30pm.

Pinacoteca (Art Gallery)
Palazzo Buonsignori
Via San Pietro 29
Open: Tuesday-Saturday, 9am-2pm,
Sunday, 9am-1pm.

Botanical Garden
Open: Monday-Friday, guided visits
9am-1pm and 3-5pm.

Theatres
Teatro Impero
14 Viale Vittorio Emanuele II

Teatro Moderno
Via Calzoleria

Teatro Metropolitan
Piazza Matteotti

Teatro Odeon
31 Via Banchi di Sopra

Teatro Fiamma
141 Via Pantaneto

Teatro Alberino
4 Via del Vecchietta

Teatro Alessandro VII
Piazza dell'Abbadia

Teatro Rinnovati
Piazza del Campo

Piccolo Teatro Siena
118 Via Montanini

Teatro dei Rozzi
Piazza Indipendenza

Traditional Festivals
2 July and 16 August with preliminary trials on the three days preceding the races, Il Palio, bare-backed
horse race around the Piazza del
Campo. A Medieval procession
through the City precedes the races.

Province of Siena

Asciano
Museum of Sacred Art
Via Bartolenga
Open: Summer, 9am-12 noon and
4-6pm, Winter, 10am-1pm and 3-
5pm.

Etruscan Museum
Corso Matteotti

Abbadia San Salvadore
Azienda Autonoma di Soggiorno e
Turismo
Viale Matteotti 29
Abbadia San Salvatore
☎ 0577 778608

Swimming pool and tennis courts.

Buonconvento
Val d'Arbia Museum of Sacred Art
13 Via Soccini

Cetona
Villa Terrosi Vagnoli Gardens.

Chianciano Terme
Azienda Autonoma di Cura
Via G. Sabatini
Chianciano Terme
☎ 0578 63538

Information on Thermal Cures
Direzione Generale delle Terme
Via Roma

Museum
Museum of Sacred Art
Palazzo dell'Arcipretura
38 Via Solferino

Chiusi
Etruscan National Museum
Via Porsenna
Open: Tuesday-Saturday, 8.30am-
12.30pm, Sunday, 9am-1pm.
Teatro Comunale P, Mascagni.

Montalcino
Museum of Sacred Art
31 Via Ricasoli
Open: 9am-12 noon and 4-6pm.
Civic Museum and Archaeological
Museum
10 Piazza Cavour
Open: 10am-1pm and 3-6pm.

Montepulciano
Civic Museum
Palazzo Neri Orselli Bombagli
11 Via Ricci
Open: 9am-12.30pm and 2.30-7pm.

Piancastagnaio
Private museum
Rocca degli Aldobrandeschi

Pienza
Cathedral Museum
Piazza Pio II 1
Open: March-October, 10am-1pm
and
3-6pm; November-February, 10am-
1pm and 2-4pm.
Palazzo Piccolomini and Hanging
Gardens, Piazza Pio II.
Open: 10am-12.30pm and 3-6pm.

San Gimignano
Museum of Sacred Art
1 Piazza Pecori

Civic Art Gallery
Piazza del Duomo
Open: (times for both museums)
summer, 9am-1pm and 3-6pm;
winter,9am-1pm and 3-5pm.

Tarquinia
Ente Provinciale per il Turismo
Piazza dei Caduti
Viterbo
☎ 0761 226161
Museums
Palazzo Vitelleschi Museo
Nazionale

Open Tuesday-Sunday, 9am-2pm
☎ 0766 856036

Necropoli Etruschi
Open: November-March, 9am-
2pm. April-May, 9am-1 hour
before sunset. June-August, 9am-
7pm. September-October, 9am-1
hour before sunset.

Tuscania (Near Tarquinia)
Museo Nazionale
Santa Maria del Riposo
Open: April-September 9am-2pm
and 2.30-6pm. October-March 9am-
2pm and 2.30-4pm.
☎ 0761 436209

Necropoli Etruschi
Open: April-September 9am-2pm
and 2.30-6pm. October-March,
enquire at Museum.

Urbino

Azienda Soggiorno e Turismo
Piazza Duca Federico 35
☎ 0722 2441

Museums
Galleria Nazionale delle Marche
Palazzo Ducale
Open: Tuesday-Saturday, 9am-
2pm, Sunday, 9am-1pm.

House of Raphael
Via Raffaello
Open: April-September, Monday-
Saturday, 9am-1pm and 3-7pm,
Sunday, 9am-1pm; November-
March, Tuesday-Sunday, 9am-
1pm. Closed in February.

Oratorio di San Giovanni
Via Barocci
Open: Monday-Saturday, 10am-
12.30pm and 3-5pm.

Oratorio di San Giuseppe
Via Barocci
Open: Monday-Saturday, 10am-
12.30pm and 3-5pm.

Museo Albani
Via P. Maia
Open: 9am-12.30pm and 3-7pm.

Fortezza Albornoz
Open: May-September, 9am-1pm
and 4-7pm.

Ducal Mausoleum
Church of San Bernardino
Open: 3-7pm.

Theatres
Teatro Sanzio
Corso Garibaldi

Cinema Teatro Ducale
Via Budassi

Sports Facilities
Mondolce
ISEF Covered Swimming Pool

Palestra F. lli Cervi
Covered Swimming Pool, Varea.

Via SS Urbinate
Tennis courts.

Colle dei Cappucini
Tennis courts.

Via Nazionale 73b
Tennis courts.

Festivals
Late July (annually), course of
Antique Music.

August 15, Passegiata Storica.
Historical Procession.

August, Corteo Storico.
Historical procession recreating
Medieval events.

1 September, Festa del Aquilone.
Urbino's annual Festival.

Urbania (Near Urbino)
Museo Civico
Palazzo Ducale
Via Piccini
Open: afternoons on request.

Useful Addresses

ENIT (Italian Tourist) Offices
Great Britain
1 Princes Street
London W1R 8AY
☎ 071 408 1254

USA
500 North Michigan Avenue
Chicago 1, Illinois
☎ 0312 6440990

Suite 1565
630 Fifth Avenue
New York
☎ 0212 245 4961/4

Suite 801
360 Post Street, San Francisco
☎ 0415 392 6206/7

also, c/o Alitalia at:

Suite 530
223 Permieter Center-Parkway
Atlanta, Georgia
☎ 0404 2239770

8350 Central Expressway
Dallas, Texas
☎ 0214 6928761

Canada
Store 56
Plaza 3, Place Ville Marie
Montreal, Quebec
☎ 0514 8667667/9

also, c/o Alitalia at:

120 Adelaide Street West
Toronto
☎ 0416 3631348

INDEX

A Note to the Reader

We hope you have found this book informative, helpful and enjoyable. It is always our aim to make our publications as accurate and up to date as possible. With this in mind, we would appreciate any comments that you might have. If you come across any information to update this book or discover something new about the area we have covered, please let us know so that your notes may be incorporated in future editions.

As it is MPC's principal aim to keep our publications lively and responsive to change, any information that readers provide will be a valuable asset to us in maintaining the highest possible standards for our books.

Please write to:
Senior Editor
Moorland Publishing Co Ltd
Free Post
Ashbourne
Derbyshire
DE6 9BR